Sponsored by

MovingObjects →

30 Years of
Vehicle
at the F

→ James Dyson

James Dyson was a student at the Royal
College of Art from 1966 to 1970. Dyson currently
employs 300 design engineers, including 25
RCA graduates, engaged in developing
technology for innovative products.

01|31

Designers –

Your Country

Needs You

→ Truly creative products like cars evolve as part of a holistic design process: the technology on the inside informs the way they look on the outside.

It's not just about turning out the same thing decade after decade. It's about looking at every-day things with new eyes, and working out how they can be made better. It's about challenging existing technology and improving the products and technologies we use every day.

Good design and technology is vitally important to the future of Britain. It generates successful manufacturing, which is the driving engine of the economy, and is a socially cohesive force uniting people in a creative act.

Therefore, Britain needs to work hard to create innovative products which work better than anything else before them. We need to learn to make planes, cars, electrical goods and ships again, instead of importing them. We need to rediscover our creativity and know-how. We need to inspire and empower our designers and excite passion in manufacturers so they develop products they love with sensitivity to the market.

Britain should realise how crucially important science, engineering and design are to this country. We should redirect talent from secondary and higher education to the core task of creating and developing products the world wants, rather than into those secondary services built on the back of industries that make real things.

Radical new ideas can then be generated by these young designers and engineers who have nothing to lose by surprising the market – they have no status or image at risk. In turn, this will stimulate challenging new industries enabling Britain to succeed in the worldwide market.

→ Brian Sewell

WELCOME to YOUNG STREET
CAR PARK

Brian Sewell

02|31

The Car is

Here to Stay

→ The car, entirely through the penny-pinching of governments, the blindness of architects and the idiocy of local government officers, has had appalling effects on architecture, town planning and the countryside. We have built the most boring motorways in Europe, the least related to the contours and natural beauties of the landscape, hideously bridged by minor roads. We have turned our cities into mephitic maelstroms, tied them in knots and put roads on stilts through suburbs, past third-floor bedroom windows and the clerestories of parish churches.

On roads that should be smooth, we have laid humps and bumps, on back-street intersections we have installed toytown roundabouts, and every main street junction we make hideous with yellow grids. We fence pedestrians with ugly railings and on every main street delay both them and traffic with island crossings that compel opposing streams of people to force their way against each other through traps that are too small and narrow. We have subordinated the townscape to the parked car, painted red and yellow lines to scare it, littered streets with hideous meters and machines for it, uprooted trees and paved front gardens for it, and devised for it that most hideous of all architectural embellishments, the garage door.

We are now being conditioned to hate the car. Instead of recognising that it is the instrument of free will and democratic choice, we must recite the mantra that motoring is a filthy, anti-social habit. Perhaps, in present conditions, it is, but present conditions are as they are because governments, architects, town planners and local authorities have always lacked imagination and chosen the cheapskate remedy that remedies nothing in the long run.

For a whole century, these authorities have lagged behind the car, wringing their hands, taxing, punishing and preaching the benefits of the bicycle – and still we motor on. Motoring is like masturbation – unstoppable and here to stay: authority should get used to that idea.

→ # Contents

010 Vehicle Design at the Royal College of Art – How it all began.

016 A Twisty Road Ahead for Car Design – What's up for Car Designers.

018 Now, we're in the Entertainment Business too – How Ford sees it.

020 Introduction: Shaped by a Century – Car Design Until 1969.

030 Gallery – Great Pictures of Great Cars…

046 Art or Science? 1: The Process of Car Design as seen by Geoff Lawson of Jaguar.

056 Art or Science? 2: The Process of Car Design as seen by production engineers.

062 What Inspires Car Designers?

070 Managing a Portfolio of Marques: Where Next for Ford?

076 Details – A Photographic study of Peter Stevens' Ultimate Creation, the McLaren F1.

082 Language of Form – Can Cars be Truly Beautiful? And are they Art?

090 Colour – A Hue and Cry for Designers. Let alone your Steering Wheel.

098 Gender – Phallic Symbol, Male Myth. Plus, the Male View.

108 Six Screens, a Table and a Nice View – designing the Volvo S80 and what Volvo means to its admirers.

118   Connections – How Cars link into the Design World.

128   The Perfect Car Designer's Career – Martin Smith at Opel.

136   Old Dogs, Brand New Tricks – Gerry McGovern at Rover.

144   Reviving a Great tradition – Simon Cox at GM. Plus Gordon Murray on 'showy suits'.

152   The Essence of National Identity – Murat Günak at DaimlerChrysler.

160   Making up Ground – Donato Coco at Citroën.

168   Porsche 911 – The Genetically Modified Machine.

176   Made in France – Patrick Le Quément at Renault.

184   Sharing Platforms – Hartmut Warkuss at Volkswagen.

192   One car, a Dozen Design Objectives – from Across the World – Peter Birtwhistle at Mazda.

202   Predictions – Working Backwards from the Future.

210   Course Philosophy and RCA Vehicle Design Graduates.

224   Glossary – Car Design Jargon for Experts and Beginners.

232   Bibliography – Essential further Reading on Car Design.

236   Index – Where to Find What.

→ | # Credits

Royal College of Art
Postgraduate Art & Design

MovingObjects is published in
July 1999 to coincide with the exhibition
'**Moving**Objects' at the Royal College of Art,
London, celebrating the 30th anniversary of
the college's Vehicle Design course and the
achievements of its graduates in the automotive
industry. Both this book and the exhibition
are sponsored by Ford.

Published by **Eye-Q Ltd**, 176 Kennington
Park Road, Kennington, London SE11 4BT, UK.
Tel: 0171 820 8899.

A British Library Catalogue listing for this
book has been applied for, and can be obtained
from the publisher or the British Library.

ISBN: 0-9536281-0-8

— Printed in the UK by BAS, England.
— Colour origination by CDI, England.
— Exhibition Design - Land Design Studio

Editors
Stephen Bayley & Giles Chapman
Design/Art direction
Paul Farrington/Tonne & Joseph Burrin/BCD
Portrait, Cover and other Photography
Christine Lalla
Assistance
Jessica Barrington-Smuts
Production
Alice Whately & Gavin Conway
Picture Research
Giles Chapman, Suzanne Hodgart & Shely Bryan
Drawings for Glossary – p225-231
Peter Stevens – RCA graduate No 1

Photographic credits
Photographs used in this book have come
from a wide variety of sources, including:
Arcaid, Barraclough Hall Woolston Gray,
Bertone, Bridgeman Art Library, Giles Chapman
Library, Citroen, DaimlerChrysler, Dyson, Ford
Motor Co, General Motors Media Archives,
Robert Harding Picture Library, Hulton Getty,
Peter Keetman, Ludvigsen Library, Moto Cinelli,
National Motor Museum, Porsche, Redferns
Music Picture Library, Renault, Rover, Science
& Society Picture Library, Seymour Powell,
Studio X, Peter Vann & Nicky Wright.

Contributors
— Stephen Bayley is a design consultant
and director of **Moving**Objects.
— Laura Blossfeld lists BMW, Audi and
Opel's colour and trim department among
her car design clients.
— Richard Bremner is a contributor to and
former editor of Car magazine.
— Russell Bulgin has been Britain's motoring
writer of the year three times.
— Giles Chapman is closely involved in the
car media as writer, editor and consultant.
— Gavin Conway is a leading motoring writer
and award-winning TV news producer.
— Matthew Gwyther is editor at large of
Management Today and contributing editor to *GQ*
— Michael Harvey writes for *The Financial Times*
and is a former editor of *Autocar*.
— Keith Howard is technical consultant to
Autocar and audio consulting editor for
Gramophone.
— Martin Pawley writes about architecture and
design, particularly for the *Architects' Journal*.
— Brian Sewell is art critic of the London
Evening Standard.
— Haig Simonian is chief correspondent in
Germany for *The Financial Times*.
— Penny Sparke is dean, Faculty of Art
& Design at Kingston University.
— Kate Trant is curator of the '**Moving**Objects'
exhibition.
— Bettina von Hase is a member of the
advisory council of the German British Forum.

00

→ Christopher Frayling

Professor Christopher Frayling
is Rector of the Royal College of Art

Professor Christopher Frayling

03|31

Vehicle Design

at the Royal College of Art

01

2

Tweedy critics once sneered at car 'styling'. But get this: 98.3% of graduates of the RCA's Vehicle Design course now celebrating its 30th birthday – partly with this book – have important jobs in the worldwide motor industry. No other RCA course has quite achieved that. Here's how it happened

→ When the Hovercraft was first launched, the version that went from Calais to Dover was named after the French engineering designer responsible for the project; the craft that went from Dover to Calais was named after a member of the Royal Family. When the 'automotive design unit' at the Royal College of Art was given the green light in October 1967, a similar form of snobbery surrounded the designers of cars in the UK. They were not eligible for Design Council Awards – the Council's director at the time, Paul Riley, thought of their work as 'styling' rather than 'design': chrome wrapped around the outside rather than form follows function – their magazines were reckoned to be full of flash-harry graphics rather than cool Bauhaus-style typography and 'renderings' rather than drawings, while the finished products were invariably associated in the public mind with the company that manufactured them rather than the designers who conceived them. Unless they happened to be Alec Issigonis.

Put another way, for every Mr Toad who designed for the open road, there was an army of Ratties, Moles and Badgers lining up along the riverbank to make their growls of disapproval heard.

So when Professor Misha Black and his second-in-command Frank Height put out feelers to the motor industry in 1967 through the Society of Motor Manufacturers & Traders, they were consciously moving into the fast lane and over-taking the tweedy design establishment. Frank Height still remembers there was "much opposition from the more traditional elements within the College Council". Like most new design subjects at the Royal College of Art, 'automotive design' grew organically out of a parent discipline – in this case, the School of Industrial Design (Engineering). Black and Height had noticed an increasing number of ID(E) students tended to select thesis projects on topics relating to transport and some of them even designed vehicles. At the same time, Black and Height were aware the industry was in much need of visually-aware designers.

The traditional routes of training on the job – re-training engineering or art school graduates, or recruiting outside consultants 'usually of Italian origin' (and this in the era of Swinging London and 'I'm Buying British') were not producing the suitable goods. For the new course to work, it would have to attract the co-operation of the industry it aimed to stimulate. Hence the initial approach to the Society.

Eventually, a series of meetings with design director Roy Brown of the Ford Motor Company (UK), who ran his own small design school at Dagenham, resulted in an agreement that, in future, the School of Industrial Design (Engineering) at the RCA was better placed to take on this educational role; the 'automotive design unit' was the consequence, the first such unit in any British art *or* engineering school. At last there was to be a European rival to the Zoom-Zoom School in California. That same summer, the Royal College of Art had become a chartered university institution, the only wholly post-graduate university of art and design on the planet. So 'automotive design' was from now on an accredited university subject.

Ford agreed to sponsor two students each year, and provide some equipment such as an American clay oven and a modelling bridge, and the two-year course would cover 'ergonomics, engineering, and the environmental and aesthetic aspects of vehicle design.' The immediate purpose of the course, according to the literature, was to 'enable students, preferably with some previous design training, to enter the motor industry with a working knowledge and expertise in the specific skills, disciplines and procedures involved in the practice of automotive design and styling.'

The prospectus added wisely: 'it is a central tenet of the course philosophy that transportation as we know it, together with the attitudes and procedures associated with its design, is undergoing a constant process of change.' The conclusion was that the course would benefit hugely from being embedded in a College which practised and studied design in an art environment and art in a design environment. Carel Weight, the Professor of Painting, in the late 1960s, called this process a 'two-way traffic.'

Chrysler UK joined the partnership in October 1969, with two more sponsored students each year – bringing the grand total to eight. There was no budget for running costs, so workshop manager Peter Walker-Taylor did the best he could with that clay oven and bridge.

The first two post-graduate students were Peter Stevens and Dawson Sellar, who had just completed their Industrial Design (Engineering) Course. Sellar recalls:

"We had enjoyed ourselves so much at the RCA, we were reluctant to leave the place, so a further two years looked attractive… There was no real structure at first, but we managed to keep ourselves busy. We were found a little corner on the fourth floor of the Darwin Building next to an outfit called the Design Research Unit [which, under Bruce Archer, was busy researching the principles involved in designing an all-purpose hospital bed for the NHS]. We built a full-size drawing board and secured it to the wall, although I can't remember if we ever used it. Tom Karen [of Ogle, a company which, unusually at the time, had a transport design office comparable to the Italian studios] came in and introduced himself as our tutor… we had some horrific model-making experiences, trying to make a 1:5 scale GRP model from plaster moulds. An unforgettable two-week course in vehicle engineering at Cranfield. The professor drove a Morris Minor and stated his utter contempt for anything rear-engined."

Tom Karen, who was indeed the first specialised tutor to join the staff – on a one-day-a-week basis – on the recommendation of Ford, adds: "I was the first and only tutor for the first two years, with two students in the first year and two or three in the second. An enduring memory was of taking Peter Stevens and Dawson Sellar to the Tate to look at Henry Moore sculptures and relating this to car body design."

Moore himself had been a graduate of the College in the mid-1920s: although he did dabble in textile design, it's doubtful whether sculptures on wheels were precisely what he had in mind.

When Tom Karen discovered that "to do the job properly I needed more time than I could afford, with a growing office," he recommended ex-colleague Carl Olsen [later head of Citroën design] to take his place. Nigel Chapman, an Industrial Design graduate of the early 1950s and a second-year tutor since 1968, 'moved across' as tutor to the unit at much the same time.

Meanwhile, the first two pioneering students completed their course in summer 1969 – which is why we are celebrating the 30th birthday of car design at the College in July 1999 – and graduated in the same year Misha Black mounted a major exhibition IDE(10) in the Gulbenkian Hall, which marked the discipline's first 10 years at the College by featuring a range of professional work done by ex-students: an electrically-propelled wheelchair by Ken Sadler, hi-fi amplifiers by Roy Gray, the Reliance 1000 tractor by Peter Ralph (who was to teach automotive design and especially the design of mechanised handling vehicles, on a visiting basis) plus, of course, the optimal hospital bed by Kenneth Agnew – the product of Bruce Archer's trail-blazing research.

In the early 1970s, Nigel Chapman secured the use of a garage in Jay Mews – since demolished – which became the model workshop. Each year, at degree show time, the garage doors would be opened to reveal an Aladdin's cave of car models in-progress and, of course, to let out the fumes.

"The rest is history," as Tom Karen rightly says. Visiting lecturers in the early years – in addition to Olsen – included Peter Ralph and Patrick Le Quément (now head of design at Renault). Frank Height took over as Professor from Misha Black in 1975, and dropped the (Engineering) from Industrial Design, since by then the title had become the internationally recognised generic term for the subject – and, besides, the Engineering bit had caused confusion (especially among engineers). Four years later, Chapman hired John Heffernan (recently returned from working at Audi in Germany) to run a design project with the class of 1979 which included Peter Schreyer (now design director of Audi). In March 1981, Chapman hired Ken Greenley from General Motors who was, in the fullness of time, to take over as tutor in charge.

Then the unit became a department in its own right, no longer a subset of Industrial Design: as it expanded, Lester Allen was hired from General Motors and Dale Harrow from Seymour Powell. Finally, three years ago, Ken Greenley became the first professor of the subject in the country, ably supported by the team of Allen, Harrow and Heffernan. Meanwhile, the department was completely re-equipped with the latest digital technology, often thanks to the generosity of the motor industry.

Between the mid-1970s and the mid-1990s, various titles such as Automotive Design and Transportation Design had been given a test run; the College eventually settled on Vehicle Design, since trains, boats and planes often appeared in final year shows – as well as cars – but Transportation seemed too broad and all-embracing a concept at such a specialised, post-graduate level. An Industrial Design Engineering course – resourced and taught jointly with neighbouring Imperial College of Science, Technology and Medicine – centrally concerned with engineering this time, since it aimed to transform University engineering graduates into College industrial designers, was successfully launched by Frank Height in 1980, operating side-by-side with the Industrial Design programme. It was the most significant innovation in RCA industrial design since the foundation of the 'automotive design unit' over 10 years previously.

Peter Stevens went on to become chief designer for Lotus, Dawson Sellar went on to design for Porsche. Since 1969, the course has sustained a remarkable track record for producing graduates – from Britain and overseas – who have gone on to become chief designers, senior staff designers, design team leaders and consultants in the automotive industry all over the world. A couple of years ago, we did a survey of the 'destinations' of post-graduates from the Royal College of Art between the years 1992 and 1996. It turned out an *average* of 92.5 per cent of our graduates are employed, at the right level, in the subject they practised and studied at the College.

But Vehicle Design reached the chequered flag ahead of all other College courses, overtaking Fashion on the finishing line, with an amazing 98.3 per cent of its graduates employed as designers or consultants in the industry. As Mr Chips famously observed when he said "good-bye" at the end of that tear-jerking Hollywood movie "…and all boys".

Where did the other 1.7 per cent (out of 58 graduates) go? We are still trying to track him down. Perhaps in an Audi quattro or a Land-Rover Freelander or a Land-Rover Discovery or a Ford Ka or an Aston Martin DB7 or an MGF or a Bentley Continental.

Because these cars all have one thing in common. They all had substantial, often decisive, design input from a graduate of the Royal College of Art. And since our 'destinations' survey was published in 1997, the monopoly of the boys has at last been challenged. Will the atmosphere of the studios and workshops become less masculine as a result? It already has.

A recent government report concluded that one of the biggest questions facing higher education (apart from improving the gender balance in engineering and heavy design subjects) was how to link universities more closely with business and the community in creative and innovative, rather than short-term, ways. The unit, launched in 1967, produced its first graduates in 1969 and has continued, as Tom Karen puts it, "to go from strength to strength". It's a high-octane answer to that question, and an indisputable one.

We are disgracefully proud of its students, its graduates, its staff and, above all, of its achievements on the road over the past 30 years.

→

Ken Greenley

→ The modern car is designed within a strict regulatory climate. Automotive legislation is both parochial and international, and at the same time mutual. With the possible exception of the pharmaceutical and air transport industries, no other product is subject to as many regulatory and legal protocols.

These are intended to simplify and add conformity to the product, to the detriment of the individuality and personality of the visual design. In addition, aerodynamic and ergonomic developments have tended to standardise car volumes and proportions.

Despite these restrictions, each individual car design continues to be the centre of public debate, usually without any personal experience of using the product; most car users are familiar with just one automotive product – the one they currently own and drive. Previous ownership is obviously historic, yet these same potential consumers will develop strong opinions regarding the latest designs.

Therefore, the individual opinion is based on only two sources. The first is received information, like advertising, media comment and sometimes opinions from a new owner. The second and most important is in the personal 'reading of the object.'

Professor Ken Greenley is Course Director of Vehicle Design at the Royal College of Art

04|31

A Twisty Road

Ahead for Car Design

This 'reading' is not in the language of words: the only words on a car are small and cryptic (GT, SLR, 300E) or iconic (badges, symbols or, on specialised vehicles, 'signatures' of the stylist, design house or coachbuilder). It's in the compostion of the spatial volumes of the product, the obvious, subtle or subliminal visual references within the design, the pedigree of the manufacturer, and the perceived product values – price, value, quality and technological integrity.

The visual design of the car also establishes its social associations with consumers; it is readily related to class and social status. The aesthetic values of an automotive product can also lead to assumptions related to a driver's age, gender and occupation.

Therefore, most of the 'reading' is in the language of visual design: the 'style.' The style of the vehicle is the most subtle and persuasive value responsible for the success of a modern car.

The general perception of 'styling' is that it is superficial, transient and insubstantial. This is partly the fault of the automotive design profession, which has made little effort to explain the methodology or the intellectual depth and responsibility of its endeavours.

So how does the public regard the car designer's work?

Sadly, I feel they often think he – and invariably it is 'he' – pens the design, usually on the back of an envelope or beer mat and, somehow, miraculously, three years later a car emerges through a factory door.

Yet there is increasing awareness that certain automotive designs have more merit than others. These judgements are seldom substantiated, due mainly to the absence of a critical dialogue in the public domain.

Encouragingly, however, there's growing evidence the visual messages implanted in the style of the vehicle are being read. This critical competence is not based on logical interpretation, but simply on accumulated judgemental activity.

What will cars look like in the future? The year 2020 is currently a fashionable target of enquiry. Twenty years into the future is a reasonable amount of time in an adult life cycle, but the average age of the owner of a new car in western Europe is about 45. Therefore, the new customers of the year 2020 are today's 25-year olds. These consumers of automotive products will not be invented – they already exist on this planet. Future purchasers of cars have already, or soon will have, established their tastes, preferences, prejudices and expectations.

The average age of the post-graduate students at the Royal College of Art is 27. These students represent over 40 nationalities, and there are 24 distinct art and design disciplines studied at the RCA. The exposure to the multi-cultural, multi-national and multi-disciplinary experience of a two-year programme of study at the RCA will inevitably have a long-term influence on the professional activities, opinions and future critical judgements of the graduates. These designers are representatives of their generation.

The inspirational factors assimilated by car designers cover a large spectrum. Some are in synergy with the car's technical evolution. Others are social. The body forms of modern 'people carriers', for instance, will signify safety and security, but also include visual clues relevant to family and recreational values. In most cases, it will be non-gender specific.

The modern car designer, pursuing a career with a multinational manufacturer, is faced with immense demands on his professional abilities inspirationally to conceive, execute, develop, present and convince the industrial executive of the commercial merits of the design. The economic implications of these decisions are paramount to commercial survival.

The successful car designer or stylist of the future will be, as always, a designer who can deconstruct the potential social and cultural values pertinent to the sensibilities of consumers in three years' time, and who can then create a sculptural, confident form that subliminally embraces those metaphorical values.

→ | # J Mays

J Mays is vice-president of design,
Ford Motor Company - the sponsor
of **Moving**Objects - Dearborn, USA

05|31

Now, we're in the

Entertainment Business too

→ The Ford Motor Company is proud to sponsor Moving Objects. We have been involved with the Royal College of Art's Vehicle Design course from its inception in 1969. Since the first students graduated a few years later, they began to have an influence on the design of our cars.

An astonishing amount has changed in the 30 years since the course started. In 1969, car design scarcely had credibility as an academic subject. Today it's one of the College's most culturally important and economically significant activities. Simultaneously, the consumer has acquired huge sophistication in design matters.

The motor industry may be global, but this doesn't mean there will be less variety in future. On the contrary: as component sharing increases in the quest for manufacturing efficiencies, the consumer's appetite for personal expression through his or her car becomes more keen. And that expression is going to be a matter of design.

At Ford, our own business has developed rapidly in recent years. So far from being what Henry Ford envisaged and created – the universal provider of ingeniously simple personal transport – Ford now manages a diverse portfolio of internatonal marques. As technological distinctions between manufacturers erode, so the responsibility of designers increases: it's their job to create meaningful distinctions between, say, a Ford, a Volvo, a Jaguar and an Aston Martin which animate the consumer. Cars compete for consumer attention with other products: in one sense, we are today in the entertainment business as much as road transport.

It's the job of our designers to look into the future and find the source of that entertainment. To find the source of our designers, we often start at the Royal College of Art.

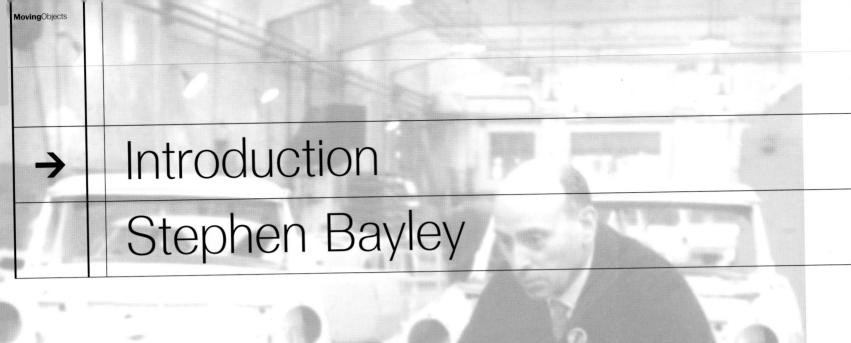

→ Introduction
Stephen Bayley

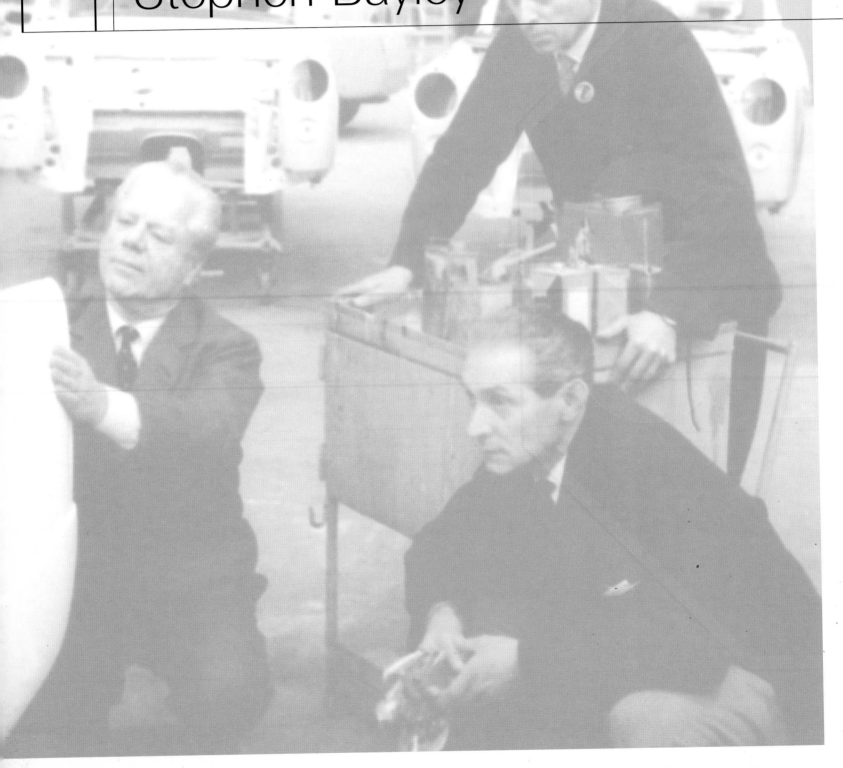

Stephen Bayley

06|31

Shaped by a Century: cars took shape at the Royal College of Art for the first time in 1969. This is the story of what had happened up to that point.

Stephen Bayley

→ Industrial design, along with rock music and movies, is one of the distinctive cultural forms of the 20th century. And the most complete expression of industrial design is the motor car. But the very first cars were not designed, at least not in the sense meant by Emilio Ambasz when he explained that design "begins once the functional and behaviourial needs have been satisfied. We create objects not only because we want to satisfy the pragmatic needs of man, but mainly because we need to satisfy the demands of our passions and imaginations. The designer's milieu may have changed, but the task, I believe, remains the same, to give poetic form to the pragmatic."

Karl Benz's German Imperial Patent 5789 may have been the first complete conception of the car, a formal record of the stuttering explosive tricycle which frightened the horses and citizens of Mannheim over the winter of 1885/6, but it was a pragmatic technical experiment, not a poetic interpretation of a belief. In those days, filling stations did not exist and, on its first outing, Benz had to stop his tricycle at an Apotheke to buy a phial of petroleum spirit. The local newspaper described the first car as 'repugnant, diabolical and dangerous.' It was experimental, ingenious, revolutionary, but not a thing of beauty. That would come later.

A restless inventor, as soon as his tricycle had come to life, Benz moved on and left the development of the car to others. Chief among these was, of course, Henry Ford. If Benz proved a self-propelled automobile was technically feasible, then Ford sensed and eventually realised the near universal appeal of such a machine. In his creation of an affordable, popular 'gasoline buggy' Ford made available a reliable car that was the expression of a profound human craving for independence and mobility. Henry Ford said he was "driven" to make his first practic car in order to escape the crushing tedium of life on a mid-Western farm. It is this essential spirit of free-dom and self-expression released by the automo-bile that is the source of mankind's passionate affair with the car (and only unthinkably totalitarian governments would ever take it away).

But Ford, too, was no aesthete, notwithstanding his most famous remark about the universality of black paint. This was, in fact, an expression of his interest in achieving manufacturing efficiencies through the standardised use of fast-drying black paint rather than an aesthetic credo: in those days, coloured paint took up to four weeks to dry. Yet while Ford himself had said he was inclined to raise his hat whenever saw a beautiful Alfa Romeo, it was a truth universally acknowledged that he took no interest in poetic design, only in pragmatic achievement.

A restless inventor, as soon as his tricycle had come to life, Karl Benz moved on and left the development of the car to others.

1920s CHEVROLET – GM INVENTED CAR DESIGN

HENRY FORD

George Walker, the industrial designer who later joined the Ford Motor Company, had been warned off presenting Mr Ford with a selection of brightwork door handles mounted lasciviously on black velvet.

In *My Life and Work* Ford wrote: 'I will build a motor car for the great multitude. It will be large enough for the family, but small enough for the individual to run and care for. It will be constructed of the best materials, by the best men, after the simplest designs modern engineering can devise. But it will be so low in price that no man making a good salary will be unable to own one – and enjoy with his family the blessing of hours of pleasure in God's great open spaces.'

Ford's "simplest design modern engineering can devise" was, of course, the Model T. Ford saw his task as continuously refining this car to approach a sort of absolute. The elementary Model T was indeed continuously refined between 1908 and 1927 and was such an epochal success Ford's ambition was largely satisfied: any American in employment could afford to buy a car. They did. A new episode in civilisation had begun.

Half a century after the birth of the Model T the car had changed the world. In her brilliant but bitter attack on the car's influence on town planning, Jane Jacobs wrote in *The Death and Life of Great American Cities* (1962) that: 'We Americans hardly need ponder a mystery that has troubled men for millennia: what is the purpose of life? For us, the answer will be clear, established, and for all practical purposes indisputable: the purpose of life is to produce and consume automobiles.'

But just as Ford had realised the social utility of Benz's invention, so it was General Motors which realised the commercial opportunities the new market of mobilised Americans offered. To Ford, the car was an absolute democratic necessity, a utilitarian tool, an expression of man's ingenuity and his freedom. To Alfred Sloan, the founder of General Motors, that same car represented an opportunity to seduce the consumer with ideas of social competition and cultural modelling which are still with us today.

It was Sloan who had no less an idea, unconsidered by Benz and Ford, that consumers might be persuaded to buy more cars, more expensively, more often if those cars were styled, if they were poetic as well as pragmatic. The beginning of this gigantic concept was when, in recognition of the same paint problem that had interested Henry Ford, General Motors formed a Paint and Enamel Committee whose brief was to 'study the question of art and color combinations in General Motors' Products.'

THE BENZ PATENT

In Italy the designers of Farina and Bertone were far more concerned with finding absolute forms of sculptural beauty, to make metal sing.

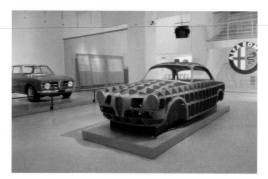

BERTONE'S ALFA ROMEO GIULIETTA SPRINT MASCHERONE

ITALIAN DESIGNER GIOVANNI MICHELOTTI AT WORK

The man ultimately chosen to do this was a flamboyant Californian called Harley Earl whose custom car business had catered to the whims of the first generation of Hollywood stars. Earl had told GM's Larry Fisher that his customising skills could make a common Chevrolet look like a Cadillac. Sloan had found his man and Harley Earl was hired to create the Art and Color Department. Car design was born.

Ten years later, Earl re-christened the department the Styling Division. Car design had come of age. Looking back we can see the creation of Art and Color in Detroit was an exact parallel to the events in New York that established consultant design as a modern professional business. Raymond Loewy, Norman Bel Geddes, Walter Dorwin Teague and Henry Dreyfuss set up their studios in Manhattan around 1927. Just as Sloan realised Ford's practical genius opened up a new market for dreams and desires, so this first generation of industrial designers worked on the assumption that the success of the American economy meant consumer demand was all but satisfied.

Consumers were moving beyond mere subsistence into the complex area of taste. Irregular desires could now be excited…by design. What they all had in common was that consumer design was construed to be a visionary process: the designer was expected to do no less than look into the future and make it happen…now.

It was under Harley Earl that General Motors established so many of the working practices which still dominate car design today. With its five manufacturing divisions, General Motors could offer not just functionally efficient automobiles but cars loaded with meaning. From the manufacturing point of view, the enormous fixed costs of production tooling meant there was an economic requirement for design to be, as it were, superficial. Earl developed the studio practice of clay modelling; before television he showed concept cars to excited customers at nationwide 'Motoramas'; he told his designers to "go all the way you can and then pull back some"; he understood and exploited evocative imagery and he reached the very top of what was then the biggest and most successful corporation on the planet.

Earl's extraordinary designs had by the 1950s whipped the industry and the customer into such a cyclone of manufacturing and consumption that the notorious 'annual model change' came about. Critics called this wasteful process (so much at odds with the European design ideal of integrity, clarity and harmony) 'planned obsolescence,' but one clever General Motors executive said: "We haven't depreciated these cars, we have appreciated your mind".

There is perhaps no more complete expression of American civilisation than, say, a 1953 Chevrolet Corvette, or the 1955 Ford Thunderbird that followed it. But an alternative tradition of car design had evolved from very different sources in Europe. While all major European countries had coachbuilding traditions, in Italy these *carrozzerie* matured into specialist car design studios whose perfectly judged executions of elegant bodywork betrayed a culture where easy style is commonplace. Outstanding among a long and distinguished list of *carrozzerie* that includes Zagato, Touring, Frua, Ghia, Michelotti and Vignale were Pininfarina and Bertone.

Their techniques were very different to the Americans. While in the US, designers were inspired by pictures of jet airplanes torn from glossy magazines and worked under the massive capitalist imperatives of gobal industries, in Italy the designers of Farina and Bertone were far more concerned with finding absolute forms of sculptural beauty, to make metal sing. Their designs were part of mankind's restless flirtation with gorgeous shapes, successive attempts to define the absolute.

As independent companies they were not restricted by precise marketing objectives, they were more simply concerned to sell a conception of automotive beauty to a manufacturer.

SIR ALEC ISSIGONIS, MINI DESIGNER

1936 FIAT 500 TOPOLINO

1953 CHEVROLET CORVETTE

Their tools and techniques resembled the studios of renaissance sculptors, as did their instincts. Ventilating louvres were made with a tool called a *gola 'd luv*, panels were beaten or formed with a *batoir* or a *tas a cheur*. And the panels were ultimately tested and formed over a full-scale wooden buck called a *mascherone*. In this way was the beautiful Alfa Romeo Giulietta Sprint made by Bertone, a vintage car that looked very modern. It was the last time Alfa Romeo supplied the *carrozzerie* with chassis ready for coachbuilt bodies. A technical antique, its lines laid the basis for all modern Alfa Romeos.

The poetics of car design are overwhelmingly influenced by style and symbolism. Occasionally, technical or statutory innovations excite change, but they're soon absorbed into the aesthetic mainstream. This is what happened with streamlining (known in the wind tunnel as aerodynamics) and, later, with safety legislation. Technically speaking, the laws of aerodynamics may be aesthetically restrictive, but the achievement of designers was to turn them into an element in the vocabulary of style.

Only very briefly was aerodynamics considered to offer a universal solution; soon experiments proved that the torpedo shape, known to have perfect 'penetration,' also had very imperfect stability. At the same time, the very first car wholly designed by aerodynamics pioneer Wunibald Kamm, the American Cunningham C-4RK of 1952, was so far from being a machine of inevitable, functional beauty, a brute of a thing. Again, after 1970s legislation required forms of crash protection, designers quickly absorbed protective imagery into their repertoire of gestures.

Sometimes great cars are brought about by engineers whose essential motivation is an engineering idea. These include Ferry Porsche, Dante Giacosa, Pierre Boulanger and Alec Issigonis. Here it is fascinating to see the functionalist truisms working through and entering the visual language: Porsche's original 356 was conceived as pure engineering, but established a style which designers are still developing 50 years on. Dante Giacosa's fabulous little Fiat 500 might have been an engineering proposition first and foremost, but its gorgeous appearance surely betrays the hand of a (sadly anonymous) but masterfully self-conscious designer well able to articulate the concepts of 'small,' 'efficient' and 'enjoyable' through meaningful shape. And the famous Citroën DS, the car that gave rise to Roland Barthes' unforgettable comparison of cars to cathedrals, might also have been fundamentally a technical conception, but its astonishing bodywork was by the sculptor (!) Flaminio Bertoni. Equally, while no 'designer' worked on Issigonis' influential car, the next generation Mini apes its style. That idiosyncratic shape has become a part of the language of design.

In Britain the premier museum of design, the Victoria & Albert, does not collect cars because, hobbled by Victorian taxonomy, its highly territorial keepers cannot decide whether an automobile is sculpture or metalwork, but as long ago as 1951 New York's Museum of Modern Art recognised the place of car design in contemporary culture, something which artists like Francis Picabia and Fernand Léger had done 20 years before. MoMA's Curator of Design, Arthur Drexler, organised a show called, simply, 'Eight Automobiles' to demonstrate his belief that cars were "rolling sculpture".

The eight included a Jeep, a Cisitalia, an MG TC, a Lincoln Continental, a Talbot with bodywork by Figoni & Falaschi, a Cord, a Mercedes-Benz SS and a Bentley. The Cisitalia, whose body was designed by Pininfarina, soon found its way into the Museum's permanent collection, where it was much later followed by a Formula 1 Ferrari racing car and, in 1996, by a Jaguar E-type, a car whose sensual, feline beauty makes 1960s sculpture look ham-fisted.

1947 CISITALIA 202 1100

"I want that line to have a Duflunky, to come across, have a little hook in it, and then do a Rashoom or a Zong" – Harley Earl

Drexler's description of the Cisitalia remains a classic of formal analysis as applied to industrial design. In the following passage at least as much aesthetic meaning is extracted from a motor car as from, say, a David Smith sculpture.

Drexler writes: '[Its] body is slipped over its chassis like a dust-jacket over a book…the openings Farina cuts into the jacket provide some of the most skillfully contrived details of automobile design… to maintain the sculptural unity of the entire shape, its surfaces are never joined with sharp edges, but are instead wrapped around and blunted. The door is minimised. The back of the car, particularly the fender, is lifted at an angle rising from the strict horizontal baseline which gives stability to the design. Thus, both ends of the car gain an extraordinary tension, as though its metal skin did not quite fit over the framework and had to be stretched into place. This accounts, in part, for that quality of animation which makes the Cisitalia seem larger than it is.'

No-one doubts cars are among the most moving objects we possess, that they are a defining expression of contemporary culture. But what of the designer? Can the designer claim the status of an artist? Like rock music and movies, car design is an essentially collaborative activity. Like rock music and movies, it is an industrial activity too complex for any individual to claim the sort of authorship which defines conventional notions of art. Harley Earl could not even draw; instead by a process of critique and recommendation (some say intimidation) this extraordinary man saw his thoughts realised in metal. One of Earl's most memorable pieces of creative direction to his studio was: 'I want that line to have a duflunky, to come across, have a little hook in it, and then do a Rashoom or a Zong.'

George Walker, the designer responsible for the '49 Ford, said you had to give credit not just to him, but to the 900 others involved. Car design is a great art form and typical of the century that gave rise to it because it is industrial and collaborative. Car designers are not necessarily great thinkers like Charles Eames or Walter Gropius, nor even great salesmen like Raymond Loewy. The universal appeal of the car makes philosophy redundant and the manufacturers have their own separate sales forces. Instead, car designers are allowed an unusual amount of concentration. Accordingly, they have developed a design language that leaves few unmoved and turned the automobile into something powerfully evocative of ideas and beliefs.

Against the visual drama and emotional appeal and collective effort of a 1964 Ford Mustang, much fine 'art' coming from individual painters' studios or 'craft' from potters' wheels seems thin or solipsistic stuff. The ordinary car is part of civilization's continuing quest for accessible meaning and beauty. As Barthes said, cars are, "The supreme creation of an era conceived with passion by unknown artists and consumed in image, if not in usage, by a whole population which appropriates them as a purely magical object".

Profiles of the Most Influential Cars.

"All cars look the same these days." Well, in fact, they always have. Line up an Austin, a Ford, a Standard and a Vauxhall from the mid-1930s, dim the lights, and you'd be hard pressed to tell them apart. But there have been firsts, cars – not just motor show specials, but cars you could actually buy – that set the trend all others followed, cars that were flattered by imitation but, perhaps, the landmark importance of which is long-forgotten. Here are the most significant, epoch-making car body designs from 1945 until 1969 – with credits to the men whose pencils made them strokes of styling genius. By Giles Chapman.

KAISER FRAZER SEDAN, 1946, BY HOWARD DARRIN.

New era, new company, new car – when the Second World War ended, Kaiser turned from making warships to motor cars, and employed Darrin to style them. His 1946 four-door sedan, undoubtedly slab-sided, set the scene for a new generation. Any suggestion of 'mudguards', separate wings, free-standing bonnet or any other carriage throwbacks were banished. This was full-width, 'pontoon' styling at its most brutal – much copied in Europe, most openly by Fiat and Singer.

FERRARI 166 BARCHETTA, 1947, BY CARLO ANDERLONI.

Imagine the impact this lithe, purposeful two-seater made in an age when Americans were snapping up MG TDs as the 'latest thing'. Almost certainly the personal work of Anderloni, elusive house stylist at Italian coachbuilder Touring, the sculpted contours and clever swage line (breaks up the 'little boat' side profile), really were the last word in simple beauty. AC's Ace and Cobra owe their inspiration to Anderloni's clear thinking but are altogether more clumsy.

CISITALIA 202 1100, 1947, BY GIOVANNI SOVUNUZZI AT PININFARINA.

The first GT of all, and quite stunningly beautiful for its day – and now. Sovunuzzi was at Fiat when he actually sketched his first ideas, finally seeing them come to fruition when he moved to Pininfarina. Details of the car were taken up in cars as diverse as the Bentley Continental and the Porsche 356.

ALFA ROMEO GIULIA SPRINT, 1954, BY FRANCO SCAGLIONE AT BERTONE.

This was the car that brought show car glamour and styling drama to the public at an affordable price…and saved Bertone from financial doom. Thousands were made until 1962. Scaglione's finest hour was spent in successfully uniting a 'straight-through' wingline with a teardrop shape, yet still allowing the car to be a practical and affordable GT.

CHRYSLER 300, 1955, BY VIRGIL EXNER.

As well as being a closet supercar in its performance, Exner's clean, lean but barrel-sided saloon – Chrysler's prestige model at the time – was also an exceptionally clean shape, especially when compared to the chromium excesses of contemporary Cadillac and Lincoln rivals. As the years went by, though, the 300 put on weight and decorative flab, and the original 300, the inspiration for such cars as the Volvo Amazon, Rover 3-litre and Peugeot 403, became a forgotten innovator.

BMW 507, 1955, BY ALBRECHT GOERTZ.

The patrician Austrian count designed a mere handful of cars including the Datsun 240Z but his first, this two-seater BMW, is perhaps his finest. That the car was a bit of a Hollywood special disguised the fact its proportions were beautifully balanced – the nose was still being copied a decade later for cars like the Iso Grifo.

LOTUS 7, 1957, BY COLIN CHAPMAN.

Lotus went back in time for the 7, to the days when a road car's bodywork was only there for the most practical of reasons – to clad the guts of the beast just lightly enough for the purpose. The fact that Chapman's budget sports-racer's handling was from a different – lighteningly quick – planet to pre-war sports car made its basic looks, with prominent headlamps and cycle-type wings, all the more acceptable to sports car lovers. It's still very much with us.

JAGUAR MK II, 1959, BY WILLIAM LYONS.

It was the custom for Jaguar's boss to take the credit for his cars' looks. And while he probably didn't do the lot, his unerring eye for great lines was what made Jaguars look so good. For the Mk II, he was updating an older car, the Mk I, but his revisions to the cabin, wing line, front and rear, made the predecessor look like a slug in comparison. Chrysler aped the rounded curve of the cabin windows for its LH sedan 33 years on.

MINI, 1959, BY ALEC ISSIGONIS.

He'd have railed at the idea that he ever just 'styled' anything, of course, but Issigonis's shape, only there for its purpose of clothing what was then the most innovative, best handling and roomiest small car in the world, undoubtedly is a design classic in its body shape alone, nonetheless. Surprisingly, imitators were few, Honda getting closest with its N360 and N600 – but they were rear-engined and cramped, which must have made Issigonis smile wryly.

CHEVROLET CORVAIR, 1960, BY NED NICKLES FOR BILL MITCHELL AT GM.

The Corvair may have been the scapegoat for an anti-Detroit safety onslaught but its simple shape, with a prominent styling 'waist' running all round the body and a deeply wrapped-around rear window, inspired a generation of car stylists in 1960s Europe; just look at the NSU Prinz, Hillman Imp, Fiat 1500 and 2100, Simca 1000…

STUDEBAKER AVANTI, 1962, BY RAYMOND LOEWY.

The car's profile gives you some idea of the futuristic details the flamboyant industrial designer incorporated into his asymmetrical '62 sports car. There was the outline of that famous Coke bottle to the side, 'leaned back' wheelarches, and a nose with all the modern crispness of a classic American fridge of the period. And you can spot a Peugeot 205 right there in the centre. Little bits of the Avanti cropped up in dozens of car in the following two decades.

JEEP WAGONEER, 1963, BY BROOKS STEVENS.

Never exactly beautiful, the chunky Wagoneer really did define the boxy, macho shape that today we take for granted (or sneer at) in the Range Rover, Mitsubishi Shogun, Isuzu Trooper and a whole raft of American terrain-busters from the Ford Bronco to the Chevy Blazer. At the time it was the most car-like 4x4 you could get, and it's helped make these kind of vehicles, together with pick-ups, easily outsell 'ordinary' cars in the US each year. Proving the longevity of the design, this is a 1984 edition.

RENAULT 16, 1965, BY PHILIPPE CHARBONNEAUX.

French 'two-box' cars (one 'box' for the engine and another for the passengers and their apparel) had been around for ages. Think of the Citroën 2CV and DS, the Renault 4CV and Peugeot 203. But the 16 not only made a virtue of its shape with a proper hatchback and folding rear seat, but gave French owners a little glamour with its razor-edged lines and thrust-forward stance. Not as big a seller as it might have been, nevertheless, it was a symbol: a practical car for the bourgeoisie. And Charbonneaux had been responsible for some of the most glorious of post-war coachbuilt French prestige cars.

OLDSMOBILE TORONADO, 1966, BY BILL MITCHELL.

The Olds Toronado was like no American car before it – there were no fins and chrome – and yet too few 1970s Stateside designs made use of its squeaky clean nose, flared wheelarches and neat, simple flanks. Today's big coupes derive more from it than their immediate predecessors – but that's almost three decades on.

NSU RO80, 1967, BY KLAUS LUTHE.

In these days of constantly good, modern saloon car designs, it would be difficult to repeat the impact caused by the Ro80. Never mind its fascinating rotary Wankel engineering, the looks, futuristic, sure, but never impractical, light, fluid and airy, made the Ro80 a true landmark. When the 'aerodynamic' Audi 100 appeared in 1982, it didn't appear to have progressed, the Ro80 is that good. And, remember, for four years it was in production at the same time as the Austin A60 Cambridge. Spooky!

AUSTIN-MORRIS 1100/1800 PROTOTYPES, 1968. BY LEONARDO FIORAVANTI AT PININFARINA.

If only BMC had made these superbly designed and practical machines instead of the embarrassing Allegro and Princess. Still, Fioravanti – whose latest masterpiece is the Ferrari 456GT – had the satisfaction of not seeing his hard work consigned to the wastepaper basket: both the small and large developments of a smooth-nosed, gracefully-sloped saloon were adopted, then adapted, and became the Citroën GS and CX respectively.

RELIANT SCIMITAR GTE, 1968, BY TOM KAREN AT OGLE.

A British innovation that sprang from a group of independent engineers and industrialists, plus Tom Karen's styling vision, this was the first ever 'sports estate,' meaning you could carry your sacks with a bit of sex. From a company that dealt with designing radios and truck cabs, the detail styling was quite something but the concept – widely aped by Volvo, Lancia, BMW, Lotus and Toyota – was what made a sometimes imperfect car a great one.

07|31

Great Pictures of

Great Cars

031

VOLKSWAGEN PARTS STACKED IN THE WOLFSBURG FACTORY

VOLKSWAGEN PARTS STACKED IN THE WOLFSBURG FACTORY

033

VOLKSWAGEN PARTS STACKED IN THE WOLFSBURG FACTORY

VOLKSWAGENS UNDER CONSTRUCTION IN THE WOLFSBURG FACTORY

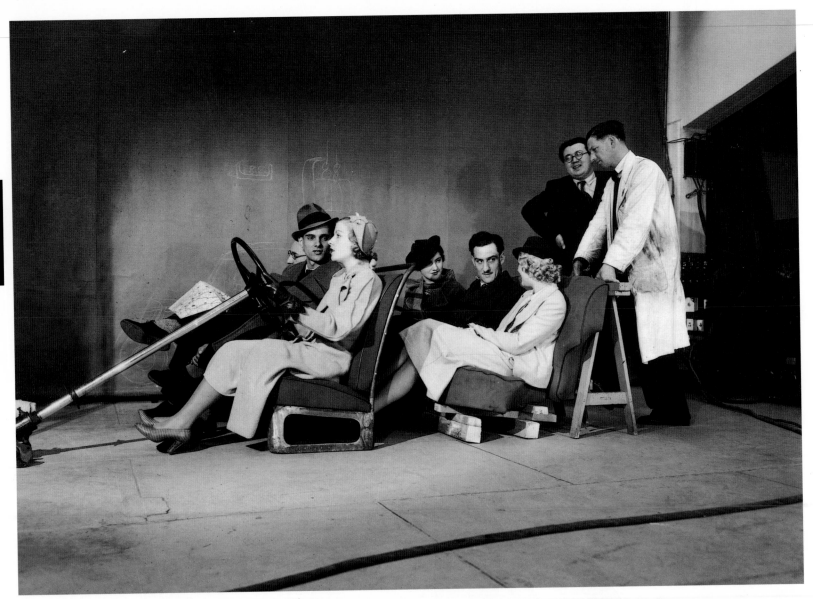

RENAULT SEATING MOCK-UP PHOTOGRAPHED BY ROBERT DOISNEAU IN 1936

MODEL OF THE 1951 BUICK LE SABRE SHOW CAR

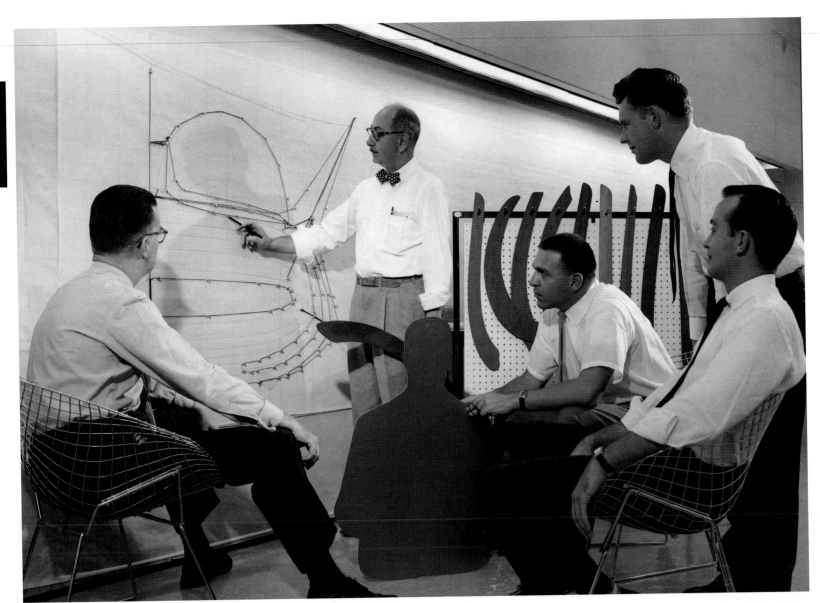

FISHER BODY DRAUGHTSMEN DISCUSS THE DESIGN OF THE GENERAL MOTORS FIREBIRD III SHOW CAR CIRCA 1957

FISHER BODY DRAUGHTSMAN AT WORK

GENERAL MOTORS DESIGNERS DISCUSS A BUICK BUMPER, CIRCA 1952

GM'S FIREBIRD 3 SHOW CAR UNDERGOING WIND TUNNEL TESTS

GM XP-39 FIREBIRD 3 SHOW CAR

PARIS SALON DE L'AUTO, 1955, WITH CARS WAITING TO BE UNVEILED

I think that cars today are almost the exact equivalents of the great gothic cathedrals. I mean the supreme creation of an era conceived with passion by unknown artists and consumed in image, if not in usage, by a whole population which appreciates them as a purely magical object.

Roland Barthes

1957

Over the years I have learned not to react too quickly when shocked by a design proposal. The very best designs, the freshest and most audacious, are often hard for a non-designer to integrate. Appreciating them takes 'soak time'.

Robert Lutz

Former President, Chrysler Corporation

1998

CONTEMPORARY EVOLUTIONARY

FORWARD REACHING INNOVATIVE

08|31

Art or Science?

Geoff Lawson, Design Director of Jaguar, Describes the Process of Car Design.

Michael Harvey

"Designing a car is like making a movie… Most of it ends up on the cutting room floor" – Geoff Lawson

→ The very first ideas come not, as you might expect, with the stroke of a pencil or magic marker, but with words. This is, you must understand, the very kernel of creation. Sure, suits will have talked to suits, put in place a plan, raised money and considered strategies. But until a design director sits down, scribbled notes in one hand, cigarette in the other and, with a small team of designers, plays around with those words, a new car remains an abstract notion.

This then is the very first meeting, the week-one, Monday morning 08.30 one. It's a prologue to one of the great industrial processes of our time; a process that once took a decade and now takes as little as two years; it is the starting gun for the collective endeavours of as many as 2000 men and women, of whom maybe only five per cent are designers.

"The board knew what kind of car the S-type was going to be. They had no idea what it should look like," says Geoff Lawson, director of design at Jaguar Cars for over 15 years. Large, likeable, and more laid back than any of his peers, be they the graduates of the Royal College of the 1970s who have dominated debate over car design since the 1980s, or the few studio chiefs the art school in Kensington has not fostered.

A graduate in furniture design from the RCA, Lawson is a passionate advocate of the designer as problem solver. To illustrate his argument he will lift a Fender Stratocaster off his office wall, or pull a replica Colt .45 out of a drawer. The design of either the guitar or the gun is a lesson in applied intelligence in Lawson's hands. Possessed of a beauty wholly dependent on their functionality, to Lawson, the man who creates Jaguars, these are as much about great designs of our time as any E-type or XK140.

"Until we began the process, the S-type was no more than 'a smaller, sportier saloon in a sector of the market we had not been in since the 1960s'. And that was understood, it wasn't a written brief. It doesn't begin to describe the car and that is deliberate; any more detail and there would be a danger of pushing a design in just one direction. That's not what we wanted at this stage. We don't want to approach any new design with our eyes already closed.

"So from that we all sit down together, probably about 12 of us, and we start to thrash out some of our own words to describe the car."

For the S-type that meant a series of themes. It's a process no different to any of the mainstream production cars Lawson has supervised the creation of – the current XJ8 and its earlier XJ6 derivatives, the XK8 and XKR. Five themes were chosen for the S-type, selected to encompass the range of emotions the new car should evoke.

JAGUAR S-TYPE SKETCH, DATED 1995

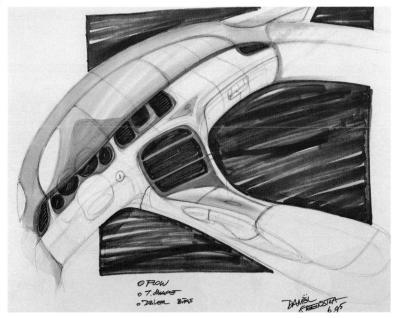

EARLY THOUGHTS FOR THE S-TYPE INTERIOR

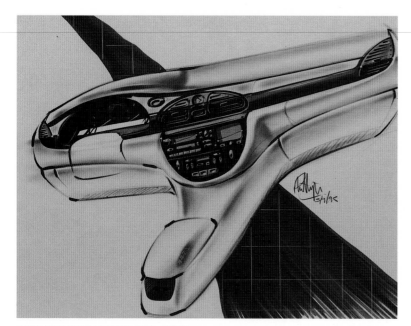

S-TYPE DASH DESIGN CLOSE TO FINAL CHOICE

S-TYPE REAR LIGHT CLUSTER

"We said, let's do one car that is evolutionary and takes its cue from the XJ," says Lawson. "Then we said let's do another, only this time let's take the XK as a lead. Then we said let's do one that captures some of the feel of the old Mk II. Since the BMW 5 Series was the main target for the car, we said let's look at that car and design a response. And finally, because we always do, we said let's just forget all that we know and do something that comes out of nowhere."

The latter is important. Jaguar's profile is evolutionary. The company's powerful sense of product identity comes from the relationship each new car has to its predecessors. That, however, must not be allowed to limit Jaguar's evolution. For one reason or another – mostly budgetary – Jaguar has never enjoyed the benefits of an advanced studio; a team dedicated exclusively to discovering future design directions for the company, through internal reviews and the public exhibition of 'concept' cars. So with each new car, Lawson encourages at least one design that takes the Jaguar shape out of the context of the past. "You can never tell what the right time might be to move on," he says.

With their themes agreed, there is an intensive six-week period of sketching. It is at this stage the collaborative process that is modern car design begins to show. Designers don't exactly finish each others' drawings, but they are encouraged to be cuckoos; everybody knows they will, at some stage, end up working together on one design. Now is not the time to be proud. There are 84 people working inside Jaguar's design department, roughly split into two teams. Within those teams it is almost impossible to detect one designer's signature on a vehicle.

Some companies, notably Jaguar's parent Ford, are already encouraging young designers to throw away their markers and sketch on screen. Lawson doesn't discourage his teams from using computers, but believes they are more useful later in the process.

No department inside Jaguar logs as much overtime as Lawson's. The sheer energy of the sketching stage is in itself remarkable, yet there is usually some consensus as to where to go next. The following step is to make full-sized models of all the developed themes in the soft, malleable clay whose aroma has pervaded design studios around the world since it was first used by the legendary General Motors designer Bill Mitchell in the 1950s. This, to Lawson's eye, is where the car really begins to appear.

"Sketches are only really useful for the graphics," says Lawson. To a designer, a car's graphics are the hard lines and shapes made on the surface of the vehicle by the headlamps and the grille, for example. Then there are the shut-lines of the doors, the bonnet and the boot; the DLO or day-light opening graphic made by the windows; the various horizontal lines along the side of a car, a feature line or swage line in the middle of the doors, the belt line across their top, or the cant line of the lower edge of the roof.

That the graphics should be the most powerful element to come out of the sketching stage should be no surprise. So many of the hard points of a modern car – the position of the base of the windscreen, the relationship of the doors to each other, for example – are pre-determined. It was no different with the S-type. This is platform technology at work and is nothing to be afraid of.

Platform technology is widely misunderstood. A 'platform' is not a physical thing. It is not some vast internal framework for a car that dictates the distance between its wheels, the overall length, the shape of the doors. A well-engineered platform need not limit the imagination of the designers, leaving them with no more scope than a seamstress charged with tailoring a ready-made suit to better fit an individual. Such thinking is already 15 years out of date.

No, platforms are an abstract notion based more around manufacturing requirements than engineering. Building a factory in which to assemble a new car is roughly two-thirds of the cost of any new car programme. A platform, then, is a selection of key components which cars can share, thus enabling them to be built more economically by using similar manufacturing technology. It is a good thing. Many of the modern icons of the road are built on shared platforms. The S-type in one of them.

It is relevant because of the way Jaguar builds its clay models.

"Designing a car is like making a movie. You might see two hours of movie, but they shot two years of film. Most of it ends up on the cutting room floor," says Lawson. For Jaguar, this means tightly controlling the process so as not to waste time later. In terms of the clay models, 90 per cent of those built are feasible. "What's the point," asks Lawson, "in creating something that looks fantastic, but which you know will have to change somewhere down the line because there's only room for a couple of very small children in the back?"

JAGUAR DESIGNERS DEFINE S-TYPE PROFILE

So Jaguar clays look like real Jaguars. They are built around an imaginary three-dimensional frame that includes all the hard points the real production car will share with its platform cousins. And there's more. Clay Jaguars have normal-sized wheels on normal-sized tyres with normal-sized gaps between the tyre and the bodywork. (Increasing the size of the wheel or reducing the size of the clearance has a dramatic impact on the look of a vehicle since, from the side, 25 per cent of what you see is wheel and tyre.) Designers use Dinoc, a heavy plastic coating, to cover the clay and simulate the look of a painted silver surface. Black Dinoc is applied to the DLO of the clay to simulate the window openings.

Information technology is forcing its way into the process relentlessly, and particularly dramatically, in the review stage. The Ford Puma was seen and approved in the US on the basis of a virtual, three-dimensional model projected on to a screen for managers to review. The car was created in the UK. The software used by Ford and others is so powerful it can not only render a lifelike, full-sized image of a car on a screen, with all the play of light and shadow that makes surfaces work or fail, but can also rotate the image, so viewers have the notion of walking around the vehicle.

It is not to Lawson's taste, nor one suspects particularly appropriate for Jaguar, although the door to IT is wide open at Jaguar's design centre. The collaboration that is intrinsic to designing a modern car means that from the very earliest stages – as soon as there's a shape in three dimensions – all information is shared, digitally, with internal departments and external suppliers. For example, the Japanese company that builds Jaguar's press tools can tell, immediately, if a headlamp eyebrow is technically achievable. Similarly, the lighting supplier can fast-prototype a new design of lamp, so it can be fitted to the clay the following day.

But we are getting ahead of ourselves. The creation of a full-sized clay model is a remarkable act of alchemy. Modellers, the unsung heroes of the process, are charged with turning two dimensions into three. Few designers – although Lawson is not one of them – will go near a clay model or the modeller's kit of knives and scrapers. With only his imagination to go on, it is the modeller's lot to interpret a designer's sketches. It is, once again, a collaborative process, the designer working with the modeller to develop and redevelop surfaces. But make no mistake, it is the modeller that fills the sheets of steel that cover a Jaguar with tension and life. "Clay never gets added to a Jaguar," says Lawson. "We only ever take it off."

051

FULL-SIZE S-TYPE IN JAGUAR'S DESIGN STUDIO

S-TYPE MODEL WITH ALTERNATIVE NOSE TREATMENT

S-TYPE STYLING MODEL CLOSE TO REALITY

It's something that has a great tradition at Jaguar. "It is so important to me that Jaguar surfaces actually look like they are fabricated in steel and not some sort of plastic material," says Lawson. "That's such an important part of the Jaguar character." Lawson is, in one sense, only the second design director Jaguar has had since the company's founder and *de facto* design director Sir William Lyons was completely involved in the process, up until his death in 1986.

"Sir William never used clay," says Lawson, who was greatly respected by the autocratic old man. "He would get panelbeaters to knock the shape out of tin instead. And these are shapes like the XK140 and the E-type, don't forget…"

It is a testament to the impact and lasting beauty of the E-type – the product of Lyons' judgement and Malcolm Sayer's largely cod aerodynamic science. But would you describe its design as art or science?

Lawson is under no illusions: it boils down to problem-solving initiative and good judgement – 10 per cent inspiration and 90 per cent perspiration. He doesn't agree with the notion, expounded by the Mannerists during the Renaissance, that a sculpture already lay within a block of marble and it was the artist's job to find it. Car design is no less inspirational, yet it remains rooted in the mundane.

"It's why criticism never bothers me," says Lawson. "I'm neutral to the point of not caring. It's the same with most of the older guys. We do our best within a constraining process. Invariably, when some aspect of a design is criticised you've been aware of the problem for two years or more. By that stage you only see what's wrong with it. You might regret not fighting harder. You know you've tried everything you can to make it go away, but for some manufacturing, budgetary or ergonomic reason, it has not been possible. So you tend to be more resigned than hurt."

For Lawson, and one suspects he speaks for all contemporary automotive designers, the only critic that really matters is the customer. It might not be what inspired his generation to design cars in the first place, but it is what the job is about. In that sense, car design is most definitely a science and not an art. Like the Fender or the Colt, the S-type is a success because its beauty lies in its ability to consistently perform over and above an owner's expectations, rather than provoke passion in passers-by.

And yet Lawson is happy to admit, with regard to the E-type, exhibited at the Museum of Modern Art, that "to be involved with a design project that is perceived as art would give greater personal satisfaction than anything that could ever be written." The spirit of the artist, at least, still survives then. At Jaguar, anyway.

"The only critic
that really matters
is the customer" –
Geoff Lawson

RADICAL LOOK DECIDED AGAINST FOR S-TYPE PRODUCTION

053

DESIGN PROCESS EVOLUTION FOR DEFINITIVE S-TYPE SHAPE

09|31

Art or Science?
Product Planners
and Production Engineers
Describe the Process
of Car Design
Keith Howard

ROVER 75 VIRTUAL BODY-IN-WHITE ASSEMBLY

JAGUAR S-TYPE BODY-IN-WHITE ASSEMBLY
BEING COMPUTER-GENERATED

JAGUAR S-TYPE ENGINE ASSEMBLY

JAGUAR S-TYPE PROTOTYPE

→ Artist or artisan? In the world of fine arts, the distinction is essentially meaningless. The painter paints, the sculptor sculpts, and their skills of execution become as integral a part of the finished work as its underlying conception.

Industrial design in general, and car design in particular, is fundamentally different. The final object is a piece of engineering that must meet stringent performance requirements, set by either an ever more demanding consumer or, increasingly, an ever more insistent legislator. So the functions of conceptualisation (appearance design) and realisation (engineering and manufacture) are inevitably distinct.

You could infer from this that car designers and car engineers live in detached ivory towers without so much as an interconnecting door between them. But that's a fanciful view, old-fashioned at best. The compression of car development cycles that has taken place in recent years, coupled with ever sterner require-ments to produce better products, has actually caused the design and engineering processes to become more integrated than ever. Simultaneous engineering is what the industry calls it: the progression of a project along many parallel paths rather than sequentially, one step at a time. It isn't only engineering that's involved, however: styling is caught up in the process too.

In fact, the first three-dimensional model of a new car, whether displayed on a CAD screen or moulded from clay, acts as an important catalyst to the whole engineering team. Richard Woolley, studio director at Rover Cars Design, had overall responsibility for the appearance design of the new Rover 75. He says of the process: "As the design progresses it gains its own momentum of inputs from other areas within the business. A 2D sketch you may only share with your peers in the design group. You don't really get engineering or any other input until you've something in three dimensions. Then a dialogue starts up – a broad brush dialogue at first but it becomes more specific as the 3D model matures. It's almost like an input to the design brief itself. As soon as the design becomes tangible – you can look at it and talk about it – that crystallises people's thoughts."

Engineering involvement, far from waiting in the wings while the appearance design is refined, is on stage from the earliest scenes. "Working alongside the designers are a team of concept engineers to give you guidance. A typical question might be: How much bumper coverage will I need on the car to pass the low speed impact test and ensure a good insurance rating? They might say start off with 50 or 60mm. Then as we get a better idea of the finished weight of the car we may have to increase that or may be able to reduce it a little. That dialogue happens continuously on any number of design issues."

THE VIRTUAL ROVER 75

JAGUAR S-TYPE PROTOTYPE WATER TESTING

Alan Elliot, manager of Manufacturing Engineering at Jaguar, who was part of the development team for the new S-type, describes the process as coming to the design table with a list of needs and wants. "If you were in total control of the design and development of the car, what would you put in it to make life easier for you? If the car was square, had no feature lines and snapped together like a big Airfix kit, that would be first prize for a manufacturing man like me, but from a stylist's point of view it would be a nightmare. From a manufacturing viewpoint I'd also like there to be modular assemblies where possible so that instead of spending time putting bits together I can bolt a big lump to the vehicle. But my service colleague wants the opposite because, were a part to fail during ownership, he wants to be able to offer the smallest, most cost-effective replacement part. So when a multi-functional design team gets together you immediately have a variety of requirements which conflict."

And who acts as referee? "You have a programme manager who acts as arbitrator, having listened to everyone's point of view."

Simply making the car manufacturable is the first engineering concern. "The issues that need to be resolved are gaps between panels, the shape of panels, whether there are contours that are impossible to press. A shape might look pretty on the clay but you have to think: If I press that in metal, can I get it off the tool? Alignment of and relationship between panels is important, too. On the S-type, for example, we have a rather large plastic front end and lots of styling feature around the headlamps. At the initial design stage you have to ask: what are the manufacturing tolerances we can expect from the sheet metal and the plastic injection moulding? And what can the headlamp supplier deliver? This way you evolve a shape that's feasible to make. The next stage is: We know we can make it but how are we going to join all the bits together?"

Iteratively, a point is reached where the initial design satisfies at least the needs of everyone around the table, if not all their wants, at which juncture the engineering input becomes more heavyweight. Richard Woolley again: "Once we have a working clay model we are persuaded by our aerodynamics colleagues to take it up to the wind tunnel to get the first feeling for what the aerodynamic behaviour of the car will be in terms of drag, lift and crosswind stability. Because clay is a medium that works best in a temperature-controlled environment, taking it up to the wind tunnel and blasting October air over it at high speed is not something we relish doing because it damages the clay somewhat. So we try to do it early in the programme so that any damage can be repaired in good time."

What happens next depends on whether the 3D design has been done 'on the tube', using computer aided design (CAD) software, or in the traditional way by sculpting a full-size clay model. In the former case, a digital description of the car's surface already exists; in the latter, it has to be generated in a process called digitisation.

"There are various ways of defining the shape of the clay. You can use a physical contact probe that actually touches the clay surface, or a non-contact laser probe can be used, instead. Either will give you x,y,z coordinates for each measurement point. Where a lot of information is required - at a panel junction, for instance - a lot of data is taken. Whereas if you have a fairly planar surface you can take measurements every 50mm or so. Typically you'll have about 6-7000 points in total. Generally, you only have to digitise one side of the car, of course, except where you've taken the opportunity to look at two subtly different styles on either side of the clay. Sometimes we do that to save producing two separate models."

The supplier knows your expectations in terms of dimensional control and functionality and puts testing in place to ensure they are met. Part of the prototype build phase includes a fit and function assessment.

FRONT SUSPENSION AND HYDROFORMED SUB-FRAME

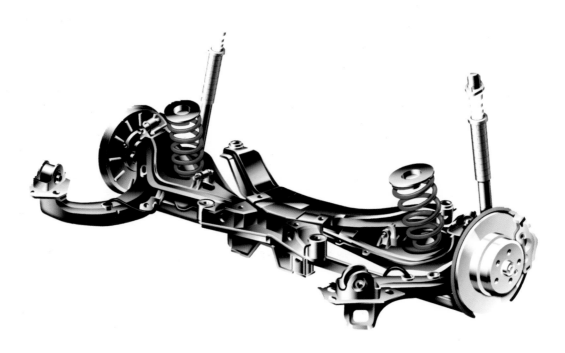

ROVER 75 REAR SUSPENSION, INCLUDING Z-AXLE

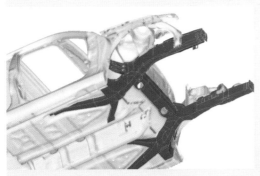

ROVER 75 FRONT LONGERONS USE LASER-WELDED
BLANKS TO ABSORB FRONT END IMPACTS

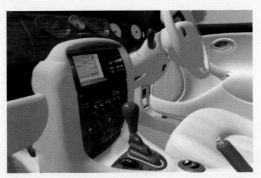

ROVER 75 VIRTUAL INTERIOR WITH SATELLITE NAVIGATION

JAGUAR S-TYPE PROTOTYPE PAVE-TESTING

Once the digitised data has been converted into a full CAD surface model – a process which typically takes six to eight weeks – engineering can begin to take a hard look at the mechanical performance of the body using computer-based simulation tools. "Structural elements of the car – sill sections, pillar sections – will have been looked at fairly early but once we've a working three-dimensional design we are happy with we can build a finite element model of the car in the computer to check its stiffness and crash performance. As a result of that you may have to incorporate some extra strength in the car. A good example of that would be windscreen pillars or door sills having to be stiffened, or sometimes made less stiff, which can affect the outward appearance of the car."

With the car's surfaces now digitised, further full-size or scale models can be machined as required from foam or hard resin, for example, to allow more detailed development by the aerodynamics team.

Engineers from the manufacturing side also take a keen interest, particularly in any complex panel forms. "The press tool people will want to know whether the panel will hold its shape after pressing long enough for it to be welded to other parts. Spring-back in the panel is also taken into account so that when the part emerges from the press it will relax into the final form we want. A roof panel is a good example of that. A lot of this analysis is done using CAD today, whereas in the past we relied on people's experience."

As Alan Elliott says: "There's a lot of simultaneous activity in simultaneous engineering," all of which is fed back into the car's detailed design. By about 18 months before Job One – the first production car – is due to roll off the production line, a design freeze is imposed. A meeting of all the groups involved in the car's development – design, aerodynamics, manufacturing, costing, marketing – agrees to 'sign off' the design for production.

Now the key component suppliers, many of whom have been involved in the design process from an early stage, can begin to make pre-production tooling. Major car-makers today insist their principal suppliers use the same CAD tools as them, so everyone involved can work from the same master database of dimensional information. By now the appearance designer's job ought to be finished, but even after design freeze there may be engineering-related styling issues to resolve. Richard Woolley: "When suppliers get into the nitty-gritty of tooling they may encounter problems when taking first shots from the tool which require an aesthetic design change. Even at the tail end of the development process on the 75 I'm still involved gathering feedback from early users of test-build cars, which again may require some small changes. As you approach volume production, though, the changes become smaller and smaller."

Assembly of the car is the focus of attention now, but once again it's an issue that's been addressed from much earlier in the project. Alan Elliott: "In the early days of the S-type programme we selected 10 assembly guys and brought them into the planning team. We called them Product Specialists. They know more than anyone about the problems of doing a repetitive assembly job 25 times an hour, eight hours a day. It was a bit of a culture shock for them but they soon settled in. They went around the different programme activity teams, wherever the need was greatest, to give their opinion on asembly issues.

"I've already stated my desire for modularity but there's an optimum size of sub-assembly above which the thing becomes unmanageable. So items like the instrument panel will be modelled on computer. Can I get it through the door aperture? Can I then fix it in position? All those issues are checked on the tube long before you ever build the part. Then we try out the procedure during a prototype build phase, using a lift assister – a counter-balanced lifting device which the operator helps develop. All this has to be part of the early development programme. It's no good getting to the end of the process and then identifying an ergonomic issue in assembly – it's an up-front consideration."

JAGUAR S-TYPE FINAL BODY ASSEMBLY

JAGUAR S-TYPE IS MATED TO ITS DRIVETRAIN

JAGUAR S-TYPE ASSEMBLY

"We have a predefined series of prototype builds during which we also write the process sheet – the instruction booklet which tells the operator how to put the car together. We validate both this and the prototype parts during the prototype builds. From that process we'll identify a number of issues and put corrective action in place. As the tooling is developed and refined and the parts become more and more representative of production, the prototype engineer backs off and the production engineer moves in. There's a progressive handover to the people who will be building the car in volume."

A key aspect of modern car production is the use of just-in-time (JIT) component delivery, direct to the side of the production line. Warehousing of components is a thing of the past, an unnecessary expense. "Reducing inventory is of paramount importance to us. We have notionally two to four hours' worth of materials on site, that's all. You have to get your suppliers on board early, give them a robust schedule – delivery every two to four hours – and then they can develop their manufacturing processes around our requirements. There are large cost-saving opportunities for them too."

Thought also has to be given at an early stage to transport issues inherent in the JIT manufacturing system. In the case of Jaguar's Castle Bromwich factory, where the S-type is assembled, a new road – the A47 Birmingham Heartlands Spine Route – had to be built in conjunction with the local authority to accommodate the increased volume of traffic travelling to and fro.

Because there's no warehousing at the factory there can be no test and inspection of incoming parts - modern production practice expects them to be 100 per cent right on arrival. "The idea that you should test parts as they come into the plant is archaic. The supplier knows your expectations in terms of dimensional control and functionality and puts testing in place to ensure they are met. Part of the prototype build phase includes a fit and function assessment. The component is assembled to the car at simulated line speed to check that it fits where it's supposed to and does what it's supposed to do.

"Personally, I've tried to stop using the word 'test' altogether – it implies you don't quite know what you are going to find. I encourage people to use the word 'validation' instead. You know what's going to come out at the end because you put your process controls in place months before you started production. There are going to be no nasty surprises, and just to give myself a warm feeling here's the validation that confirms it. You're designing for quality, not selecting or adjusting for it after something's assembled. In today's car industry it's a given that things will work correctly, it's not discretionary."

'Train hard, fight easy', said Marshal Zhukov. In the intense fight for survival that characterises today's car industry, it would make a highly appropriate motto.

ROVER 75 POWERTRAIN AND SUSPENSION

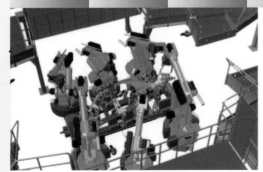

ROVER 75 VIRTUAL ASSEMBLY LINE

COMPUTERS TESTED ROVER 75 MANUFACTURING TECHNIQUES
PRIOR TO BUILDING THE PRODUCTION LINE

VIRTUAL SYSTEMS ENSURE ROVER 75 LINE OPERATORS
CAN WORK WITH MINIMAL PHYSICAL STRAIN

10|31

0

What Inspires
Car Designers?
Russell Bulgin

Inspiration? These guys have it in abundance. Pre-packaged, left-field, intuitive, emotional, rational, radical, off (this, that or) the (other) wall – this is the stuff from which tomorrow's cars spring.

Ask these 10 questions of 10 designers and they deliver 100 slivers of what makes them tick, from a one-word answer to the odd pocket treatise, some funny, most wise, a few just plain out there.

Yet these responses are unified by intelligence and passion (plus a deeply-held dislike of penny-pinching suits lodged high in the corporate ziggurat).

Cars have never been better than they are today: in quality, concept and in slicing the world into fine niches which were off the radar just five years ago. Car design became much more sharply realised as this decade stretched out.

Read these answers to find out why that's no surprise.

01 _ Is there one particular object, item or thing which has directly inspired a car design – or part of a car design – of yours?

02 _ Where should a designer look for inspiration – and is this an intellectual or an emotional process?

03 _ Are there any key non-automotive products which you find yourself referring back to?

04 _ What's the first product you can remember being impressed by as a child?

05 _ Referring to an inspiration – or ripping it off? What's the difference?

06 _ Are there any records or songs which inspired you?

07 _ What kind of work environment fosters inspiration?

08 _ What absolutely fails to inspire you?

09 _ What's the most inspirational advice you have received?

10 _ What is the least inspirational piece of car design you have ever seen?

GUGGENHEIM MUSEUM

PINKY LAI,
DESIGN MANAGER, PORSCHE AG, STUTTGART.
RCA GRADUATE 1980. RESPONSIBLE FOR EXTERIOR
DESIGN/PORSCHE 996 COUPE, CABRIO AND TURBO
DESIGNER/BMW 3-SERIES E36

01 _ Modern sculptures and animal forms inspired my college projects – they still play a major role in inspiring my work.

02 _ I always pick up most of my ideas while out running – maybe that's why I became a passionate marathon runner after discovering the 'runner's high'… I see nature inspiring contemporary car design, modern design and architecture around the world.

03 _ Basketball shoes, running shoes, ski-boots and sports gear have a very strong emotional and design impact on me. Occasionally, architecture makes me feel lost in an unknown time and dimension – the Guggenheim museum in Bilbao took my breath away, instantly.

04 _ The Peak Tram in Hong Kong; the Morris Minor; old Mercedes-Benz 190, especially with the strong plastic smell from transparent seat covers; elevators and escalators.

05 _ Inspiration can be linked to good interpretation – whereas a rip-off has no interpretation.

06 _ My top album for years has been *As falls Wichita so falls Wichitafalls* by Pat Metheny.

07 _ I don't find the work environment inspirational – inspiration is a very personal experience. At work I focus on a 'shopping list' of themes and features I put together while running, sketching them on paper or on the workstation.

08 _ Technical and management meetings fail to inspire me.

09 _ No answer.

10 _ No answer.

DAVID WOODHOUSE, 30, ASSISTANT CHIEF DESIGNER,
CONCEPT VEHICLES, GENERAL MOTORS NORTH
AMERICAN OPERATIONS, ENGLAND.
RCA GRADUATE 1992 DESIGNER/MGF SUPERSPORTS
CONCEPT CAR DESIGNER/MGF EXE BONNEVILLE RECORD
CAR EXTERIOR DESIGNER/LAND-ROVER FREELANDER
DESIGNER/LAND ROVER MEGACITY CAB, *JUDGE DREDD*
MOVIE

01 _ Those sinister and intimidating ice hockey helmets for the stance and face of the MegaCity Cab.

02 _ Sources of inspiration are unlimited – auto heritage, architecture, product design, fashion, jewellery, plus natural forms and science fiction from Jules Verne to *Gattaca*. Inspiration is essentially emotional, the usefulness of the product intellectual.

03 _ Aircraft, fish, watches, race cars and, in particular, transformer toys.

04 _ Meccano, Lego… the Ferrari Dino 246.

05 _ It's in the execution, the cleverness of interpretation.

06 _ Blur's *Song 2* for the MGF SuperSports concept car.

07 _ The RCA was the most inspirational environment I've experienced – mixing with other art and design disciplines. Most car company environments are very poor.

08 _ Sadly, most mass-produced cars of the last three decades, with few exceptions. Why don't they reflect show cars and design studies more closely?

09 _ "To attempt to challenge, surprise and have as much fun with work as possible." Luigi Colani.

10 _ Far too many to count – the fault of conservative companies and their bean-counters

A WIND-UP GRAMOPHONE

MORRIS COMMERCIAL J-TYPE

HANS-HARALD HANSON, 43, GENERAL MANAGER/
DIRECTOR DAIMLER-BENZ ADVANCED DESIGN ITALIA.
RCA GRADUATE 1984

01 _ No.

02 _ Both. Intellectually, you should look at trends
in products, furniture and customer needs;
emotionally, you might get inspired by fashion,
people, nature or just an empty white room.

03 _ All designs by Phillipe Starck.

04 _ Driving in a neighbour's Mercedes-Benz and
seeing that long hood with the star in the middle.

05 _ No idea.

06 _ I feel quite creative with classical music.

07 _ Clean, ordinary, nothing unnecessary.

08 _ Too much noise.

09 _ Sitting in an empty room.

10 _ The Lancia Dialogos.

FERGUS POLLOCK, 49, PROJECT MANAGER, STYLING
DEPARTMENT, JAGUAR CARS. RCA GRADUATE 1975
WORKED ON/JAGUAR XKR AND XK8. WORKED
ON/CITROËN CX AND AX. WORKED ON/CHRYSLER
SUNBEAM, ALPINE AND AVENGER. WORKED
ON/CHRYSLER SUPERVAN

01 _ Through college I was obsessed with the
Morris Commercial J-type van. When I returned
from the US, the idea of a one-box people-carrier
– which became the Renault Espace – was
developed. Really, it was my schoolboy crush on
the J-type, and a bit of lateral thinking.

02 _ Initially, of course, it's emotional – like being
drawn to a beautiful woman. But I don't think you
get inspiration: that tends to be 10 per cent of the
equation while the rest is perspiration, working on
details.

03 _ Simple, beautiful objects you love can be the
backdrop – but you don't 'use' them cold. It's
more a collective appreciation of form and design
which you apply as honestly as possible.

04 _ My brother's Austin-Healey 100/4, running
on Castrol R: every sense worked overtime to
keep pace with that lovely car

05 _ A Ferrari GTO versus a Ford Focus – the
latter is a Fiat Tipo jigsaw with three pieces
upside down.

06 _ None.

07 _ Solitude for original thinking and the buzz of
an animated studio for speed with resolution.

08 _ Nothing.

09 _ "You'll never be any good as long as you've
got a hole in your arse"

10 _ 'Least inspired' is doing an injustice to the
language – it has to be the unbearably bog-awful
Fiat Multipla

GILES TAYLOR, 31, PRINCIPAL STYLIST, JAGUAR CARS.
RCA GRADUATE 1992. DESIGN AND PRODUCTION
DEVELOPMENT/CITROËN XSARA SCALE CONCEPT
MODEL/CITROËN C3 CONCEPT CAR

01 _ The shape of the Citroën Xsara exterior door
handles is taken from the hard rubber Ace pocket
comb – a design classic which was simply
enlarged for the car. I bought one in LA in 1990
and thought its simple, recognisable shape went
well with the exterior graphics.

02 _ Fashion, shoes, domestic furniture and
appliances for visual forms which consumers
associate with progress, quality and reliability. A
specific feel should be intrinsic to shapes and
forms in automotive sculpting – computer-aided
design can remove the ability to relate to a 3D
object at human scale during its development.

03 _ Architecture: Frank Lloyd Wright interiors,
New York's Chrysler building, Lord's Pavilion.
Watches. Military design – engineering for
function. I own an ex-RAF lightweight Land-Rover
for its thorough honesty of form.

04 _ A replica Colt .45 cap gun: for its smell,
noise, weight, shiny metal, tactile qualities…
Nothing to do with killing, of course.

BARCELONA (GAUDI'S LA SAGRADA FAMILIA)

05 _ Totally original creativity is rare – and all auto designers subconsciously absorb stuff all the time, often coupled with the phrase 'the head-lamps are too small…' If shapes are totally recognisable from another product, it's a rip-off and shows a lack of vision and passion.

06 _ None.

07 _ An open environment, with debate and open critique. Competitiveness to be encouraged only when necessary.

08 _ Tight budgets – all those nice 'touchy' interior details are always too expensive. Most Japanese car interiors – bad plastic treatments, colours, and trim.

09 _ No answer.

10 _ No answer.

GRAHAM HULL, 47, CHIEF STYLIST ROLLS-ROYCE AND BENTLEY MOTOR CARS, CREWE. RCA GRADUATE 1971. CHIEF STYLIST/ROLLS-ROYCE SILVER SERAPH AND BENTLEY ARNAGE, CHIEF STYLIST/BENTLEY CONTINENTAL SC SEDANCA, CHIEF STYLIST/BENTLEY CONTINENTAL CHIEF STYLIST/PINNACLE ROLLS-ROYCE SILVER SPUR AND PINNACLE BENTLEY RT

01 _ Yacht aesthetics, I believe, are a fundamental part of Rolls-Royce body language. I looked to their stance and purity of line as an element of Silver Seraph. It is a shared manifestation of civilised man's expression.

02 _ It depends on the subject being designed. I see Rolls-Royce as a man-made artefact, hence the stainless steel model of a Greek temple on the front. Bentley is more of an organic machine – a thoroughbred horse, awesome predator or warrior. It is an intellectual process which establishes the design brief background to the design task.

03 _ I tend to like design at the extremes where compromise is minimal – aircraft are great for this, and boats. A racing bicycle is an icon of design beauty. Any tightly focused design brief inevitably leads to a convincing solution.

04 _ A wind-up gramophone at my grandfather's: sight, smell and sound equals an indelible sensory delight.

05 _ Maybe not a lot, but you can be inspired and reflect with affection or cynically exploit an idea.

06 _ Virtually anything with a melody, most classics and some electronic *Claire de lune* through The Beatles *Yes it is*; Keith Richards' *You've Got the Silver*; The Kinks *Waterloo Sunset*; Paul Brady's *The world is What you Make It*; and so on…

07 _ Any circumstance that lets you tap into the creative ether – low ambient noise with a personal choice of music is pretty good. It helps if there is an atmosphere of fun and permission to fail and, most of all, wise top management.

08 _ Programmes based on an unrealistic premise: 'inspiration will arrive in week 36…' Soul-less environments – such as barren town planning – with no recognition of the human spirit.

09 _ Peter Cambridge, an ex-Ford tutor at the Central School of Design, Holborn, who worked on the original Lotus Elite, showed me how art and engineering can be joined in 30 minutes talking through my boring mobile spray unit. Also 'never get too many feature lines meeting in the same place', and present really slick models.

10 _ The rear ends of Mercedes-Benz saloons demonstrate how hard it is to finish the thick end of the wedge in any three-box style. The outer corner of the front apron on the first Lexus makes me wince, especially in gold. I've always admired Ford's professionalism but prolonged exposure to the rear of a Scorpio can make me lose the will to live.

BRUCE SPRINGSTEEN

IAN CALLUM, 44, CHIEF DESIGNER, TWR DESIGN,
ENGLAND. RCA GRADUATE 1979
WORKED ON/ASTON MARTIN DB7. WORKED ON/ASTON
MARTIN PROJECT VANTAGE SHOW CAR. WORKED
ON/VOLVO C70. WORKED ON/FORD PUMA

01 _ My main reference to designing cars is generally my love and understanding of cars themselves. I enjoy all aspects of product design but my influences tend to be automotive.

02 _ Inspiration can come from anywhere and the more lateral-thinking designers can find it from the most obscure sources. I often try to think of random forms to see what evolves, but generally most of my design is evolutionary, driven by the need to simplify and strengthen rather than complicate.

03 _ I admire the simplicity and ingenuity of some products – this is often as a result of strong graphics and sensitive masses or forms such as Frank Lloyd Wright architecture or a Loewe television. In themselves they offer an inspiration of purity but little in specific references.

04 _ The first product I remember being aware of at a very young age was our Hoover and I thought how ugly it was – then seeing a Porsche 356 coupe and thinking how beautiful that was. My impression that car design is more masterly has remained.

05 _ Being inspired by something is being made aware that an object can be beautiful or have an emotional effect for certain reasons. It is these reasons that must be understood, translated and used – not the design itself.

06 _ Listening to music while working is inspirational – artists ranging from Captain Beefheart to Van Morrison. A couple of tracks from Bruce Springsteen usually works – *Born to Run* loosens the baggage!

07 _ A simple room, full of music, or a modelling studio full of good clay modellers.

08 _ Office environments are generally deadly. Not only are they distracting but impose behaviour patterns that are not conducive to creative work.

09 _ Never give up on the purity of the original thought. This requires tenacity and hard work – but it's worth it.

10 _ There are many cars that fall into this category but I nominate the first Ford Mondeo mainly because this was such an important product and lines our streets in thousands. It should have been more inspiring for its viewers. Every design should be the best it can be.

KENNETH MELVILLE, 39, DDI CHEF DE PROJECT,
RENAULT DESIGN, PARIS. RCA GRADUATE 1984. INTERIOR
DESIGNER/CITROËN ACTIVA CONCEPT CAR INTERIOR
DESIGNER/MERCEDES-BENZ SLK INTERIOR
DESIGNER/RENAULT CLIO 2 INTERIOR
DESIGNER/RENAULT ZO CONCEPT CAR

01 _ The interior of the ZO concept car was influenced by the animal world – in particular the scarab beetle.

02 _ A designer should look for inspiration every-where – in my opinion, the world is our inspiration. We cannot create in a vacuum and a designer chained to his drawing board will inevitably lack creativity.

03 _ There's not one product in particular – but architecture and fashion design are a strong influence.

04 _ Lego bricks – because I could create with them. It was a precursor to automotive styling clay.

05 _ Ripping off is taking an idea or a style and making a few changes to cover up the crime. Inspiration is taking the idea several steps further. It's a bit like the development of pop music styles – many bands built their careers on the success of the Beatles without ripping them off. The Beatles, however, sparked a new movement.

06 _ *Born to be Wild.*

07 _ An environment where there is mutual respect between designers and engineers.

08 _ Engineers with blinkers on.

09 _ 'The biggest risk in life is never to take risks' – Patrick Le Quément.

10 _ Second generation Ford Scorpio.

JUDGE DREDD LAND-ROVER

TONY HATTER, 44, DESIGNER, PORSCHE AG, STUTTGART
RCA GRADUATE 1981. DESIGNER/1993 PORSCHE 911
DESIGNER/1996 PORSCHE 911 GT1 DESIGNER/1997
PORSCHE 911 GT1 DESIGNER/1998 PORSCHE 911 GT1

01 _ I will admit to being inspired by certain sports cars of the 1950s and '60s – and not necessarily all Porsches. Italian design houses were prolific and influential in that period and I feel a mix of that feeling and traditional Porsche functionalism can be very rewarding.

02 _ This depends on the project – don't go to Le Mans to look for inspiration for a city car. The brief should be clear whether evolutionary traits or a certain style is required. Car designers are very narrow-sighted – I'm particularly badly afflicted by this – and it's important to be aware of what's happening in art and design.

03 _ I just love machines. Watches, or John Harrison's wooden maritime timepiece. Or an old machine shop where the lathes are driven from a central power source by leather belts. It's all fascinating to me.

04 _ My younger sister's tricycle. It had small-diameter, thick white tyres and looked just great compared to my thin-tyred bike.

05 _ One cannot help being influenced by others. A design evolves in a design department, intentionally or not, drawing on the influences of the whole department. I don't think anyone wants to rip off designs. Then again, I could name one Japanese luxury manufacturer…

06 _ Music is important to me, although the hectic studio atmosphere is not conducive to listening to music. Occasionally I can be absorbed listening to blues or jazz on headphones. Current favourite? Jan Garbarek's *Officium*.

07 _ Happy designers do good work. Keep him/her warm, well-fed and at the centre of the action. Send him/her to California or Barcelona. At Porsche it's possible to follow products through to production virtually on one site; that generates motivation.

08 _ Motor shows – an overdose of unnecessary hype.

09 _ 'Would you really want to be seen driving around in that?' A kind of negative inspiration which would cause a useful rethink.

10 _ I find the latest crop of Korean saloons particularly uninspiring

KEITH HELFET, 52, PRINCIPAL DESIGNER ADVANCED
PROJECTS, JAGUAR CARS. RCA GRADUATE 1977.
DESIGNER/JAGUAR XJ220 DESIGNER/JAGUAR XK180

01 _ Several of my designs have been inspired by their predecessors. The XJ220 was inspired directly by the XJ13, the XK180 by the D-type and the XJ41 by the E-type.

02 _ Inspiration, for me, is the stimulus that triggers a new idea, new direction, a feeling or permutations of these; ie intellectual, emotional or a combination. What in particular inspires each designer is very much dependent, and part of his/her individual 'design style'.

03 _ Along with many other designers and artists, my point of reference is the human body. In particular, the female body has form that can be functional, beautiful and sensual – that combination of pure function with desire is, for me, an inspiration and the true challenge of design.

04 _ Can't remember!

05 _ As stated in question four, inspiration is a source for new ideas or applications; anything else is a rip-off.

06 _ Too many to remember!

07 _ A relaxing and indulgent environment such as lying on a beach in Portugal or Cape Town, plugged into a Walkman, admiring the scenery.

08 _ Corporate politics and career managers.

09 _ Can't remember either!

10 _ I just don't have time to sort out the list…

The weighty legacy of the Model T hovers in the wings; Lincoln, Jaguar, Aston Martin and Volvo flourish in their carefully nurtured images. Set against this is Chris Bird's task: define and design the Fords of the future.

11|31

Managing a
Portfolio of Brands
Stephen Bayley

Astonishingly, for a company founded by a solitary genius who disdained aesthetics, the future of Ford is to be determined by design as much as manufacturing economies

→ For Chris Bird, the design of new Fords is a priority. Yet Henry Ford had little use for designers (although with an entirely natural perversity familiar to all parents, his son Edsel, with his catalogue of novel motifs for the Lincoln marque developed through the 1940s, was to become one of styling's great innovators). Instead, Ford's achievements were to appreciate the most fundamental needs of the consumer and then to devise the most ingenious and economical way of satisfying them. In his 1922 autobiography he wrote: 'My effort is in the direction of simplicity.'

His mentality and his morals were rooted in the self-improving ethical climate of 19th-century rural America. Not a great reader, he perhaps did not know Samuel Smiles' *Self Help*, but the notion of democratic progress through hard work was a shared ideal. In 1909, he said: "The car of the future must be a car of the people… the market for a low-priced car is unlimited."

Ford's great innovation was not simply to make this inexpensive car. At the time the Model T went into production, there were many other cheap cars available. Instead, Henry Ford decided precisely what a mass-market car would be, and only when this formula was clearly established in his mind did he set about finding a way of manufacturing the essential car at the lowest cost. The Model T took 12 years to develop. Ford said: "Rushing into manufacturing without being certain of the product is the unrecognised cause of many business failures." This was not the case.

Like Coca-Cola, with which Ford shares so much, the Ford Motor Company for many years produced only a single product. The consumer found it amply satisfying. If design is, as Le Corbusier believed, intelligence made visible, then Henry Ford was, indeed, a designer.

Design credits for the Model T were shared with his colleagues Childe Harold Wills and Joseph Galamb (among many others). It was a car that was crude only in the sense that a *haiku* can be described as a simple poem. True, its idiosyncratic control system centring on a foot-operated, two-speed gearshift led to some US states requiring special licences for Model T drivers, but these quirks did not frustrate an astonishing popularity that defines American consumer capitalism in its early phase.

The Model T went on the market in 1908 at a price of $850, although Ford was convinced that to achieve true popularity that price had to be brought down to about $600. The production methods were thus further refined. In 1913 a conveyor belt system was used for assembling magnetos and that led, the year after, to the full-moving assembly line for the whole car. The Ford Motor Company developed the just-in-time production system more than 50 years before the Japanese copied it.

Ford's invention of 'mass-production' (a term he coined only in the 1920s) was one of the great organisational achievements in human history. The moving production line was so efficient the price of the Model T had fallen to $360 by 1916. Over the car's life (Ford himself sometimes had difficulty spelling the word 'model') 16m copies were sold, built in 50 different factories in 19 different countries spread over every continent. During this period the concept of the Model T changed little; the means of manufacturing it changed enormously.

FORD PUMA

FORD FOCUS

The immense influence of the Model T had a hobbling effect on Ford's development. Henry Ford's fixed belief in an unalterable product, inexpensively manufactured and universally available, did not take account of the sort of social and cultural whims which motivate consumers once they have passed that condition of mere subsistence, his own starting point.

More subtle, less scientific notions enter the consumer's imagination when his basic needs have been satisfied. Henry Ford's practical character did not lend itself to whim.

However, these were just the sort of qualities so succinctly labelled 'Art and Color' which General Motors was to provide. The prophetic genius of Henry Ford in supplying basic immediate needs took no account of future unexplained wants. And, with almost mystical poetic significance, this pioneering design department of General Motors was set up in 1927… the last year of Model T production.

A vast intellectual inheritance from Henry Ford has influenced the company that carries the family name ever since. Wherever they are sold, Ford cars represent honest value and provide decent solutions for basic transport needs. Ford cars are not glamorous and exclusive, they are workaday and decent. If they have character, it is a reliable, steadfast one. The formula remains successful, but Ford's commitment to building a global business had to develop to satisfy the ever more sophisticated aspirations of those very consumers Ford's genius had originally liberated from the static condition of staying at home.

Ford is ordinary in the best possible sense, but second-generation consumers sometimes wanted the extraordinary. Mere transport was not, in itself, any longer enough.

Brand values are built on a basis of memory and expectation. In this sense, Ford's brand was limited to the satisfaction of certain basic needs. 'Blue collar' is one way of putting it. Ford needed to diversify. The design-conscious Edsel Ford created the Lincoln division (named after the late President). Later, Ford toyed with buying Ferrari and, when Fiat intervened, Ford decided its own success in motor racing would achieve as much.

In a period beginning in 1965, very distant descendants of the gasoline buggy won all the most remarkable awards in international motor racing: the Indianapolis 500, the Le Mans 24 Hours and the Formula 1 World Championship.

The accrued lustre from success in competition allowed Ford to produce cars which had a racy character that Henry Ford would never have understood, but still the solid weight of so profound a tradition limited Ford's development in an international market place, becoming daily more sophisticated.

After flirtations with Fiat and Alfa Romeo, Ford bought the quintessentially English Jaguar in 1989. Purchasing and production disciplines inherited from Dearborn saved this characterful but chaotic British company from oblivion and extended the Ford franchise into hitherto unexplored consumer territory.

FORD KA

FORD GALAXY

Another British firm, Aston Martin, soon followed. With the acquisition of Volvo in 1999, the Ford Motor Company now manages a bulging portfolio of marques, not just a car company.

Today, the business of running a vast multinational company like Ford is as much concerned with managing such a portfolio as it is with making refinements in production technology. When a Jaguar may be using components shared with, say, a Lincoln, then the designer's ability to make definitions and distinctions that are meaningful to the consumer is disproportionately significant. Equally, future Volvos will inevitably share components with Ford and Jaguar.

Ford wanted Jaguar, Aston Martin and Volvo for their character. But how can this ineluctable but immensely valuable, character be maintained – let alone enhanced – when the heart and skeleton of a new car are commodities shared between Coventry, Gothenburg and Newport Pagnell? This now is what designers do.

Astonishing for a company founded by a solitary genius who disdained the triviality of aesthetics, the future of Ford is going to be determined by design as much as by manufacturing economies.

And even stranger to say, this applies to the main Ford brand more than to any others in the portfolio.

Lincoln is easy. Lincoln means American cars with a distinctive design language, influenced by a sense of 'continental' flair.

Jaguar is no problem. Jaguar means British comfort and refinement and an unmistakable sense of well-bred style.

Aston Martin is a gentlemanly version of very high performance.

Volvo means family values, environmental responsibility, the outdoors and practicality.

But the big question remains – what then does Ford actually mean?

Chris Bird is the Royal College of Art graduate whose job it is to decide. After more than 10 years at Audi where he participated in some of the most attractive and distinctive car designs of recent years – which have translated Audis from being Volkswagens in drag into genuine rivals for BMW and Mercedes-Benz – he knows a great deal about how design can direct the consumer's expectations.

He says Ford is about "accessibility and simple values". The Ford tradition is not based on an aesthetic inheritance, but on a philosophical one. Within the limits of the consumer's tolerance (which it is the designer's job to understand, interpret and then extend) Ford can, aesthetically speaking, do anything. Freed even from any requirement to make luxury or sporting products, Ford's amazing corporate portfolio now allows the designers of the basic marque to explore every opportunity of building a modern interpretation of Henry Ford's vision in the future cars that bear his name.

Yet this very inheritance of functionality carries certain obligations. Bird has to consider, in exploring new territory, just how far he can lead the consumer. Any new design has to reach that sensitive point beyond excitement, but fall short of utter alienation.

Too much cautious research and 'clinic-ing' may have made the Mondeo bland, but the Ka (developed without the immediate supervision of management) may have gone too far. It was hugely admired by the design profession for its bravery and novelty, but there are signs it may be too daring for the public. Yet.

Bird understands the nuances. Mercedes-Benz works top-down. At Mercedes-Benz another Royal College of Art graduate, Murat Günak, knows the top-of-the-range S Class will donate style parts to lesser cars. Ford, on the other hand, must work bottom-up.

The creative challenge for a Ford designer is to define the absolutely basic essentials. In a sense it's much easier for Mercedes-Benz. It's similar to the relationship between Philips and Bang & Olufsen. At the prestige end, it is easier to be experimental with Bang & Olufsen. Establishing a convincing aesthetic for Philips has been more of a problem.

Ford's invention of
'mass production' was one
of the great organisational
achievements in human history

FORD FOCUS – EDGE DESIGN

DESIGNING THE FORD PUMA ON COMPUTER

Here are the issues Chris Bird is
considering at Ford:

NEW FORMATS: a type of car presently just a sub-
category, might soon evolve into the mainstream.
Thus the Ka, which has leapt the species barrier
and become a consumer product. The
adventurous Ka has more in common with a
Walkman than a Ferrari. The Ka was first seen not
in a garage, but in the Conran Shop. What might
a second- or third-generation Ka be like?

OLD FORMATS: there will always be a conservative
part of the mass market. The MPV format will
evolve: already the Focus (with its very high H-
point) is evidence of the one-box mentality
entering the mainstream. Women enjoy MPVs
because they are less claustrophobic and have a
sense of security. Their slower windscreens and
reduced tumblehome articulate this. But some
customers still like a boot: the rear overhang is
one of the most powerful ways of articulating a
car's character. The saloon will survive.

PRESTIGE: increasingly important even for the
mass market customer, but while the sort of
social prestige enjoyed by Mercedes-Benz takes
a century to acquire, the design prestige enjoyed
by Audi can be more rapidly acquired. The signs
are that future customers will be more product-
conscious than status-conscious. This is good
news for designers.

MEDIA: advertising and design are getting much
closer. The moment when you could fool the
public for even a little bit of the time has long
passed. Today, there are no bad cars. Advertising
is not a crude sales pitch, but an additional
element in building up an entire belief system
which supports the product. There was a time
when advertising had to involve a deal of post-
hoc rationalisation to sell inconsistently developed
cars. Chris Bird says that, today, we know what
we are doing from the start: we are much more
focused and aimed.

COMPETITION: with city traffic conditions
deteriorating to absurdity point, the car's original
function may be compromised, but its appeal
endures, even as it's changed. The private car
now competes in the consumer's imagination with
other products. Design is increasingly important.

At Ford, future design must find interesting ways
of re-interpreting ideas of utility. The company has
an inestimably valuable inheritance of democratic
ideas to stimulate the studios: its best-selling
vehicle is still the F150 truck. Bird says: "Only
Ford can build a Ford".

According to Chris Bird, the challenge for Ford is
to find "a future new design language which
maintains a functional base". And if there is to be
a Model T of the future, what would it be like? "My
brief to the designers would simply be to cite
Henry Ford's belief that: 'Nearly everything we
make is more complex than it needs to be'."

Chris Bird believes: "Our core competency is
our brains."

Just as well, since design is a matter of thinking.

The McLaren F1 costs
£540,000, does 240MPH
and is designed by Peter
Stevens – the RCA's First
Car Design Graduate.
Photographic Study by
Christine Lalla

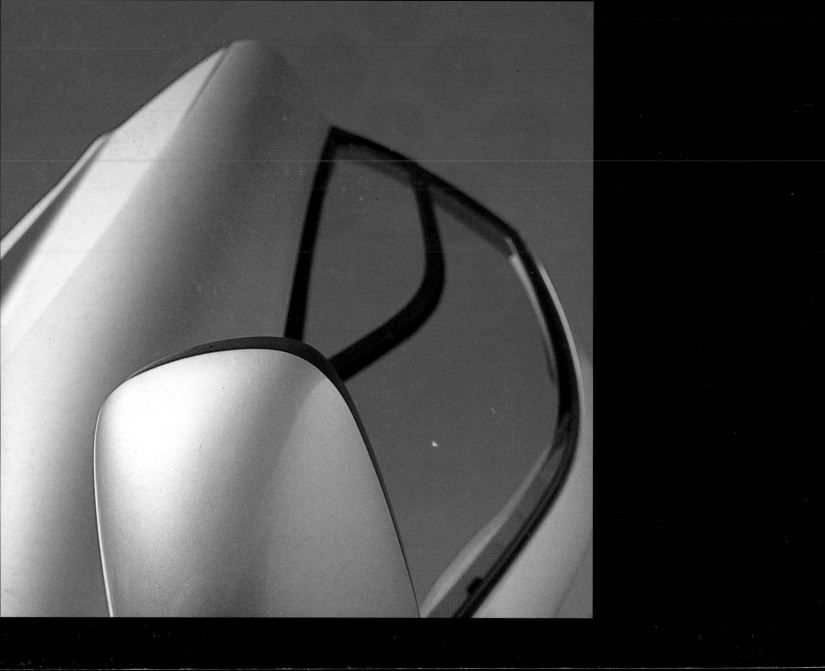

13|31

The Language of Form

'Beautiful' is a difficult word: when we attach it to the word 'car' we seek to lift the automobile out of the category of tool or object and convert it into art.

Brian Sewell

TATRA T77 PROTOTYPE – VOLKSWAGEN CONTEMPORARY

→ When the car first took to the roads a century or so ago it was no more than a mechanical means of personal transportation, a replacement for the horse, but once the simple principles of transferring power from an engine to the road wheels were established, it became a creature of the imagination, soon recognised by the Italian futurists as an image, icon and allegory of speed and freedom, or power and dominance, as effective as the human body had been in personifying such abstractions since the days of ancient Greece.

Line, form and colour came into play as surely as in painting and sculpture – to discover under its bonnet the repeated forms of the four racing carburettors of a Bugatti straight-eight engine of the 1930s is to see the embodiment of a painting by Balla or Boccioni, to contemplate a coachbuilt body by Saoutchik or Figoni & Falaschi is to see sculptural forms to match those of Gabo, Pevsner and Brancusi, and after cudgelling one's brains over the rivets that hold together the wayward inventions of Richard Deacon now, it is with relief the motor-maniac turns to the precisely spaced rivets on the bonnet of a Railton or Invicta.

The fourth clause of Filippo Marinetti's *Futurist Manifesto* of February 1909 proclaimed 'that the magnificence of the world has been enhanced by a new beauty: the beauty of speed. A racing car with enormous exhaust pipes like fire-spitting serpents…a roaring racing car running like a machine-gun is more beautiful than the Winged Victory of Samothrace'.

The source of Marinetti's dramatic imagery lay in the great veteran competition cars made by Fiat – the 100hp, 100mph Corsa of 1905, the 110hp Gordon Bennett (the origin of the exclamation – and the background to the following page spread) Corsa of the same year and the 130hp Grand Prix de France Corsa of 1907, all with an engine of 16,286 ccs, and the even larger and faster SB4 Corsa of 1908, with an engine of 18,146 ccs that developed 175bhp and sped around Brooklands at 120mph.

These were cars with the aesthetic appeal, if any, of the tractor and the shunting engine, not horse-less carriages for they were carriageless too, comfortless bare bones machines to be driven by modern heroes in a week from Paris to Peking, or overnight from Trondheim to Taronto, and it was in their aggressive characteristics of noise, speed and kicked-up dust that Marinetti perceived new beauties to usurp the past – 'To admire an old painting is as much use as pouring our sensibilities into a funerary urn…the heart of the young man burns with fire, hate and speed.'

We should not, perhaps, take too much notice of the Futurists – even Vasily Kandinsky, who has some claim to be the father of abstract art, used the perjorative 'daft' of them, and Marinetti's *Manifesto* was very much a nonsense of its time, anticipated in this country by Kenneth Grahame's Open Road chapter in *The Wind in the Willows* of 1908, where the car is apocalyptically described as a 'cloud of dust with a dark centre of energy, advancing…at incredible speed…with a blast of wind and a whirl of sound…with a brazen shout in their ears, they had a moment's glimpse of an interior of glittering plate glass and rich morocco, and the magnificent motor car, immense, breath-snatching, passionate…possessed all earth and air…'

That the Futurists had no influence on the design of cars is obvious in the passenger vehicles made by Fiat at the time, of which Grahame, with plate glass, morocco and magnificence, offers the perfect description; these, as with marques all over Europe and America, inherited from the era of the horse and the Grand Tour the aristocratic mode and style of the 19th century carriage, and were lofty capsules of polished wood and buttoned leather that even in their names – the Rolls Phaeton, Cadillac Brougham, Mercedes Sedanca and Daimler Landaulette – retained entrenched class distinctions and set bench-marks for social aspiration.

This is the trap for all who wish to consider the car as an aesthetic object, for such is the vanity of men that the big car at once became, and is still, the Ship of Fools, the silly self-flattery of all who choose to see it less as a fine functional machine than as a proclamation of wealth, power and status.

DUESENBERG MODEL SJ SPEEDSTER WITH BODY BY BOHMAN & SCHWARZ

Not even Damien Hirst could use a car as a ready-made constituent of art

CADILLAC STRETCHED LIMOUSINE – ABSURD

Fifty years ago, the aesthetic argument was centred on the belief held by some followers of Le Corbusier that, for a machine to be beautiful its form must be dictated by its function; ancient denizens of the Institute of Contemporary Art may recall the view passionately propounded by Reyner Banham that the aesthetic beauty of the car lay less in streamlining (as aerodynamics was then known) than in clarity of purpose and simplicity of function within that purpose – he thus maintained an Edwardian Silver Ghost Roi des Belges was infinitely more beautiful than a Talbot-Lago roadster of the late 1930s with the front wheels fully enclosed in teardrop wings, and that a polished aluminium bonnet built like a box made better functional sense than one fared into the wings and heavily cellulosed in two colours separated by a hand-drawn coachline. Banham has eventually been proved right, although not quite in the way he proposed, for despite the fact we still judge cars by the social baggage they display – even to absurdity, as with Citroën's 2CV and the stretched American limousine – and the enchantments of 1930s streamlining, eroded by science, have been abandoned as the means of a seduction in the showroom, true aerodynamic form is now regarded as an essential element of function and performance.

Chrysler engineers discovered in 1927 that a conventional D-backed saloon driven backwards was far less wind resistant; in the early 1930s Wunibald Kamm observed that an erect and sharply cut-off tail brought a marked increase in maximum speed compared with an elegant tapering tail; collating this information, Renault should have produced its Espace in 1935, but today's people-carrier is decades behind its time.

Aerodynamic thinking in the 1930s was further confused by Auto Union engineers, who bodied their victorious racing cars with rounded capsules that enclosed the driver and the rear-mounted engine in a single form, and it was the rear engine in the small family car than enabled Porsche to develop the hump-backed and droop-snooted Volkswagen – ideas he had first put to Zündapp in 1931-2, although they were very much part of central European thinking, as evinced by Tatra designer Hans Ledwinka.

Slowly, slowly, from these tentative beginnings, the short low snout and high rump of today evolved, and with the conventions of beauty that once dictated a flowing line and slender form abandoned, nothing of the grace, elegance or devil-may-care rakishness of the Lagonda V12, Mercedes 500K, Bugatti T57 Atalante, Lincoln Continental, Cord 810 Beverly sedan and Packard Darrin Victoria, all of 1935-40, survives in late 20th century designs; nothing, even by Mercedes and Bentley, now recalls the coachbuilt magnificence of Duesenbergs of 1929-35, the boat-tailed J Torpedo by Walter Murphy and the unique open two-seater by Bohman & Schwarz on the 7-litre SJ chassis, cars that demonstrated the sudden and swift change from the veteran tradition at its most dashing, but still a car for Paul Revere, to concepts that for the first time in its history brought the coachwork of the car into the forefront of 20th century design.

This Bohman & Schwarz body, with its long, high bonnet, swept tail and quadruple exhausts in chrome could well be the epitome of the Futurist vision of the car, yet its wingline is svelte, merging with running-boards that imperceptibly blend with spatted rear wings to give an astonishingly smooth profile and a surface suggesting uncluttered solid form; the most intriguing touches are the three parallel curved slashes in the bonnet sides, as elegant as any canvas slashed in the 1960s by Lucio Fontana. No more beautiful car in the American idiom was ever made.

The difficulty with the word beautiful in this context is that in using it we seek to lift the car out of the category of tool or object and convert it into art. Art in the ancestral traditions of the west is imbued with gravitas and terribilitá, with abstract resonances and emotional associations, with lofty and spiritual qualities that are beyond explanation but at which we stand in awe, and the car has none of these.

Not even Damien Hirst could use a car as a ready-made constituent of art – if he can present as art a cupboard filled with manufactured surgical instruments, it is we, the audience, who perform the alchemy with our response to the emotional and painfully tactile implications that they carry in their use; our response to their design is secondary, no matter how exquisite it may be, and of a different nature.

RENAULT 14GTL - SHODDY AND MISSHAPEN

The big car became the silly self-flattery of all who chose to see it less as a fine functional machine than as a proclamation of wealth and status.

ROLLS-ROYCE SILVER GHOST – ELEGANT

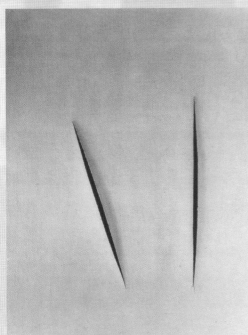

CANVAS SLASHED BY LUCIO FONTANA SUGGESTS LOUVRES

Every discussion of the car as a work of aesthetic value is bedevilled by its function and by the social aspirations of ownership; style has too often been the deceitful transformation of car architecture to conform with public perceptions of modernity while camouflaging a car's lack of engineering and technological progress, and hand-in-hand with 'badge engineering' has been a means of manipulating the market and keeping up demand – the annual imposition of astonishing gaucheries and aberrations in the interest of change for change's sake has meant the absolute denial and rejection of the mantra 'form follows function'. GM has been guilty of all these sins, and even Rolls-Royce of some of them.

If anything is to be said for this mantra, it must be with the caveat that as the function of the car has changed, so has the form, with the consequence that cars have always had their clones, whether they be the Lanchester Brothers' boat-like object of mannered elegance supporting two settees of buttoned leather in 1895 or today's high–performance coupes with back seats fit only for dachshunds. The complaint that 'all cars look alike nowadays' is as old as the industry: they have always looked alike and they always will, for they borrow styling cues from each other and are as subject to period affectations as any work of furniture or decoration. Zeitgeist and monkey-see, monkey-do syndrome were always as much to blame as function and science for the sameness of formal language in the car in decades past; at the end of the car's first century our demands for economy, efficiency, refinement, passenger accommodation and high speed even in the smallest cars compel manufacturers to treat all these as prime functions, and their response has been to combine as many as they can, perhaps giving primacy to one.

The result is that, within each genre, form – to some considerable extent – follows the prime function, and most cars bear obvious taints of incest and adultery.

Perhaps among the few that do not we may find a car or two that can be defined, if not as sculpture, then as sculptural in form. Consider the Bentley S1 Continental fastback saloon by HJ Mulliner, a thing of flowing forms exquisitely inter-related, devoid of decorative detail and crude embellishment; consider the overriders on its bumpers, perfectly functional yet employing the formal language of early abstract sculpture.

Consider the Cisitalia Gran Sport Coupe 202 of 1947, the first car ever to be recognised as having a sculptural identity and be exhibited, in New York's Museum of Modern Art, as a work of art, a Pininfarina design that profoundly influenced Ferrari, in whose hands it became sublime, perfect and spectacular. Alas, when the wise men of the Centre Pompidou, the museum of contemporary art in Paris, decided the car could be and occasionally had been art, it was not the Cisitalia that they hung from their rafters as a static mobile, nor Mulliner's Bentley, nor a Bugatti by Kellner or Van Vooren, nor a Delage by Chapron, nor any of the futuristic Talbot Lagos by Figoni & Falaschi, nor the maverick Fiat Topolino, Lancia Aprilia and Citroën Traction Avant, all of the 1930s, nor even those style icons of the 1960s, the Citroën DS and the pure Issigonis Mini, but the shoddy and misshapen Renault 14 family hatchback of 1976, thus utterly defeating the proposal.

The idea of elevating the car to become an art form presupposes art is somehow higher than design. It is certainly more 'difficult' for both artist and observer, but that does not make design lower, or any less worthy.

Cars are not Art.
…says Peter Stevens

Peter Stevens is a freelance designer, responsible for the Lotus Excel, Esprit and Elan, Jaguar XJR-15, McLaren F1, several ERF trucks, the 1995 GT race series-winning McLaren and BMW's 1999 Le Mans car. He was also one of the first two graduates of the Royal College of Art's Vehicle Design course.

→ It is absurd to see the car as 'art', yet it has recently become common for writers and critics to do so. Few, if any, designers view the car this way, although I have yet to hear their voice raised in disagreement with this premise.

A recent editorial in *Auto & Design* magazine quoted Malraux: 'Art is the medium through which forms become style'; in Italy a few years ago, old Ferraris were displayed as modern art in sealed glass cases on a hillside above Florence in Piazza Michelangelo.

This pretentious nonsense appears to allow its supporters to express an appreciation of car design without appearing to be 'petrolheads', 'anoraks', or socially irresponsible.

The difference between sculpture and industrial design is similar to the difference between art and illustration.

In the first case, the artist either challenges or expands our perception and understanding of life or attempts to communicate his experience or belief through his work.

In the second case, the designer, in either clothing or combining the visual appearance of an object with its technical elements, reflects the technology and style of the present moment, just as the illustrator invites us to share his perception of a moment in time rather than experience his philosophy of life.

The idea of elevating the car to become an art form presupposes art is somehow higher than design. It is certainly more 'difficult' for both artist and observer, but that does not make design lower, or any less worthy.

So why not celebrate automobile design for its style, creativity and craftsmanship, if that is what it deserves. Probably because style and its practise, styling, is seen as a superficial pastime. Creativity is considered self-indulgent. Craftsmanship is difficult to spot in the modern car because we associate it with wood-carving or hand-stitched leather. This is why wood trim and rich-smelling hide are used to help define a quality car.

Actually, the craftsmanship is in the design, the manufacturing technology and the assembly. Creativity is in the originality of the concept. Style is in the shaping of the form and the freshness of the details.

Certainly, like art, design can stir emotions, generate furious debate, delight the eye and intrigue the mind. But so can sport or furniture design and, apart from the back page of *The Sun*, sport is not considered 'art'. Nor is even the finest of furniture.

Charles Rennie Mackintosh or Charles Eames would never have considered what they did to be art. It was a mixture of design and craft and quite bloody marvellous – like the Clifton Suspension Bridge, the Field Marshall Tractor, the Jeep, the Spitfire, the J-class yacht or the Jaguar E-type.

Let's not obscure the elegant solution to an engineering problem with inappropriate labels.

Rainbow Worrier

Two-tone Chevrolets
used to look like land yachts;
now a single coat of paint
can turn from lilac to beige
at the flicker of an eyelash.
This is about a colourful past
that keeps re-inventing itself

Laura Blossfeld

Some 80 per cent of the colour trends are the same between America and Europe; where they differ is in the area of neutrals. In America, neutrals rule.

Colour has played an important role in the story of the car from the very beginning.

When cars were first raced in Europe at the start of the century, each country was designated a specific colour for their racing cars. Thus, Britain ended up with 'British Racing' green, France with blue, Italy with a 'Bordeaux' red (later evolved into Ferrari's *Rosso Corsa*) and Belgium with orange. At first, Germany had white racing cars: then some bright engineer at Mercedes-Benz realised leaving the paint off altogether to reduce overall weight, giving us the first *Silber Pfeil* – Silver Arrow. To this day, German cars on the street remain predominantly white or silver or black.

American and European coachbuilding companies of the 1920s and '30s built car bodies that were usually of a luxurious character. Carefully refined interior/exterior colour combinations were developed that carry on to this day: silver or gunmetal bodies combined with red; navy or black with beige or tan; red exteriors with cream or white interiors, and vice versa.

What, sadly, hasn't survived, are the fantastic two-tone exterior paint combinations from this period. You can only admire the two shades of blue adorning a fantastic Talbot Lago Type 26 or Bugatti Type 57SC, or the striking black and blue of the Bugatti Type 41 Royale.

Classically subtle combinations were the beige, tan and wood exterior of the Isotta-Fraschini Tipo 8A, and the tomato-fendered, claret-bodied 1930 Cord L-29 with a peachy tan convertible top and wheelcover, and the silver and titanium of the Pierce-Arrow Silver Arrow from 1933.

Even braver was the black and yellow of the 1937 Bugatti Atalante, and the famously coloured-light-coded – bright orange paintwork twinned with intensely orange leather upholstery) 1936 Duesenberg SJ owned by India's Maharahjah Bahadur.

In the US, by the mid-1930s the mantle of styling leadership had passed to General Motors. Its Art and Color Department was formed in 1927 by Harley Earl, to dictate colour and styling to the entire GM car line-up. Along with the yearly style changes came annual colour changes.

Cadillac usually led with new colours, eventually trickling down through the Buick and Oldsmobile lines and finally end up on the lower-end Pontiacs and Chevrolets.

In Europe, manufacturers didn't change colours or styles every year; their customers kept cars longer because they represented, by comparison, a significantly bigger personal investment.

Post-war, 1940s austerity prefaced a conservative approach to car colours. Their colours were as grey as the prevailing economic outlook – light warm greys, beige-greys, tan greys, greyed creams; the only relief was, surprisingly, emerald green…and even that was a highly toxic paint!

Apart from the lavishly timbered Chrysler Town & Country (twin-tone woods with cream or beige paint), a Hollywood favourite, the first post-war cars America saw were swathed in conservative beige and silver and white. Then the USA, in the flush of its post-war boom, went styling- and colour-crazy. High contrast, two-tone combinations came to the fore: primrose/white, red/white, sky blue/white, black/silver, black/red, black/creme – the palette seemed endless.

A decade of excess ended with the epochal pink 1959 Cadillac combined with a black interior. But not all cars of the 1950s were so outlandish: the Ford Thunderbird and Chevrolet Corvette remain design classics, and the vivid colour combinations worked quite well on them, whereas they made the bigger cars somehow resemble land yachts.

From the mid-1960s to the mid-1970s very bright solid colours had their time. Remember the Beetle's orange, the Ferrari Dino's intense high-cadmium yellow called 'Giallo Fly' and Audi's almost fluorescent 'Mars red'?

VANDEN PLAS 1300

SAAB 900

VAUXHALL CARLTON

VOLKSWAGEN GOLF

MERCEDES-BENZ 280CE

BRISTOL 411

FIAT BARCHETTA

NISSAN MICRA

SAAB 99

TRIUMPH HERALD

FORD ESCORT

CADILLAC DEVILLE

ROVER METRO

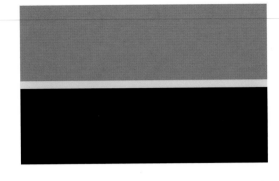

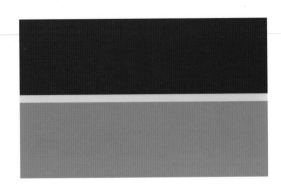

The mid-1960s was also the era of metallic paints going mainstream. Paint suppliers tried to make metallic colours as bright as solids but faced endless technical barriers. For instance, if paint was applied in one coat, only a few aluminum particles came to the surface and, over time, they oxidised and darkened markedly. By 1970, VW introduced a two-coat metallic – a thin coat of aluminium metal flakes covered by a clear coat to protect them and prevent oxidisation. Having cracked the problem, popular metallic colours for the new American 'muscle cars' like Mustangs, Camaros and Barracudas were gold-greens, metallic bottle greens, blue-greens like turquoise and aqua marine, and truly elemental copper, gold and silver. Paint was a design element on Bill Mitchell's 'Mako Shark' series of Corvette show cars, their subtle gradiations of grey progressing from white underbodies to dark blue-grey roofs.

The 1980s meant a different aesthetic, 'high tech'. At times of economic downturn architecture, product and design colours become more conservative. This was true of the car industry then. We saw a predominance of safe, resaleable car colours rocketing in popularity: silver or titanium with a black interior; white with black; red with black; black with black. The 'key' colour was red – it acted as an influence on all the colours around it. We saw greys and blues tinged with red, (aubergines and grey-violets then evolved) and colours that used red as an accent. True greens faded away (in the early '80s, legions of green VWs, Audis and Porsches were piling up in the New York harbours – no one wanted green) or evolved into turquoise, shades from 'dark petrol' to 'Carribic'.

Burgeoning environmental awareness led to restrictions on cadmium-based and even more toxic chromium-based paints, so yellows, yellow-greens, oranges and really bright reds died out. Friendlier, water-based, organic pigments replaced them. But they have drawbacks; they're more transparent, they don't hide the base coat and they need more layers. Instead of the pure, bright colours of the past produced with the help of cadmium, we see milky or mustardy yellows, depending on whether white or black is added to the pigment to increase its hiding properties.

Colours, like fashion, rotate in 15- or 20-year cycles. The market gets saturated with a trend or colour, it fades away, and 20 years later it reappears looking fresh again.

The mid-1990s saw a resurgence of colour, in parallel, amusingly, with the upswing of the stock market. Porsche – which could always afford to be avant garde – introduced a bright cobalt blue, a fuschia pink and a fluorescent mint green into its standard colour range in 1991. By 1995, yellow had returned, this time as a 'key' that influences or tinges all other colours; greys become warm greys, green reappears and becomes yellower, and the redness goes out of the blues so they become more neutral.

Red moves to orange and copper tones, so we see orange reappearing, notably this time on the Fiat Barchetta. Offshoots of orange, colours like 'Siena' brown or 'Russet' red appear in up-level sports car interiors – the Aston Martin DB7 and Audi TT Cabrio show car.

Bright colours work well on small and sporty cars, but designers must be careful with size. When we were working on Porsche colours, we discovered a bright yellow, which worked well on a 911, made a 944 or 968 look like a big banana. It's for this very reason that most large or expensive cars are produced in dark colours or neutral metallics.

Renault, always a colour-innovative manufacturer, went against the small car/bright colour platitude, and introduced 'greyed-down' colours harking back to the 1940s when it launched the Twingo. Yet the company was forced to introduce brighter colours a year or so later due to unfavourable customer response.

New paint technologies are coming to the market and are on the horizon. The plastic door panels of the new Smart city car are painted bright red, or yellow-orange, or cobalt blue or a new splatter-type effect where yellow and lime green flow into each other. They're interchangeable on their black frames, giving two-tone paint effects in Europe once again after a long absence.

'Micas', with their changeable, flip-flop iridescent effects, in the past feasible only for show cars, are now being used for production cars. The new Opel/Vauxhall Zafira has a silver in its colour palette called 'Mirage': micronised titanium dioxide particles mean this paint can flip from silver to pale gold to pale ceramic blue depending on the prevailing light and your viewing position.

VW has launched a technical-looking, satiny silver for its new car shapes as it moves away from the ovular shapes of the last decade, and becomes more design-edgy. Evolving oranges are getting darker and moving into the brown range – but unlike the browns we know now. The mica process gives them lots of fire and life. Brown will reposition itself in the colour palette as green has done already.

For show cars, there are pigments known as 'Chrome Flare', borrowed from the banknote-printing industry. This was used on the Opel Speedster, where the colour 'flopped' from a silvery lilac grey-blue to a beige-brown. This technology allows for unimaginably shrill colour flops – deep turquoise to ruby red, for example. The big drawback, however, is the prohibitive cost – a litre is 1250DM.

How do the car colourists, the designers in the colour and trim areas of car companies, manage to keep abreast of trends and new developments? How do they predict what the customer will go for in the next five years?

It's hard.

It's not simply a case of picking an exterior colour at random or of personal choice. An interior colour usually has to work well with several exterior colours. All the materials used in the interior – fabric, leather, vinyl, carpet, wood, headliner and package shelving material – must be colour-matched or colour-co-ordinated to make a complete whole.

There are many organisations in Europe and the US that give presentations and offer seminars and workshops to aid designers in their elusive quest for the next hot colour trend: the International Colour Authority in America, and the Colour Marketing Group, just getting a foothold in Europe, and in England the Colour Group workshops at the Royal Society of Art.

These all try to get designers from interiors, products and cars together to work out a sort of concensus of coming colour trends. Very helpful, too, is France's *View* magazine series and the Italian *Trend Collezione*. Conventions and shows – Heimtextil, Pitti Filati, Bologna Leather Fair, Premier Vision and Neocon – are a must.

But most helpful of all, because they relate directly to cars, are paint company presentations.

BASF, Dupont, Herberts, PPG and Nippon Paint often hire experts to scour the world for the next coming thing, and the most globally-focused are the most informative. Some 80 per cent of the colour trends are the same between America and Europe; where they differ is in neutrals. In America, neutrals rule. Which says a lot about America. Then again, this is a country where the Mary Kay cosmetics company *still* awards its top saleswomen pink Cadillacs…

Your Steering Wheel: To Hold it is to Love it
Giles Chapman

→ If you're a car designer at Mercedes-Benz you can let your imagination run free. But tamper at your peril with the steering wheel.

Owners like them big, chunky and leathery, imparting power and pomp to even the humblest of C Class-driving salesmen. Now they're packed with technology too – airbags, mobile phone, hi-fi controls. It all makes Cathryn Epinosa sigh. "Really, there's very little you can do with it today", she says. "Once the airbag's been designed in and the engineer's worked out the structure, you end up with something very conservative".

Until recently, Cathryn designed conceptual interiors for Mercedes-Benz cars of the future. "You have to be very careful with the angle and position of the wheel, how it feels to grip it", she says. "Your first impression is how it looks but your second and most important is how it feels. It has to be comfortable to be near".

A recent Mercedes show car, the F200, did away with a wheel altogether, providing the driver instead with an aircraft-style joystick. It didn't work. But why not?

"A steering wheel is such a universal idea that it would be hard to sell a car without one", Cathryn says. "I think it's a lot like music: play a series of notes to Aborigines and they'll get the same sense of joy from them as someone in Sweden would feel".

Ex-RCA car designer John Heffernan, who with partner Ken Greenley designed the Aston Martin Vantage and Bentley Continental R, began his career designing steering wheels for Bedford and Leyland trucks.

"They tend to be at a different angle and much more utilitarian because of the engineering of a truck cab", he says. "However, even when we worked out ways to make them more car-like, lorry drivers didn't like them – they thought they were too effete, not manly enough. Strange, though, when you think of the back problems truck drivers suffer because of it…"

Heffernan is a great admirer of the classic wood-and-aluminium steering wheels fitted to Ferraris of the 1950s and '60s. He also rates BMW wheels as ergonomically excellent, particularly the 7 Series. Yet the steering wheel has often been the curse of his own work.

"While we were designing the Vantage it became obvious we'd have to include an airbag. Unfortunately, there was no money to pay for a new design that would suit an Aston so we ended up adapting one from an American Ford. It didn't look too good but there was so much going on inside it that we had no choice".

Your steering wheel, in fact, is much more important to you than you probably realise. Conrad King, a transport psychologist working for the RAC, says it actually becomes part of you when you drive.

"A steering wheel has a transitory status – when you hold it, it's part-human, part machine. When you're in your car, it's one of the few points where you can express control on the outside world. It allows you to make your own way – direct your own progress. It gives you power, influence.

"It's a very evocative symbol in its own right; a circle signals wholeness, continuity, death and rebirth. A steering wheel offers familiarity, comfort and autonomy".

Indeed, according to King, there's something "puritanical" about your approach to a new steering wheel.

"At first, you always make sure you've placed your hands on it in the correct way. You start at the '10-to-two' position and then, gradually, you explore other positions as you get to know your wheel more intimately".

LOVED: MERCEDES WITH A STEERING WHEEL...   ...AND, LOATHED, WITH JUST A 'JOY' STICK

80

15|31

Reflections of
Cars and Gender

Feminists say the
car is a phallic symbol.
This is a male myth

Professor Penny Sparke

FORD MODEL T WITH, INSET, HENRY FORD

SONIA DELAUNAY: BUGATTI MATCHED HER COAT

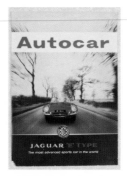

JAGUAR E-TYPE – PHALLIC?

The only time women express an opinion about cars is when they feel their bodies are being used to sell them. This injects guilt and unease into some men's relationships with their cars.

Few people, I suspect, would deny car culture is perceived to be overwhelmingly masculine. The majority of men in the western world interact with cars from the Dinky Toy stage onwards, acquiring a relationship with cars largely denied to women. However, now women are increasingly allowed access to the 'car experience', as drivers as well as passengers, it's worth reflecting about the ways in which the two genders interact with these dynamic objects.

Are the dominant themes appearing to underpin the male psychic response to cars through this century – speed, sexuality and power – the same ones that motivate women in this context, or is there another set of 'feminine' relationships? I recently witnessed a group of young male auto-motive designers drooling over a shiny new Fiat saloon, just purchased by one of their peers. Cries of "Wow!" were accompanied by caresses of the car's soft curves and a ceremonial circling around it to allow scrutiny from every angle. It was a group ritual which would have delighted an anthropologist analysing tribal behaviour.

As an observer of this ceremony I found it hard to identify with the reverence and adoration expressed towards the car. A striking design, sure, but I wasn't drawn to it physically as the men were. So just what lay behind this overtly masculine ritual?

Clearly, on one level, the group was confirming its shared values and, by extension, its sense of belonging. This, mostly non-verbal behaviour, was an expression of sharing – in the way a wink when a well-developed girl walks past is – the participants' perception of masculinity.

An obvious explanation is of the car as a substitute female sex object, complete with curves and aesthetic appeal, drawing men towards it like bees to a honeypot. There is, however, something unsatisfactory about this reading. It fails to account for the fact that many women not only buy cars but actually enjoy looking at them and driving them, or why, when a man is at the wheel, cars are often seen as physical extensions of the male body.

The popular cliches that come to mind are those of the penile-inadequate man driving a bulbous E-type Jaguar, or another encased in a muscular Mercedes in the hopes of enhancing their masculinity in the eyes of others. (The corollary of this would mean, of course, women E-type drivers are expressing penis-envy, while female Mercedes drivers want to be men!)

The gendered relationships between people and their cars is more complex. They operate on a number of levels and cannot be reduced to a limited discussion about masculinity, sex, speed, and power, although these have a role to play in the bigger picture.

Rather, men and women look at and use cars in the same complex ways they look at each other and themselves. Motivating factors, include desire, narcissism, envy, and a quest for self-identification – social, psychological and cultural needs that are deeply rooted. The masculine paradigm has tended to dominate literature on the subject, while the feminine side of car culture has been largely ignored.

Women have been well served as passengers in cars through most of this century – with front-seat vanity mirrors, glove compartments and patterned upholstery all catered for. Even matching luggage has appeared, in the hope of pleasing the female passenger, herself an accessory. (This involvement between women, cars and aesthetics goes back to the early 1900s, with the artist Sonia Delaunay decorating the body of her car to match a coat she designed. Similarly, interior decorator Elsie de Wolfe created a car interior for an American manufacturer.)

It is, however, taking a long time for women to be considered equal to male drivers where practicalities are concerned, despite growing numbers of women behind the wheel. For example, getting into most cars when pregnant is still uncomfortable, while reaching back between the front seats to comfort a crying baby remains a tricky manoeuvre.

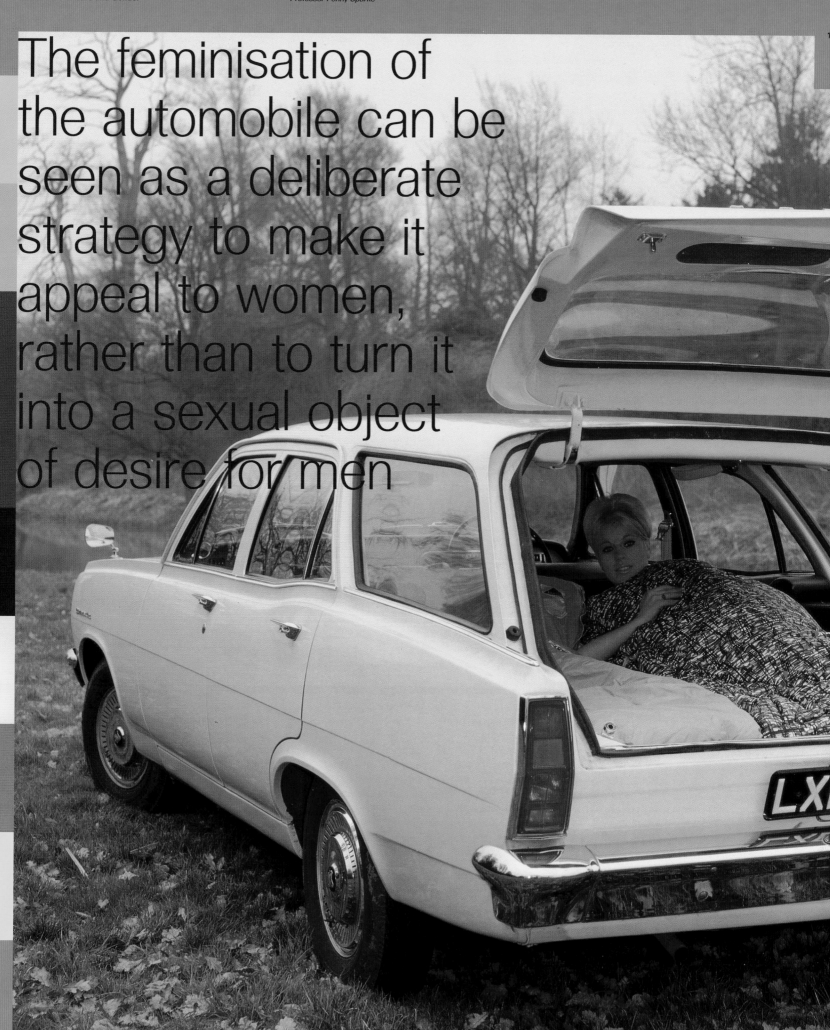

The feminisation of the automobile can be seen as a deliberate strategy to make it appeal to women, rather than to turn it into a sexual object of desire for men

PLAYING WITH TOY CARS – THE MARK OF A BOY

The familiar notion of half-dressed females festooning bonnets at motor shows, has been seen by many women as just another form of male domination

The reason for this is simple. The vast majority of car designers are male and these practicalities have not occurred to them. The cultural link between men, the workplace and the world of technology has been in place for many years, and the dominance of men in the world of car design is no surprise. Nor does the fact that the few women in automotive manufacture have been, for the most part, designers of the interior – an area linked to the traditional feminine sphere of domesticity.

Where the gendered symbolism of cars and its relationship with consumers is concerned, it's much harder to be clear-cut about the ways men and women relate to their mobile possessions. Why do these lumps of metal, which were created to take us from A to B, relate so closely to our inner psychic beings? Why have they become containers of our dreams, our desires and our innermost fears?

One reason must be the fact we trust them in situations of potential danger. Only items of aggression, such as guns, fall into the same category and they also carry strongly gendered messages. In addition to their role as life-threatening objects, cars also allow us to parade ourselves in public while remaining partly hidden, with the object taking over the main role of display.

Driving represents a rare instance of the private being expressed in terms of the public. Cars can be seen as extensions of our clothes, the most body-expressive objects of all. This role is extended to accessories such as handbags, watches, spectacles and jewellery which, like clothing, are imbued with numerous gender characteristics in order to express sexuality.

Cars encase our bodies as yet another layer outside our clothes and accessories. Unlike clothes, however, they have bodies of their own – their own faces, for instance, and their own muscular structures. Unlike most machines their forms are organic rather than rectilinear, and their bodies can be seen as extensions, or replacements, of our own. Given their role as substitutes, it is not surprising that we invest them with our identities so easily.

Taking the link between cars, our bodies and our identities into account, it is inevitable that gender and sexuality play a key role in our relationships with them. To date, the only context this has been discussed in is the exploitation of women. The familiar notion of sexy girls in car ads, and half-dressed females festooning shimmering bonnets at motor shows, has been seen by many women as just another form of male domination.

This works on the simple assumption that men want to buy sexy women and subordinate them. What it does not take into account is the fact that women also look at other women, mainly for reasons of self-identification, or that men look at women not only with libidinous desire but also with the need to locate their femininity through them. Without entering into Freudian psychology, it is possible to say the male and female 'gazes' are neither fixed nor univalent, and that the gendered meanings of cars are, thus, complex.

To what extent can cars be understood as primarily feminine objects in our culture? To see cars as feminine is to put aside their status as items of advanced technology, items defined primarily by their performance, and to see them as manifesting characteristics viewed as stereotypically feminine – ie as fashionable objects of desire; as objects relating more closely to the organic world of nature than to the geometric world of the machine; as objects which depend upon aesthetics for their identity; as mobile living rooms and hence extensions of the domestic sphere; and as icons of popular, rather than high, culture.

Seen in this light, from the moment General Motors usurped the utilitarian Ford Model T with its style-conscious models of the late 1920s, cars have been androgynous objects encapsulating values the culture of our century has positioned within both the masculine and the feminine spheres. This distances them from other technological items like washing machines, televisions and video recorders which make few concessions to femininity, even though they're destined for the domestic sphere.

DID THE CAR REALLY HELP 1950S MAN TO GET IN TOUCH WITH HIS FEMININE SIDES?

It also makes disentangling the way men and women look at, and use, cars very complex. All the possible gender relations that exist between men and women, men and men, and women and women can be expressed in car design. While the male car designers I observed were using the Fiat to affirm their masculinity, women could relate to the same car as a way to confirm their femininity. The difference lies in their respective behaviours: while men need to demonstrate their masculinity through visible rituals, women tend to watch other women in an undemonstrative way.

The fact women identify themselves as feminine by looking at other women, and by extension at cars which have been 'feminised' (either through aesthetic language – remember the pink Cadillac of the 1950s – or by a sexy woman in an ad), is supported by the sociologist David Gartman in his impressive book *Auto Opium*. From the 1920s onwards, women were seen as the main consumers of cars, Gartman claims: 'While men buy cars, women choose them…' He writes: 'More than half the people attending the 1929 New York Motor Show were women'.

The feminisation of the car can be seen as a deliberate strategy to make it appeal to women, rather than to turn it into a sexual object of desire for men. 'The feminine demand for line and colour has overborne the mere masculine insistence on practicality, durability, power and such dull and commonplace things', Gartman explains – an entirely different story from that relayed by feminists of female exploitation.

Gartman also has a view about men's relationship with cars in the middle years of the century. He calls it a 'dirty little secret' claiming that the feminised car enabled men to get in touch with their female sides but that in the homophobic 1950s this could not be admitted openly, hence the need to take the wife along as 'apparent' consumer. Indeed, the exaggerated feminisation of cars in 1950s America can be seen as a reflection of the polarised gender stereotypes during that time – the need for men and women to know exactly what their roles were.

The following decade saw a dramatic shift both in women's self-image and in the gendering of cars. While stereotypes continued to exist at either end of the spectrum, a new, agendered car was created for 'liberated' women who had entered the public space of the workplace and the city. The Mini was a neutral little box which offered female drivers a new, open-ended image as they stepped into the world, increasingly independent of men.

Inevitably, this was quickly sabotaged by the arrival of the racy little Mini Cooper with its powerful engine, its deep roar and its chunky wheels, which served to reinstate the male/female polarity, and to keep the threat of women invading the male sphere at bay. It was an interesting experiment, and one which changed things irrevocably.

The 1980s and '90s have seen the most dramatic shift in our gender identities this century. Women's liberation has transformed gendered roles; the idea that men and women have both feminine and masculine sides has become a truism and homosexuality is widely accepted. The ensuing confusion has led both to a revision of the way we relate to consumer objects in terms of gender, and the way in which those objects both mirror and create the stereotypes with which we communicate our gender identities.

The new androgyny, manifested in products such as Calvin Klein's cleverly packaged perfume CK1, is based on neutrality, ie: the idea of neither gender rather than both genders. It has inevitably hit car culture as well: Ford's Ka, for instance, resembles a well-toned body but there are no clues as to whether it is the physique of a man or a woman. The variety of drivers at its wheel reinforces this sense of gendered openness. As women in the 1990s enter the world of masculinity with ease, driving 'macho' cars, such as Mercedes, BMWs, and four-wheel drives, so men are zipping around the city in little Peugeots and Fiat 500s, without fear of metaphorical castration. (Some boundaries remain, however, and I have yet to see a man behind the wheel of a small Japanese people-mover.)

It has become easier *and* harder for marketing men to sell cars through their gender symbolism, because today almost anything goes. The ground is undoubtedly shifting, but a reaction is inevitable. In the meantime, women are having lots of fun playing with toys which used to be an impenetrable reserve of the 'boys'.

A Man on Women and Cars
Stephen Bayley

→ There's a sexual element in owning a car. Questions of power and control are as influential in driving as they are in relationships. Then there's the element of look-at-me narcissism involved. You'd have to have an undentable ego to deny that, in the breach as much as in the observance, the car you drive expresses an aspect of your character. Daewoo Fan Club members may have a problem with this, but it's a rule that applies to the rest of us.

A female account executive in the agency handling BMW's famously ballsy advertising once explained that any woman driving a BMW with an engine larger than 1.6 litres and possessing more than six cylinders, was making an overt statement about her predatory, and possibly even feral, sexual nature. Yes, I know some of them. There's something suggestively erotic in the notion of controlling excess power, an implication that "I want to be pleased, but the threshold is very high".

The conventional view that women are less interested in cars than men is under siege from every quarter. Five years ago Caroline Charles, Britain's leading designer of serious-but-sexy women's clothes, said to me: "I've just bought a new car". When I asked what it was, she replied ingenuously and triumphantly, "It's black". But at her last two catwalk shows during British Fashion Week, Charles was promoting Vauxhall's cute Tigra as a desirable fashion accessory for the urban woman.

Still, no woman has ever actually designed a car, although nearly 40 years ago in Detroit a select group got pretty close. For his 1959 Motorama, an automobile fashion show, General Motors' Harley Earl – the Barnum & Bailey stylist who gave the world chromium plate, tail fins and two-tone paint – commissioned some privileged young women with names like Vanderbilt and Ford to do what they could with GM's current production. These 'damsels of design,' as the local press called them with quaint condescension, produced a Corvette called Fancy Free with loose covers, an Impala called Martinique with fitted glassfibre luggage and pastel striped upholstery, and a Cadillac with black mouton carpet, a phone, pillows and lap robe in black seal fur. Forty years on, a woman has – thankfully, on this evidence – still not designed an entire car, although manufacturers acknowledge increasing feminine influence in purchasing decisions.

Condé Nast, publishers of *Vogue* and *Vanity Fair*, recently conducted a survey among 3500 women readers and found 89 per cent were interested in more than colour in their car, and none expressed a preference for black seal fur. These same women drove 10,000 miles a year and listed safety, design and power as the most important characteristics in the car they wanted. Last year, nearly half the two million cars sold in Britain were chosen and bought by women. But what would a car designed by, and for, women actually be like?

There's no question shape has a sexual identity. Thirty five years ago the E-type Jaguar was launched at the Geneva Motor Show. Styled by an aerodynamicist in a white lab coat called Malcolm Sayer, the magnificent E-type flushed a gargantuan load of Freudian and Jungian junk out of car industry psyches. Here was a car of astonishing elegance and technical refinement, but you didn't have to be under hypnosis to concede that here too was a car whose morphology acknowledged the extraordinary, expressive power of the phallus. Who can say what precise influence this had on the car's social impact, but few would contest the proposition that the E-type exerts an exceptional physical appeal.

But this question of morphology works both ways. A few years before Jaguar's E-type, Ford of America introduced the Edsel after a programme of detailed market research. Despite Ford's meticulous probing of the nooks and crannies of consumer preference with the most penetrating instruments, despite its offering the customer a car that was advanced by contemporary American standards, the Edsel was a catastrophic sales failure. One curious mid-Western psychiatrist conducted an experiment on Edsel customers: he found that in various tests his subjects admitted the Edsel was disturbing because its garishly plated vertical ellipse of a radiator grille, like a chrome horse's collar, reminded them of a woman's sexual organs.

It's curious how male symbolism worked for the Jaguar and female symbolism failed on the Ford. The expectation at Jaguar was that the new XK8, athletic and muscular, would appeal to women as much as men.

The XK8 was designed in Coventry by a team led by Geoff Lawson and Fergus Pollock. The team included a female upholstery specialist, but there's no evidence any gyno-centric brief was being slavishly respected. The XK8 is a handsome car, with massive, rounded haunches and bulges like Mr Motivator in his Lycra cycling shorts, but in some senses it's a less confident design than the old E-type since its form and details raid our memory of the lovely 1961 car for their effect. I wouldn't say the XK8, for all its attractiveness, is a car that's specially feminine in appearance, so what can Jaguar mean?

Well, research shows women are enjoying sports cars. Fully 48 per cent of people who drive Mazda's successful MX-5 roadster have bras in their wardrobes. With its new 4-litre 300bhp V8 engine, the new Jaguar XK8 is not to be confused with a woman's car in the sense that a Nissan Micra 1.0 with automatic and decorative Sainsbury trolley dents is a woman's car. Maybe Jaguar is trying to tell us contemporary women enjoy manipulating excessive power. But we know that already.

→ I think that unless we know

more about machines and

their use, unless we better

understand the mechanical

portion of life, we cannot have

the time to enjoy the trees,

and the birds, and the flowers,

and the green hills.

Henry Ford

1922

→	Two generations of Americans	
	really know more about the	
	Ford coil than the clitoris,	
	about the planetary system	
	of gears than the solar system	
	John Steinbeck	
	1945	

With these simple elements, Peter Horbury and his close-knit team forged the Volvo look for the next century with the S80. It also took talent. And was achieved against all odds. Here's how

16|31

Volvo
Six Screens,
a Table and a Nice View
Giles Chapman

Design, says Horbury,
is the number one reason
people choose a particular car.

CALIFORNIAN INSPIRATION BEHIND S80 ETHOS

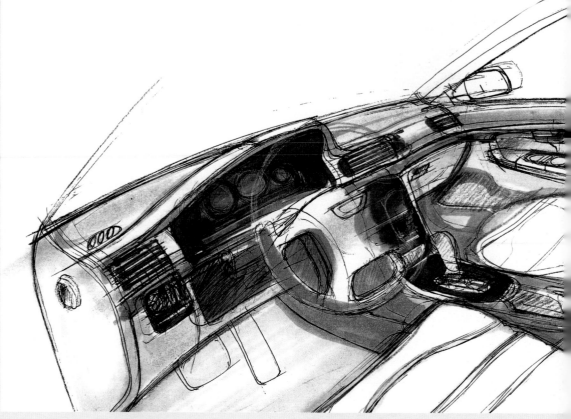

VOLVO S80 INTERIOR DESIGN SKETCH

OLD SCHOOL: VOLVO 760

NEW BROOM: CAREFULLY REVISED 960

→ On his first day as design director of Volvo, in the autumn of 1991, Peter Horbury reported for work at the company's Gothenburg design complex. Wearing his characteristic grin and rubbing his hands, he was itching to get to work on fashioning the future generation of Volvo cars.

The smile gradually faded when he saw what was on the drawing board.

Code-named R800, it was the new large Volvo saloon, and essentially the old 960 with a new body.

"I thought: 'Christ, this is bad news if it's going to be our big car for the next 10 years'", he recalls. "It was handsome in a traditional Volvo way, and softer than the 850. It had some nice details. But it was *very* Volvo – and, worst of all for me as a new design director, it was virtually finished."

Like a gift from the Gods, however, events were to turn suddenly in his favour. Volvo and Renault announced they were in advanced merger talks. That meant pooling their design thinking. A krona-pinching rehash of a design already a decade old was no longer the right car for a federal future.

"I had to tell the guys in the studio, who'd been perfecting this particular model, that I'm really sorry but we're stopping the job" – Horbury's eyes gleam – "with, of course, my fingers crossed behind my back!"

Horbury, an RCA graduate, had worked for Volvo in the past. In Sweden in 1979-80 and for the company's Dutch division in 1981-86, he'd learnt a great deal about how a small manufacturer could achieve its design aims by eking the most from paltry design resources. A spell with independent design consultancy MGA in Coventry preceded his appointment as holder of Volvo's platinum Rotring.

Now, here was the prospect of designing a new Volvo on a shared platform, confidently assumed to equate to that of Renault's bland but relatively new Safrane executive saloon, complete with its V6 engine. Still, something had to be done with the increasingly stale 900 series.

Gathering his new team around him – acknowledged by Horbury as "incredibly enthusiastic about Volvo, real car freaks" – the new design chief rejected the idea of shoving a new nose on the old-timer's uncompromisingly square-cut collosus. Instead, the grille was slimmed down, the bumper line was lifted, new wings were designed and several other clever modernising tricks pulled off. Best of all, in investment terms, it cost no more than designing and engineering a new bonnet.

"Then we turned our thoughts to a new car," says Horbury. "We'd settled upon Safrane size but with the floorpan modified to incorporate all the 'Volvo-ness' we'd need to put in."

VOLVO S80

"I thought we could try out
some new designs in public –
it's always useful if you're going
to change the image of a company
dramatically to test the water."

112

RENAULT SAFRANE – ONCE THE BASIS FOR A NEW LARGE VOLVO

VOLVO S80 INTERIOR

Meanwhile, Horbury had got wind of a petrol-electric hybrid prototype being developed by Volvo's technical team. The base car was a Volvo production saloon, but he envisioned clothing this interesting new technology as an ideal opportunity to stretch the company's creativity.

"I thought we could try out some new designs in public – it's always useful if you're going to change the image of a company dramatically to test the water."

It was intended as a quick design project entrusted to Volvo's small Californian design studio ("five or six screens, a table and a nice view"). The results were epoch-making.

"Immediately I saw the directions we should take. They were using Volvo design cues in a brand new way. It was a simple marker and pastel sketch by one of the designers there, Doug Frasier, pinned on the wall that made me think: 'This is it – this is what we'll do'".

Frasier's proposal for a smooth new saloon car featured a nose that was extremely low-set for a Volvo, a flush-fronted car with a grille, still recognisable as the traditional Volvo frontispiece, set deep into its bumper/front apron. All the car's lines then flowed back from it, while the leading edges of the wings formed a 'shoulder' that also flowed right back to the sharply cut-off tail.

Thus was born the ground-breaking shape of the 1992 ECC – the Environmental Concept Car. "This was not supposed to be a design exercise," says Horbury wistfully, "but here was a potential new Volvo – it was an immediate guide to the future."

"I wanted to get this 'look' into production so, when we started work on the Renault joint-venture car, I told my designers just to do the ECC again over the new platform!"

Four different full-size models were then constructed for evaluation, one in Holland and three in the US, some more sheer and sharper-lined than the ECC, some almost identical to the original. Horbury was happy to plunder the Volvo family album for inspiration.

"I actually hate 'retro'. That's not what we're about. But the positive arc from the front lamp to the back one was there since the Volvo PV444 of 1947. Then there was the shoulder that didn't 'fall away' immediately from the bottom of the side windows. It's solid, strong, a flat-top shoulder that came from the 140 and 240. On top was what we call the 'Volvo bridge' – three side windows with a dog-leg shape at the back. The 400, 800 and 900 series – they all had that.

"It was the basic architecture of a Volvo in a very new way. I felt we'd managed almost a sub-conscious recognition. Unlike previous Volvos, though, we didn't want the car's safety to be in-your-face."

Horbury was discovering that large-corporation working practices could easily infect design purity.

"I learned a lot as we began to work internationally. Our engineering department is in Gothenburg; our American designers, about six of them then, were in California. They're there because America is Volvo's biggest market, bigger even than Sweden. The designers represent the market and must live in it."

"But as the designers' work was given to the engineers I realised, quite frankly, that we were losing it. It was proving very difficult to retain the essence of the ECC, and that was the car I wanted to bring to life. It's one of the problems of giving one person's work to another."

As Horbury fretted about the design compromises, something unexpected happened. The deal to merge Renault and Volvo, two companies that had enjoyed cordial collaboration, mostly on engines, since the 1970s, was off. With moss starting to grow on the 960 in Volvo's showrooms and a concept car whetting the public's appetite for a radical replacement, it was panic stations. Volvo, despite its robust reputation, was one of the smallest mainstream car makers, and had no choice but to go it alone.

Far from demoralising the creative minds within the company, Volvo designers were jump-started into action. Like no model before it, Volvo's future rested on the new car's successful genesis.

Throughout the Christmas holidays of 1993 and 1994 Volvo's engineers worked 24-seven to create a uniquely Volvo platform, codenamed P2, for the new model, using the 850 mechanical base as a starting point. This was, after several false starts, the birth of the S80.

"It was amazing, absolutely wonderful, the way we gelled to create something new. But, without the Renault V6 engine, what the hell could we do? True, we had our straight-six engine but we knew that, by 1998, we'd need front-wheel drive to be competitive in packaging terms."

113

THE VOLVO S80 'SHOULDER'

VOLVO S80

The only solution, with the clock ticking, was to mount the straight-six engine longitudinally between the front wheels – a layout only attempted once before in Australia with a bizarre Anglo hybrid called the Austin Kimberley, based on the unappetising Austin 1800. As the engineers wrestled with the challenge of adapting an engine designed to send power to rear wheels into a front-wheel drive powerpack, Horbury's styling team pondered the impact on their baby.

"We knew that, at 1810mm, the S80 would have to be wide. That makes for a pretty big car. But our design, once we'd adjusted the models, actually helped with the width.

"We wanted the windscreen well forward and now, with the engine well out of the way, we had the room to do it – it's a 'thinner' engine than a V6, and was now mounted further forward. We had proportions that worked: the shoulders took up the width and we avoided a stubby, wide front end because the grille extended down into the bumper and the 'V' of the bonnet split the nose into three manageable sections."

The mammoth effort from all involved also brought the Californian designers and Swedish engineers closer together although, says Horbury, "It was like going back a year to find out what had happened to our design – the roofline had got too flattened, the pillars too straightened." However, with the sunny California studio now feeding its data via computer links straight to gloomy Sweden, the designers were effectively working alongside the team at the sharp end. New full-size S80 models, for example, were machined in Gothenburg directly from California-supplied data.

"I was so protective of the original design because I wanted a car that wouldn't date quickly," Horbury reflects. "In terms of purity of form, I wanted it as Swedish as possible. If you do something less than simple and pure it starts to date quicker.

"Take good Swedish furniture, for example. You can't date it. A decent Swedish chair could have been made yesterday or in the 1920s. They design with no excess, no decoration, no flowery bits.

Horbury points to the tail lights as a good example of his ethos.

"The lamp is only a change of material and surface, a block on which we draw lines; it turns a corner and another panel takes over. Nothing else happens apart from that change. It's a feature by virtue of not being designed as one."

The interior is something totally new for Volvo. There's a feeling of security and serenity you get from sitting in the driver or passenger seat without the feeling you're cowering behind a vertical protective mass. Horbury grandly likens it to the difference between standing behind a prison wall and standing on top of a mountain.

The top of the dashboard is perpendicular to the passenger's eyeline – you look straight at a surface with a 90deg elevation. It's not falling in on you and nor, unlike in Citroëns like the CX, do you feel you could be thrown across it.

"We repeated the theme into the doors and around the interior. It gives a harmony throughout the whole car."

In fact, having created an exceptionally roomy cabin, in conjunction with chief interior designer José Diaz de la Vega, Horbury then set about filling it. The comfortable seats, a Volvo hallmark, were a given, but the high and broad centre console was inspired from an unlikely source.

"Well, both José and myself love those 1960s GT supercars – Aston Martins, Ferraris, Maseratis. You reclined into them and they all had a massive central transmission tunnel. The S80 is front-wheel drive, so you don't actually need it, but it looks so quality, so expensive. We decided to make a 'tunnel' between the front seats as big as possible to evoke quality and luxury – and, incidentally, to house a lot of the car's equipment. However, we were careful to make sure it didn't encroach on leg space, or 'cut off' the passengers from the driver."

The entire interior gives a feeling of comfortable security – "calmness", says Horbury. "We have softer lines, rather than rounded ones in a Renault or a Fiat. This is very Scandinavian, very controlled, with long, flat curves."

With the whole emphasis of the passenger compartment brought forward as the engine retreated to the very prow of the car, that meant lots of room in the back. This is a crucial plug-in to Volvo buyers' psyches.

EARLY VOLVO S80 CONCEPT IDEAS

Says Horbury: "I think one of the biggest benefits in the S80 is in the room it offers for business and also for family – the useful space for mum, dad and two, possibly late teenage, children. Family values are much stronger in a Volvo than in a more 'selfish' company car. The BMW 5 Series driver, for instance, buys the car for himself to drive, and the family just has to fit in around him. As society changes then I think Volvo will be supplying a kind of very discreet luxury."

Something Volvo has been supplying for a very long time indeed is the seminal large estate car. The S80, however, was designed purely as, in the American vernacular that's so important to the Volvo design community, a sedan.

There will be, emphatically, no S80 estate.

"Our sedans actually suffered because of the rules of good estate car design – the saloon had become a derivative of the station wagon, if you will."

"In a Volvo estate, wasted space is minimal compared to, say, a BMW 5 Series Touring or an Audi A4 Avant. A Volvo is much more efficient as a load carrier. The flat sides, the vertical tailgate – it's a box on wheels. Yet…it still looks good because the window line is one shape. It never looks like a conversion. However, we wanted to make a saloon that didn't look like it had been created from an estate."

You can expect, however, a new range of big Volvo estates in the future. And there will be plenty of the new Volvo look, exemplified by the S80, in them. "I'm quite confident we can keep the shouldered look on a station wagon. Its Swedish brand value is its pragmatic practicality, its functionality."

The S80 went on sale last year.

"The most memorable comment for me came when we put the car in a German customer clinic before it was launched," says Horbury. "One guy said: 'At last – I can buy a Volvo.' That was great to hear."

For Volvo, the S80 is the last of a line – the last Volvo necessarily developed on a shoestring. Now owned by Ford, future Volvos will be able to share in one of the world's biggest technology pools.

It is also the first of a line, the car that marks the change in Volvo's attitude to car design. Horbury: "We had to change. We had to aim for the upper segment of the market because that's where we could make money. Crucial to that was a need to make cars that, while fulfilling the desire in buyers to make an intelligent purchase, also offer an aesthetic attraction. We had to get away from the old Swedish idea that the best medicine was the one that tasted worst.

"You see, form following function doesn't actually sell cars."

"The I-don't-care-about-my-looks might have been OK for university dons in the 1970s, but car buyers expect to be able to match intelligence with beauty. This underlies everything we do now. Volvo has to appeal to the world, and not just to Swedish farmers who want their cars to operate at -40deg on dark mornings, and nothing else."

Design, says Horbury, is the number one reason people choose a particular car. Surveys in the early 1980s showed Volvo buyers put design at number eight or nine on their buying criteria list.

"I saw that huge gap as a potential," smiles Horbury. "There are hundreds of thousands of people buying Volvos regardless of how they look. But there must be millions not buying them because they don't have the aesthetic appeal of other cars. If you could combine the two, you could really get somewhere."

The Values of Volvo
Stephen Bayley

If a single brand summarised Surrey it's Volvo: decent, safe, prosperous, suburban and middle-class. Volvo now belongs to Ford. But does Woking Man and, especially, Woking Woman, care?

It's nearly 10 years since Ford acquired its first trophy marque. There were grumbles then that Jaguar would be turned into a badge for high-end Sierras. But it was nothing of the sort. After a scary start, when skeletons fell out of the cupboards in Coventry, Ford's stewardship of Jaguar has been exemplary.

The challenge for Ford is to do for Volvo what it has already done for the British make. Yet 1999 Volvo is in far better shape than 1989 Jaguar: Ford has acquired a badge with a monumental and probably indestructible reputation for probity and environmental responsibility.

Ever since 1927, Volvo has consistently developed. Although its engineering is conservative, the company has an audacious tradition of innovations in safety and comfort including standard seatbelts, orthopaedic seats, day notice lights and side impacts protection.

The Swedes have a superb reputation for thoughtfulness and undemonstrative elegance in architecture and interior design: Volvo annexed that tradition for the car.

No wonder the drivers of West Byfleet and Ripley, whose concept of modernism was acquired from cargo cult versions of 1950s Swedish furniture and stainless steel fish platters sold in local chainstores, found Volvo delivered both the letter and the spirit of the goods.

Indeed, put the middle-aged consumers of Surrey under deep hypnosis and ask them to do free association tests, against the prompt "Volvo" they'll rise up as one and respond "estate car".

But today Volvo does not manufacture a big estate and here is the dilemma Ford has to solve.

Woking Man in his Austin Reed cords, once inseparable from his 240GL estate, has now mutated into Gap, Ralph Lauren and Timberland. He drives Shoguns, Discoveries, Galaxies and Espaces. Four-wheel-drives and MPVs are over-crowding Volvo's territorial niche.

Simultaneously, Volvo's unique selling proposition of impregnable safety has been devalued since legislation and fashion made serious crash protection sexy. Fiestas have airbags too.

Volvo's response has been to chase other markets, with only partial success. Having invested so much design effort and advertising spend on persuading the public to have certain expectations of Volvo, the product has moved on and left its image behind.

Today Volvo makes better looking, better handling, more sophisticated cars than ever, like the C70 coupe…but no-one quite knows what they're for. No-one that is, except, Ford.

Wherever you are, Volvo's established image capital has vast amounts of unexploited value which it would be reckless to ignore. Think Volvo and you think estate car, but expect to see more large Volvo cars as well as new Volvo minivans, sports-utes and pick-ups.

How do cars link into the theory and discipline of the design world at large? Four very different designers, RCA graduates to a man, explain how it all works

17|31

Connections
Gavin Conway

Go too far and you
end up with bad taste,
"like a woman with too
much make-up"

COMMUTER TRAIN BY BERTONE

LUCIANO D'AMBROSIO – **DESIGN DIRECTOR, BERTONE**

He speaks with as much passion about mopeds and bicycles as he does about cars and toasters. And women. In his career, Luciano d'Ambrosio has styled concept cars, worked with Ford on Fiesta and Escort, designed bicycles and motorcycles. But, he says, one of the hallmarks of good design is a constant theme regardless of the subject; 'a balance of misproportion'.

"If you see a nice looking lady, with very regular, symmetric features, regularly proportioned mouth and ears, this is somehow not so good. Everything is too organised," says d'Ambrosio. "What really appeals in a nice looking lady is something that goes away a little from normal, perhaps a spot on her cheek, or a little curve on the nose. It is like that with a car, if it is too regularly proportioned, it is boring. If you are attracted by the little differences, that's half the job of design done."

He cautions, though, that a good understanding of proportion is crucial to getting the balance right. Go too far and you end up with bad taste, "like a woman with too much make-up." D'Ambrosio attended the RCA on a Ford scholarship from 1979 to 1981, an experience he says has made him a better designer. "Before, I was in college in Italy, but it was only automotive design. But at the RCA, I was surrounded by furniture and appliance design, people working with glass and jewellery," says d'Ambrosio. "Even fashion, very useful for interior design on cars. All of those influences gave me a much wider view. So when you think of designing a new car, you are not simply referring to other cars for inspiration."

D'Ambrosio's other guiding principle is simplicity: "It's an easy word to say, but achieving simplicity in design is actually very difficult. Quite often we will take a design and analyse it in model form, asking ourselves whether all those lines are actually necessary. You look at any design that's survived over time, and the key element is always simplicity." D'Ambrosio reckons two exemplars of design simplicity are Fiat's Panda and BMC's Mini. "They were designed around big packaging constraints," he says, "and yet they still achieved that simplicity of design."

Humour and irony can also figure in the mix, says d'Ambrosio. "You can take anything – a toaster or a chair – and it does its job, it is purely functional. But life is not to be taken so seriously, and function is not the final target. When you want toast, you are attracted by the action if the appliance has a little humour in the design. It becomes less of a routine, more an enjoyment."

But there is a serious element here, too. D'Ambrosio says designers hate being called stylists because it implies superficiality. Not what today's designers are about, according to him: "Car styling can sometimes be considered nothing more than covering something that already exists with new clothes. But really, your solution should be to improve the package, make the cabin more useful, advance and evolve the design. That is what designers do today. Not simply making another shape, but going under the skin to create something new."

DUCATI SUPERMONO

DUCATI 900SS

**PIERRE TERREBLANCHE –
DESIGN DIRECTOR, DUCATI MOTORCYCLES**

A clue. He collects antique refrigerators. That single fact reveals one of Pierre Terreblanche's most passionately held design philosophies. And although he is design director of Ducati – producer of some of the world's most beautiful motorcycles – he does nurse a secret desire.

"I've always wanted to design a fridge," says Terreblanche.

"At the moment, I'm restoring an old one from the 1950s. I love the way the surfaces are moulded so gently, so that running your hand over it becomes a pleasure. The materials, too, have a weight and feel to them that's hard to recapture. Smeg do a modern fridge something like that, but it still doesn't have the right tactility."

Tactility figures large in Terreblanche's world; motorcycles reveal, by design, much of their working bits. And the people who buy them want to touch. "Bike owners are constantly running their hands over the machines, so we pay a lot of attention to surface finish and materials. Things like cast aluminium, polished alloy, titanium, anodised metal, all of that is part of the tactile pleasure. After all, 90 per cent of the motorcycle experience is emotional." The trick, says Terreblanche, is not to make things look too deliberately designed. "For example, a Harley Davidson is the most designed thing out there, but a lot of the parts you see look like they came off a tractor. They look right, like they just happened." Just make sure it's good to touch; RCA graduate Terreblanche on how not to do it: "Phillipe Starck did a motorcycle very much designed in the way of a common domestic appliance. There just wasn't enough cast aluminium, and it simply wasn't tactile enough."

Terreblanche reckons the current crop of designers, many in their early forties, are also borrowing styles and forms that made an impact when they were growing up. "It's the neo-classical side of current design, with cars as well as appliances," he says. "You can see it in the new Volkswagen Beetle and Ford's Thunderbird concept. They aren't necessarily copying, but rather interpreting their memories of good design."

And keeping it simple, clean. Terreblanche reckons the other dominant design theme is a Bauhaus-inspired minimalism, demonstrated by Audi's TT coupé. "It reminds me of a 1950s customised, chopped and lowered Mercury. Very clean, uncluttered surfaces and a small, narrow greenhouse area. You see that in the latest furniture designs, too. At a recent show in Milan, one company presented a chair design that took simplicity to the very core, a sort of Le Corbusier for the Millennium."

But Terreblanche comes back to surfaces, tactility. "People are tired of plastic square boxes. Look at how popular Apple's iMac was when it came out. I'd love to see a computer made of Bakelite, perhaps with a polished aluminium keyboard." And fridges:

"I remember we had a Frigidaire for decades. It just gurgled away in the kitchen while everything around it wore out. It was beautiful to look at, with its own distinct character. It had the feel and the perception of quality."

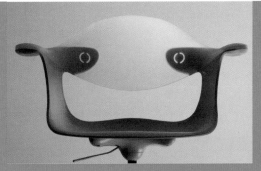

SEAT BY STUDIO X

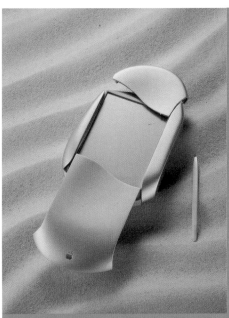

APPLE NEWTON CONCEPT BY STUDIO X

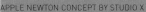

→ ROSS LOVEGROVE – INDEPENDENT INDUSTRIAL
DESIGNER AND FOUNDER OF STUDIO X

There isn't much in your world that Ross
Lovegrove hasn't touched: cameras, razors,
computers, luggage, perfume bottles, cutlery,
lamps and furniture to name a few. From the
stylish confines of his Studio X in Notting Hill,
nothing that surrounds us in the daily crush has
escaped his intense scrutiny. Not even cars.

And this Welsh-born, RCA alumnus reckons
the industry needs a good shake-up. "It's true
we live in a visual world and it's become that
way through graphics and advertising," says
Lovegrove, who has an informal relationship with
the likes of Audi and Honda. "But we are still quite
sensual beings. When I drink from a coffee cup
I don't look at it, and when I drive my car, I don't
look at it. So there are other priorities, and I think
we should put human beings first. Even before
Honda used it in their advertising, I've been saying maximise man, minimise machine. You do that
by being honest about how people actually use
cars. And because I'm not in the world of car
design, I can say what I like about it."

And he does. Lovegrove believes passionately
that car design should be informed by the real
world around it. "Why shouldn't car controls be
as beautiful as finely rendered cutlery?" he says.
"You can take the experiences of common man,
the feel of a remote control, the look of his TV,
his sofa, and bring that into his car so he'll feel
good about being there." Lovegrove believes,
too, that it's time to abandon the convention
that dictates cars are made from metal, wood
and leather: "Wood and leather! Look, we're not
building horses and carriages, we're building
absolutely modern, mass-produced products.
If you want to touch leather, you should go stroke
some cows in a field. It is plain we are living in the
age of plastic. Think of cameras; they started out
made of wood, then metal and now plastic."

Plastic cars, then? "An outfit like ours thinks
differently. I'm not stuck in a car design studio
all day, so I can bridge different worlds. For
example, rotational moulding is a really cheap
way of producing plastic products. People with
their backs to the wall look around to see the
cheapest way of doing things. But it seems
almost as though car companies have too
much money to think that way."

And with a bit of lateral thinking, Lovegrove has
even poached a bit of car design for use in the
back garden. "Lights designed for cars can resist
frost and the effects of sun and they are just
about unbreakable. So I just took that way of
thinking and came up with a new product –
garden lighting."

Ultimately, Lovegrove would love to design his
own car from the ground up. A city car that
would be light, efficiently packaged, environmentally sound and full of ideas brought across from
pure industrial design. "For example, headlights
could be unclipped and become a torch if you
break down. And they could be suckered to the
inside of the windshield. Where's the switch?
On the actual light itself. We know cellphones
aren't going away, so why not design a connector
on the steering wheel so your phone becomes
truly hands-free when you're in the car. This is
all about making the car a real extension of
your life."

IDEAL STANDARD BRIDGE TAPS BY SEYMOUR POWELL

MINOLTA SHARK CAMERA BY SEYMOUR POWELL

→ **RICHARD SEYMOUR – OF LONDON-BASED
PRODUCT DESIGN PARTNERSHIP SEYMOUR POWELL**

These guys are serious petrol heads. Walk in the front door of design house Seymour Powell and the first thing you'll trip over is a motorbike, perched on a stand in reception. It's an MZ Skorpion, not a brand you'll recognise immediately, but plainly a fully-functioning, road-registered machine. Also, a good clue to what this outfit is all about.

"There is still this persistent view that the designer is a stylist," says Richard Seymour. "But the fact is, we are a product design company, although styling is part of what we do. When MZ came to us for a new design, we didn't give them a drawing when they came back. We gave them an ignition key. That bike out front was the show bike, and it was roadworthy before it even got to the show stand."

Design and function. You hear that a lot from Seymour. This RCA graduate, through Seymour Powell, has been involved in the creation of products as diverse as palm-top computers and intercity trains. What drives him and his company, though, is the sense that the product grows out of what the user needs. And desires.

"One of the most important factors in all of this is what I call emotional ergonomics," says Seymour.

"It's the importance of the unimportant. One of the best examples of that is the car interior light that, when you get in and close the door, fades away instead of popping off. It creates excitement, it's like being in a theatre when the lights go dim before the show. Everybody loves it, and when you really get into it, you realise most things we love have those kind of qualities." Those ergonomics are one of the reasons why Seymour is so convinced car design needs to integrate much better with the world around it. "The automotive world is waking up to the fact that we don't just drive cars, we own other things. If you live with a certain type of product in your life, a computer or wristwatch, it's going to have a bearing on your expectations of all objects. For example, we were working with a Japanese train manufacturer and they were terribly excited by their electric windows, saying they were the first to have them on a train and so on.

"In the meantime, the cheapest cars you can imagine have electric windows. And consumers would be making a negative comparison, because their car window works smoothly and quickly while this one is rather clunky. The point is, we make comparisons across boundaries. And the consumer is much more attuned to detail and quality, much more design aware."

And, says Seymour, much more picky: "The consumer of the next century is about choice. And I can tell you, they'll be demanding a lot more than bloody cupholders! I mean, there are still lots of things you can do with space and shape and volume that have not been done. And things like hydrogen fuel cells will make it possible to do new things."

So the message is simple, clear. Design cars from the driver out. Sure, style is important, but it just better damn well work, growls Seymour. "We don't draw pictures, we design products," he says. "There's a big difference."

These guys
are serious
petrol heads.

The automobile makers have made, in the past few years, a greater contribution to the art of comfortable seating than chair builders had made in all of preceding history.

Walter Dorwin Teague
1940

I came into designing Rolls-Royces thinking of them as flying drawing rooms. My one passion was to perpetuate that, to keep a rather nice idea intact.

John Blatchley
Former Rolls-Royce
Chief Stylist

He's done it all – from Le Mans cars to truck cabs – and, in a 20-year stint with Audi, helped create a world-leading brand in just 20 years. Now Martin Smith, an RCA graduate in 1973, is about to get to work on General Motors' European cars. They need him

18|31

The Perfect Car Designer's Career?

Matthew Gwyther

129

We want to create a
very strong brand identity
so that people will say
"That's an Opel interior"
— Martin Smith

VAUXHALL/OPEL VECTRA – COMPETENT AS AN AUDI A4?

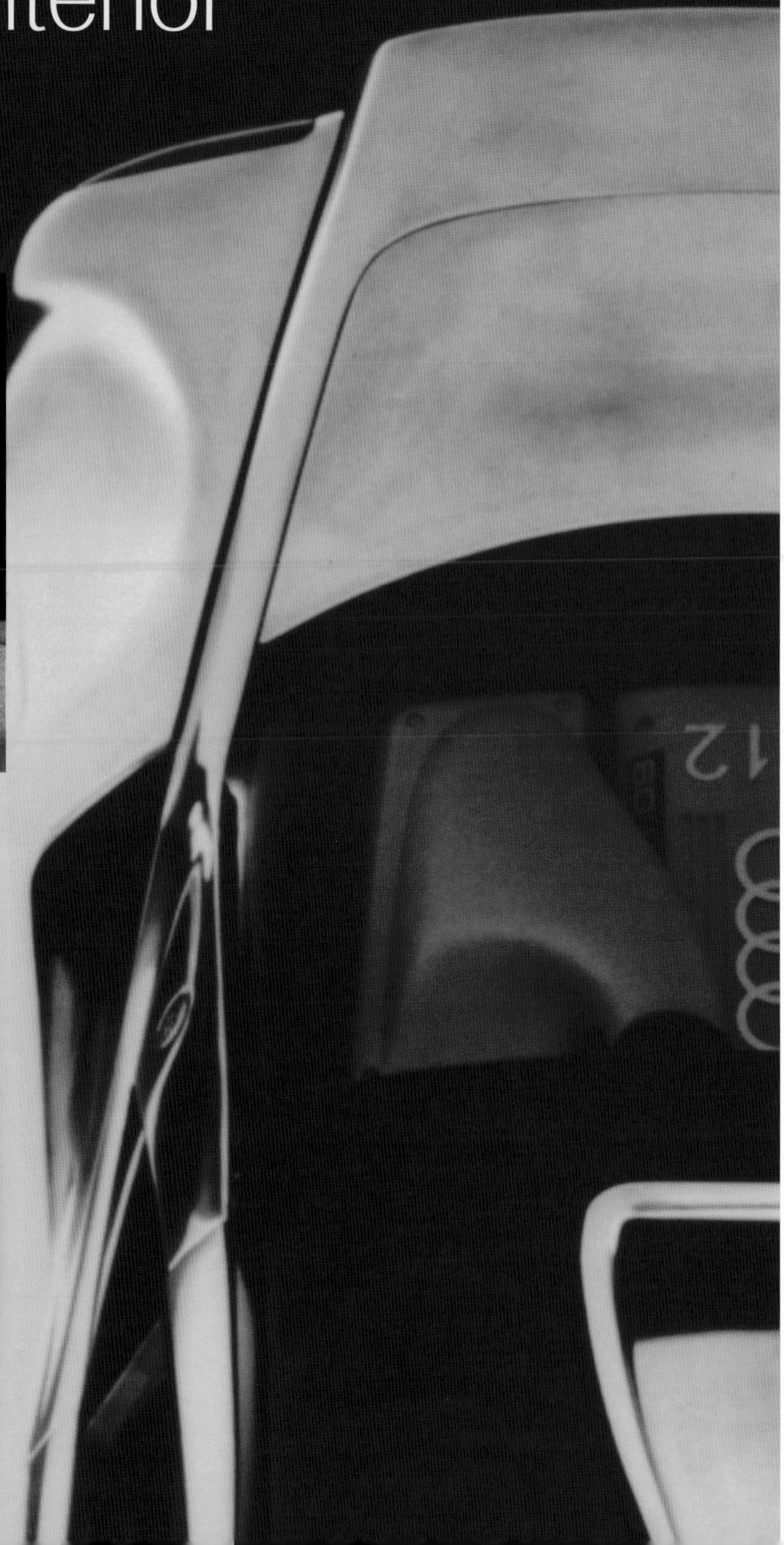

LEYLAND ROADTRAIN 'POPEMOBILE'

AUDI AVUS

→ The night Manchester United played Bayern Munich in the European Cup Final led to a painful crisis of loyalty for Martin Smith. Having worked as a team-leading designer for Audi for 20 years, Munich was his home town. In addition, his new employer, Opel, is Bayern's shirt sponsor. But despite having lived in exile in Germany for the past 27 years he still found himself urging Beckham and Giggs to victory beneath his breath. (And he is a Yorkshireman.)

The day afterwards he was keeping his head down. That is not, one suspects, a difficult posture for Smith to adopt because, despite being a key designer of European cars for the last two decades, he maintains a studiously low profile. An extremely reticent man, he is dressed not, as you may expect, in Hugo Boss, but like a Latin teacher at a minor public school. The mildest of outré additions to his garb is a pair of sunglasses on a cord around his neck.

Smith, now 50, is cautious and thoughtful. He would clearly rather be dragged by the heels behind one of his speeding Audi quattros than talk about himself. One thing that does rouse him to vocal emotion, though, is the difficulty he faced in trying to become a car designer.

If ever anyone was born to the trade it was Smith. As a boy he'd written a fan letter to Alec Issigonis, who had replied in a kindly and encouraging fashion. However, at King Edward Grammar school in his home town of Sheffield, the powers that be were not so keen.

"The top people at my school went to Oxford or Cambridge to study classics," he says ruefully. "The second string went to Oxford and Cambridge to study science. The third string went to provincial universities and the fourth went to art college. Or rather, they didn't because art college was out of the question. I went to do an engineering degree at Liverpool University and that was pretty much bottom-rung."

Pure Engineering was not what he wanted to do and before long he was on a train to London and the Royal College of Art where he had heard about the automotive design course, then in its infancy. "It was like taking a blindfold off," he recalls. "I used to draw pictures but it never occurred to me you could draw cars with magic markers and coloured chalks. This was a real revelation after thermo-dynamics and coefficients. I could hardly believe students got grants to do this." He was told to come back in a month after he'd practiced how to sketch reflections on windscreens. Then, he was accepted.

"The RCA was a typically English system," he remembers. "You didn't need to go to lectures, you were left very much to your own devices, sitting around drawing cars all day." But that was all right by Smith. He learned enough to receive job offers from Rolls-Royce, Chrysler, Vauxhall and Porsche. Unsurprisingly, perhaps, for a man in the flush of youth, he chose the German manufacturer.

131

PORSCHE 928

It was the beginning of a long spell abroad. He can see quite clearly in retrospect why it happened: "I thought the British car industry would never realise the importance of design in selling cars," he says. "Porsche understood design very well. At BL, however, I would have earned the same or less than a secretary." (And, for his pains, he would have been put to work on the Allegro.)

So in 1973 he left the RCA, emptied his flat, packed all his possessions into a 34bhp VW Beetle and set off for Stuttgart.

"When I got there I went straight into the studio and it was fantastic – there were *real* cars in clay. I was just so frustrated I had to go to the personnel department to sign all the necessary forms before I could get on with it."

His boss was the legendary Tony Lupine who had been in on the original Chevrolet Corvette. Also working for old man Porsche were Wolfgang Mobius and Dick Soderburgh. The engineering-led company was exactly what Smith was after: "If Lupine didn't like something you had drawn he'd rip it off the wall and tell you you were an idiot. Nowadays we're a bit more tactful. The 'profes-sionality' [sic] beaten into me at Porsche has stayed with me for the rest of my career."

Smith got to style the engine and the famous rear spoiler of the original 911 Turbo, contributed to the 911 Le Mans cars and helped develop the 924 and the 928. But then came disaster with the oil crisis and thirsty Porsches went rapidly out of fashion. The workforce had to be trimmed. Smith actually volunteered to leave as he "thought it was the correct thing to do." He came back to the UK for a year to Ogle Design and helped with the Leyland Roadtrain truck, a bit of a comedown after 911s.

It was at this time he designed the most unusual vehicle in his career – Luke Skywalker's Land Speeder for the first *Star Wars* film. "I met George Lucas who was making the film in the UK and he explained that he wanted a post-modern, *Dan Dare*-style vehicle," says Smith. "We made it from the chassis of the three-wheeler Bond Bug." It was Smith's one and only wheel-less car – they removed all three with photographic special effects.

It was shortly after this that he was headhunted to Audi in 1977. Audi, probably more than any other manufacturer worldwide, has undergone a perceptual change in the last 20 years. From being a rather dull but essentially worthy Euro car that some members of the British public were convinced was Belgian, it has transformed into a highly desirable marque which is quite the height of chic among the aspiring middle classes.

Smith was right in the middle of the creation of this technology-driven "new Bauhaus". He was one of a team of five that created the original quattro which caused a minor sensation with its flared fenders and aggressive technical/mech-anical look. Forms that followed function clearly made sense to this kind of frills-free Yorkshireman, and he was asked by Ferdinand Piech to create the Audi Advanced Studio in central Munich, from which came the Avus show car in 1990 that harked back to the silver Auto Union racing cars of the 1930s, and from which the roofline of the current TT is derived.

In the 1990s, after working on the interiors of the A3, A4 and the TT, now, maybe surprisingly, he finds himself working for General Motors at Russelsheim near Frankfurt. (Friends in the know say that, as an Englishman and despite his talents Smith had reached a glass ceiling at VW/Audi. They want *echt Deutschers* for the top jobs so Smith, who has spent more of his life in Germany than in the UK, had to look elsewhere for advancement.)

Coming from one of the most sexy, happening places in the car business, GM might seem a bit workaday and prosaic. Certainly, Opels and Vauxhalls are competent, well-engineered cars but they do not, at the moment, set many motorists' hearts on fire. The salesman who gets a Vectra rather than an A4 in which to pound the motorway (or autobahn) and ply his trade is, by and large, a disappointed man. Or woman.

GM invented styling and the tradition
of the company is to never have
looked backwards – Martin Smith

AUDI QUATTRO

AUDI A4 – COMPETENT AS A VAUXHALL/OPEL VECTRA?

Audi, probably more than any other manufacturer worldwide, has undergone a perceptual change in the last 20 years

Smith, loyal to his new employer, says he believes this to be highly unfair. "The Vectra is as competent a car as the A4," he protests. "It may not have the image of the A4 but in form language and design execution it's every bit as competent – the same genre."

For Smith the move is like coming home.

"My mentors for whom I worked at Porsche came from here," he says. "GM invented styling and the tradition of the company is to never have looked backwards. We created very emotional, dynamic cars in the 1970s and now we want to progress that. We want to create a contemporary European design, looking forward to the future."

So now he drives around in an Astra, especially as his Ferrari 512 Testarossa is currently in the garage with a flat battery. One of his first tasks must be to do something about Vauxhall interiors which, while they work, are nothing to write home about. Smith acknowledges that a bit of homologation across the range is now called for: "The interiors have not had that look. They have been very functional, competent ergonomically, but possibly have not used the best materials and haven't possessed an identifiable Opel brand architecture. We want to create a very strong brand identity so people will say, 'That's an Opel interior.'

In the meantime, as a hint of what might be to come, Opel has come up with the Speedster, developed with Lotus in the UK.

"The Speedster is the first big indicator of where we're going," he says. "With it we want to demonstrate our futuristic form language." It certainly does not look like what we've come to expect from Vauxhall in recent years, and is all the better for it. And it adheres to all Smith's principles of constructing cars properly rather than making them superficial styling exercises.

"It's constructed, not modelled, from the elements of body, cabin and four fenders. And their intersections. It was not modelled from solid pieces of clay." In bright yellow or orange, the Speedster is unmissable.

Another prominent yellow object in Smith's life is the Lamborghini model that sits on a shelf behind his desk. It is a 1968 Countach designed by Marcello Gandini of Bertone. "That was the car that inspired me as a student," he says. "It is one of the cleverest designs ever created. It's dynamic, constructed like a piece of architecture. The lines are hard-edged but the shapes all run into each other. It's just brilliant." For the first time in the last hour-and-a-half, Smith emits a fraction of a smile.

→ For all but a handful of car manufacturers, 'product identity' is a term heard in the design office only recently. Product identity is, in almost every sense, the set of values we have come to know as 'brand,' only viewed through the keen, discreet eye of a designer.

A brand manager – a broader-reaching, marketing role – is a position now occupied not just in those automotive groups which sell cars with more than one badge on their noses or tails, but in those rare companies with only one set of headed paper and envelopes. He or she is a custodian. They exist to ensure consistency of communications – visual and non-visual – in all areas relating to a vehicle's brand; the way BMW advertisements have looked the same for 20 years, for example. That's textbook brand management.

The look of an advertisement, the tone of its copy, the interior or exterior of a dealership – none of these brand management issues need worry a design studio head. Product identity is, in its purest form, the ability to recognise a product without its badge. In the same way, most famously, that the classic Coca-Cola bottle made reading the label redundant, so Dieter Rams created a surface treatment and a graphic organisation for the German company Braun that gives its electric shavers, blenders and coffee-makers a recognisable uniformity. The trick is to combine such visual discipline with superior functionality and a consistent reputation for quality. Pull it off, and you'll be lecturing MBAs in no time.

Just like BMW. BMW has taken the simplest route to creating a product identity: build the same sporty saloon cars, but in three different sizes. "Small tomato, medium tomato, large tomato", say those envious of BMW's strength through consistency. "You can look at them any way you like, but they're still tomatoes". The trouble comes when growing 500,000 irregular tomatoes is no longer enough. When, to take your volume to a macro-economic one million (still roughly only a quarter of the size your investors' analysts would have you be, incidentally), you decide to add 4x4s, cheaper cars, sports cars, cheap sports cars. Do you make them tomatoes, or do you look elsewhere on the greengrocer's stall?

Mercedes-Benz and BMW reached this junction in the mid-1980s. The need to grow, to achieve economies of scale and more clout with the supplier was overwhelming. Mercedes swallowed hard and decided its three-pointed star (alongside Coca-Cola and Nike the best recognised brand mark in the world) would not be devalued on the nose of a small car or a 4x4. Then again Mercedes, seemingly the supplier of every airport taxi in continental Europe and manufacturer of the Vito and Sprinter – white van man's wet dreams – has always taken an inclusive approach to growth. The Mercedes A Class failed its elk-avoidance handling test; time will tell what damage this will do to the exclusive aura that envelops an S class.

NOW – THE MGF

BMW's product identity – half the age of Benz, don't forget – has been achieved through exclusion. The most commercial vehicle BMW has ever made is a motorcycle for an upwardly-mobile courier. It has never courted continental taxi drivers. An inclusive approach to further growth could potentially destroy the carefully nurtured identity of the 3 Series, 5 Series and 7 Series family. So it bought Rover Group.

Rover Group demonstrates very clearly the value of product identity and brand names. BMW took over a culturally alien company, with sickly, ageing assembly facilities, an almost empty engineering shop, some fine examples of the worst of British management and some truly appalling dealers. By the time all of the company is back on its feet, BMW will have spent many times the cost of picking a name out of the air, designing an all-new car and an all-new factory to build it in.

Yet in reality the option of starting from scratch was not available. Unless a product offers a unique innovative proposition, like James Dyson's twin-cyclone cleaner, for example, the economics of the car industry will not give it enough time to mature into a brand buyers will trust. It will never evolve or re-generate itself enough to create any sense of product identity. And even innovation might no longer be enough. Despite its whiff of brands like Mercedes-Benz and Swatch, DaimlerChrysler is learning this the hard way with its Smart city car project.

For BMW then, this meant buying all of Rover just to get hold of the brands. And, of course, as BMW knows better than anyone, a brand that has not been lovingly managed can deteriorate to an alarming degree.

Take Rover Group as a whole and it becomes clear just how disparate the comparative strengths of brands can become within the structure of a single company, even if that company is BMW.

Rover Group, historically and culturally rooted in the West Midlands, has four active brands: Land Rover, Mini, MG and Rover. The fact that at least two of them have a product identity powerful enough to compete in the North American market should be considered something of a small miracle.

As British Leyland, Rover Group was, in the 1970s and early '80s, part of a woefully unsuccessful experiment of state ownership and central control – a period every bit as injurious to British manufacturing as the reforms under Margaret Thatcher 15 years later. BL cleansed the British motor industry of its product identity; Triumph, Morris, Riley all lost their personalities in giant assembly plants that carried numbers and not names. Austin would survive the purge only to die of its injuries later. The greatest name in British motoring, Jaguar, was reduced to an Orwellian number; the Brown's Lane factory, where cars that won Le Mans for the Queen in her coronation year were built, became Large Car Assembly Plant Number Two under BL.

SOON? THE MGF SUPER SPORTS

The brands that failed to make it were hit from both sides. Poorly equipped factories and a demoralised workforce would produce cars in conditions one manager later famously claimed were no better than those in Gorky in Russia. The quality of the cars was little better than Lada automobiles assembled there. They also looked awful. Mel Nichols, a former editor of *Car* magazine tells a story of being sneaked into BL's centralised design office in the mid-1970s to look at the future product. There, he lifted the covers of a Jaguar XJ-S prototype, but declined to photograph the scoop on the basis he could not believe Jaguar would actually build such an ugly car. They did.

And not only were the cars ugly, there was no attempt even to pay lip-service to product identity. If anybody out there can find a visual relationship between these – Metro, Allegro, Princess, Maestro – then please tell the historians who tend to the British motor industry's chamber of horrors at the Gaydon Heritage Centre.

They already know the classification begins 'Austin', it's the rest that's less clear. At the same time, it is worth remembering that BMW was already making its 2002 and 2500 Series small and large cars, and the first generation threes and fives were on the drawing board.

Today, Rover Group – with the 75 just launched, a new Mini on the cards, MG back in rude health and Land Rover hitting new sales records every month – has, at least, regained some sense of product identity. The designers have done their jobs, it's up to the others now.

Gerry McGovern is studio director at Land Rover. A graduate of the Royal College of Art in 1976, he has seen Rover through the Honda-influenced era under British Aerospace, and through the difficult years after the BMW buy-out.

"I think some brands survived the nationalised period more by luck than judgement," he says. "What would have happened if the brand boys – not that there was anything that scientific in those days – had decided to make the Metro more of a Mini than a Mini Metro?

"I think the period also shows that even if everything else has turned bad, then decent design can at least halt a brand's slide. Jaguar only produced two, two-and-a-half cars during the nationalised period and at least one of them was drop-dead beautiful. Even though the cars had a terrible reputation, at least they always continued to look like Jagaurs. That link with the past was never broken and the fewer cars there are between you and the point in history where the brand values stem from, the stronger it is. That's why Ford ended up paying so much money for Jaguar. Not for the factories, not for the dealers or the rest of the infrastructure, but for the name, for the premium brand identity."

BL concentrated on the mainstream, the niches were largely neglected. It's one of the reasons Rover still contains so many powerful product identities. It was for access to this pure automotive genetic code, this powerful sense of product identity, that BMW placed itself in a position that brought the company to the edge of crisis for the first time since its reconstruction and regeneration after the Second World War.

In 50 years there have been only five basic Land Rover shapes, and one of those is less than two years old; with Land Rover the genetic material of product identity is pure and strong. With Mini – now a brand name not a model, don't forget – it is, if anything, stronger. Give or take a little evolution and some tiny linear mutation, there has only been one Mini in 40 years. With MG, as in Michael Crichton's Jurassic Park, the DNA has been preserved through a hiatus and lives again now, wrapped successfully around the helix of another.

Gerry McGovern was part of a tiny Saturday Club of engineers and designers that brought the MG name back to life in 1995, in the appealing form of the mid-engined MGF. The F remains one of the most spectacular recent examples of 1990s industrial art of creative platform engineering. At the time of the MG's development, Rover Group was still under the control of the culturally alien British Aerospace. Driven by short-term city pressures and board level misunderstanding, the sheet of paper on which McGovern and his team would draw the F was anything but clean.

NOW – THE ROVER 75

NOW – THE LAND ROVER FREELANDER

BMW has taken the most simple route to creating a product identity. Build the same sporty saloon cars, but in three different sizes.

SOON? NEW LAND ROVER

"We had to be pragmatic there. It's difficult enough when you start with a brand that has so clearly established itself in the past. Then, when you add in the engineering constraints we had to deal with, you can see why we had to dip into the abstract and intellectualise the exercise. If you're looking for MG design cues on the *F* you won't find any other than the grille. But I think there's a more philosophical identity there; if you look at all MGs there's a perception of honesty, simplicity and affordability that the company has never tried to disguise."

Land Rover, where McGovern moved as studio director after the success of the MG*F*, is driven by a similarly pragmatic ethos. In the words of its chief engineer, Tony Baker, the very first Land Rover 1948 Series I was "never really styled. It just sort of happened". It's an approach McGovern understands clearly, but one that is no longer acceptable in the customer-driven market of today. "Working at Land Rover means you have to think more like an industrial designer than an automotive stylist," he says. "Vehicles like ours are functional above everything else. They have to be usable. Every feature should do a job while conveying what the vehicle is capable of.

"Some of the design cues associated with Land Rover's visual identity came about because of manufacturing constraints and functional reasoning applied at the time. On the original Range Rover, for example, the E-pillar was body colour but, as a result of bad surface deformation it was decided we'd cover it with vinyl. That meant all the other pillars were blackened to match, so we got the 'floating' roof effect that's now synonymous with the Range Rover."

McGovern, like a lot of automotive designers, hates the notion of 'styling' – essentially a decorative art he views as anathema to product identity. "Short term, it can create a strong image as it did for Cadillac in the 1950s," he concedes, "but then everybody was able to do exactly the same thing and the identity was lost. And look where it's left them now. Look where it's left all North American manufacturers, come to that. Their only products with true identities are their trucks, and with companies like Jeep, we are back in this 'pure DNA' thing, where only a handful of products has ever made it out of the factories. With cars, they built so many of them it became impossible to evolve any kind of identity. The Japanese made exactly the same mistake in the 1980s."

The solution, as McGovern sees it, lies in an approach pioneered by Audi over the last 20 years. He calls it a 'product design' directive, functional, certainly, with one foot in the Bauhaus school, but more closely related to the finely honed surfaces of a Braun kitchen appliance. "It's certainly less limiting than the BMW approach, you only have to look at an A3, and an A4, A6 and A8 to see that. And you can extend it more, look how the TT fits into the line-up. A Z3 relates to the mainstream identity of BMW totally differently."

It should come as no surprise that Audi has mastered the art of product identity better than most. As part of the Volkswagen Group, Audi is obliged to share most of its unseen components with other cars in the group. Not just VWs, but Seats and Skodas too. "Their design is all they've got, isn't it? They can no longer rely on the way their cars handle or the noise their engines make. You can get the same things in a VW…" says McGovern.

And there's the point. VW, like GM and Renault-Nissan, all want to one day build their cars around three basic groups of components, called platforms. As consolidation in the motor industry continues apace, more and more apparently disparate cars will be the same under the skin. In the future there could be less than 20 basic platforms. It will be left to the designers to differentiate them. Only those with the strongest identities will survive. The era of product identity might only have just begun, but it has a long future ahead of it.

GM styling chief Harley Earl said: "You will never know what the industrial products of the future are going to be like, but the secret is to keep trying to find out". That's just what Simon Cox is doing.

20|31

Reviving a
Great Tradition
Kate Trant

Probably best known for his work on 4x4s, Cox says they bring out "the product designer" in him.

→ The dream car is back thanks to designers of imagination like Simon Cox at General Motors. What's more, he does it his way.

Given the complex and mysterious alchemy of the vehicle design process, uncovered pain stakingly while piecing together the material for the Moving Objects exhibition, I shouldn't have been surprised to discover Simon Cox wasn't really what I expected.

This hit home most clearly when asked about how car designers might indulge themselves if there were no constraints and all was blue sky; rather than answering "low, sleek and red," he laid out for me, carefully and without pomp, how there is a moral way, a way which might call into question cars which have the potential to travel at speeds which can kill.

"People are becoming more sophisticated and demanding of their products and 'low, sleek and red' is not going to fulfill everyone's needs." Assumptions challenged yet again.

Sponsored by Ford while at the Royal College of Art, Cox's creative history has its roots in fine art. Encouraged early on to take a painting and sculpture path, he chose instead to go – via jewellery and silversmithing – to product design, finally arriving at vehicle design as the natural combination of his practical and sculptural talents. Since then, he has forged his way ahead through Lotus, Isuzu and now GM.

His creative spark is combined with a practical approach, and he communicates an acute sense of form, style, function and appropriateness applied across a range of design disciplines.

His gentle nature belies his reputation; Cox is known for his drive and his total commitment. Probably best known for his work on 4x4s, he says they bring out "the product designer" in him. When it appeared his fellow students were designing sports cars, he decided his graduate project should be a 4x4, and developed the vehicle type as more than just a box on wheels. He feels 4x4s require more functional detailing than other types of vehicle and, using this potential to his advantage, maximises every detail to give additional or specific appeal.

Director of Concept Vehicle Design for General Motors for a year and charged with establishing the company's concept design studio in the UK, Cox has chosen to bring with him Per Ivar Salvaag, Julian Wiltshire and David Woodhouse, all three graduates of the RCA's vehicle design course.

Cox feels the RCA course produces individuals with a sculptural sense. "The RCA offers a completely clean sheet of paper. You can put your own slant on things, you can make whatever you like. That is what college should be about; then you go out into the real world."

146

ISUZU VEHICROSS CONCEPT

ISUZU COMO CONCEPT

ISUZU VX2 CONCEPT

Although the term 'concept car' itself was not coined until the 1980s, Harley Earl's landmark Buick Y-Job of 1939 is generally acknowledged as the first. GM's Motoramas, first staged in the 1950s, heralded the international motor shows we know today, with their glitz and glamour, and predictions for the future.

While not wanting to over-emphasise his role in the continuation of GM's pioneering position in the concept car arena, Cox is in the process of regenerating the concept car for the corporation. "GM started it all off and, at that time, it was real styling. The concepts excited the public about the way things were going to look in 2000. There were cars that looked like jet fighters." He explains that it was felt the time had come for GM to start putting concept vehicles back out there.

"There have been one or two GM concepts in recent years but no concerted effort to show the direction in which the company is travelling. It will take a while before people understand what we are trying to show or the way the company is going.

"The way I do concept vehicles is very different from the way GM did them in the 1940s. We have to be seen to be more believable.

"When people think of concepts, they think of show cars. This is not necessarily the case. Some will never be seen outside the studio, but are used internally to kick off or feed a production programme. They can be used to motivate designers, or to inform them so when a concept car moves into a production programme, everyone is up to speed. Or they can be used in what are known at GM as 'clinics', shown to selected members of the public to gauge their reaction. Or at motor shows to confirm - or not - designers' speculations about what the buying public want in their cars of the future, to measure the public's response to new and sometimes radical ideas, to gauge reactions to ideas for complete vehicles or individual design details. The concept vehicle's journey does not necessarily lead to a production vehicle and, even if ultimately a concept goes into production, it might only contain elements of the original concept.

"When you start a production programme you don't want to be doodling around. When a concept car approaches production stages, the financial stakes are high and a concrete pathway is key. Concept vehicles help in some products as a clinic. The Isuzu Vehi-Cross was never intended to be a production vehicle. I was asked to do a vehicle for the Tokyo show and it was up to me to decide what vehicle we should aim for.

ISUZU COMO CONCEPT INTERIOR

"We didn't have a small 4x4. What I tried to do was not to make it an all-singing, all-dancing show car that people would just take or leave; I wanted it to have some meaning. I wanted to do something exciting and seductive enough to be at a motor show, and attract people's attention, but which had enough meaning to lead to a production vehicle. And it did in the end. Some concept vehicles are purely show cars for glitz and glamour; some are more styling-orientated and some are technology orientated. My personal aim is to do something meaningful. It's a serious endeavour. There are so many elements to a concept vehicle; I'm not doing them purely as a piece of sculpture but if they're seen as that and do something more meaningful, then that's great. Ultimately, saleable products have to be designed."

Either way, a concept car is a catalyst, generating momentum, and the international motor show circuit is now a powerful force providing a spotlight under which to unveil new directions and enthrall the public.

"I like to think a concept car is the vehicle you might be driving in the near future, that it's possible to imagine yourself in that car. A concept vehicle should have some dream-like qualities but it shouldn't be so far away from reality that it is just a dream. It should project a future that's reachable. Although a concept vehicle can be based on a form of technology that, economically, might not be available for another decade, it has to relate to the environment in which it will be driven, whether that environment is two years, five years or 10 years ahead. Designers are now considering what will be available in 2020.

"Concepts have to have some emotion, to get the buyer to say 'that's what I want' while also reflecting a strong direction of the company. A concept should have something very relevant to show, whether it's a single feature or a whole vehicle. Show cars should not be seen as just a frivolous waste of money."

The existence and nature of a concept car brief depends on the programme. Concept vehicles are conceived fairly close to when they're shown, about a year to a year-and-a-half before a show. Sometimes, work might not start until six months beforehand. So, even though production programmes are being reduced to 24 months, a production vehicle's gestation period is still longer than that of a concept vehicle.

"It's not a case of starting with a blank sheet of paper," says Cox. "I still have to work within constraints. Once we have the basic idea, we have to design it. Everything on a concept car has to be made and, even if it carries over some technology, it will be done in a new way. All those parts have to be designed and drawn. It's like trying to build an Airfix kit with no instructions. We do have some freedom but I try not to let that freedom take hold."

A brief will indicate the intended market sector and a specification of what the vehicle should contain, targets Simon Cox can either agree or argue with. Ideally, a dialogue will take place so the eventual vehicle will communicate the company's point of view; a personality, rather than just a personal point of view.

Achieving that fine balance between celebrating a company's heritage and taking it forwards into new and uncharted territories is an aim. "Sometimes it's better to forget what's gone before, while with some projects it's good to know your heritage. There are a number of ways to approach a concept vehicle, for example through technology, heritage or by trying to do something totally new that forgets the past. Our new cars might have some clues but done in a new way to appeal to a new buyer."

As the range of materials, technological and manufacturing possibilities widens and accumulates, choices made by designers become crucial. Only too aware his buyers are more and more sophisticated in their understanding of what their vehicles say about them, hence more demanding of their designers, Cox remarks: "If you have two or more vehicles that are ultimately very similar, down to the price, how do you persuade the buyer with his chequebook at the ready to buy yours rather than any of the others? The choice is based on which is going to say more about the owner.

"I hope I'm bringing a different perspective to GM. The way the American car market is going now GM has to be seen as more global. I see my studio as just part of that. It feeds some European thinking, some European culture into that market; it's not just about the vehicles that are going to be sold in the UK. I think it can have relevance for the vehicles sold in the US. As long as you have a good perspective on what you're doing, and enough emotion and passion for what you want to do, I think you can do it anywhere. But where you work has got to be useful; this is why I have set up here."

148

"Everything on a concept car has to be made and, even if it carries over some technology, it will be done in a new way"

ISUZU DESEO CONCEPT

ISUZU VX2 CONCEPT

ISUZU VX2 CONCEPT

Counterpoint:
The Shortcomings of
Showy Designer Suits

Gordon Murray

→ During my 20-year stint in Formula 1 design I visited the British motor show occasionally as a mildly interested punter, and I always found it slightly confusing, for reasons that escaped me at the time. When I entered the hallowed world of road car design in the 1980s – the year we started McLaren Cars – I was duty-bound to visit most of the shows with my friend and colleague Peter Stevens. We had many hours of fun dissecting (and usually panning) 'new' concepts and designs.

Now I am a veteran show-goer of some 10 years, I am afraid I have become even more cynical, but I have learned the reason for my confusion in the early years: I have a problem with styling.

Car design, for me, is the conceptual processs by which a new vehicle is created. Central to this process is packaging – after all, a car is always designed primarily for moving people and objects from one place to another. Sometimes the requirements are utilitarian, and sometimes there is a heavy fun factor.

Which is where styling, and my problem, begins.

We are car people. For the past 100 years we have grown more dependent on the motor car, not only for travel and personal freedom, but also as part of our lifestyle. Most of us won't buy an ugly car, and therefore styling is an important factor. It must be good enough to generate the I-want-one feeling. But, unfortunately, it is intimately interwoven with packaging, engineering and aerodynamics, which is where things start to unravel.

I have learned, in the past 10 years, that the more I know about the motor car manufacturing and marketing business, the less I like. The money and marketing perople govern so much of the process, which culminates in the end-products we purchase and drive. So many of the mass-production manufacturers operate in a way which does not integrate the design departments. This makes even the word 'styling' confusing enough, particularly for the public, as we now have a worldwide situation where stylists are called designers and car company marketing people dictate to engineering designers. This process dilutes the product to the point where we end up with a motley bunch of vehicles to choose from, and, ultimately, the pace at which car design moves forward is controlled by the wrong people and would make a snail feel like Mika Hakkinen.

151

Gordon Murray is design director of McLaren Cars and writes a column for *Car* magazine, from which this excerpt is reproduced by kind permission.

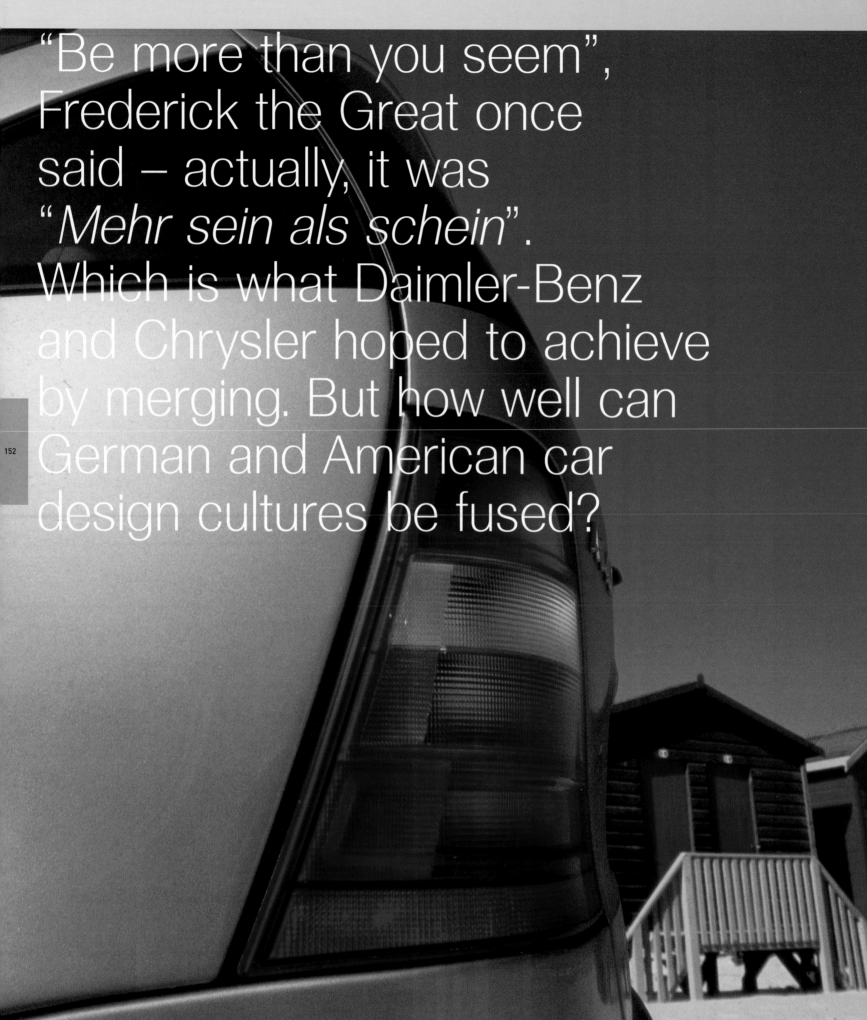

"Be more than you seem", Frederick the Great once said – actually, it was "*Mehr sein als schein*". Which is what Daimler-Benz and Chrysler hoped to achieve by merging. But how well can German and American car design cultures be fused?

DaimlerChrysler
The Essence
of National Identity
Bettina von Hase

MERCEDES-BENZ S CLASS

CHRYSLER PT CRUISER

→ To understand the significance of the recent DaimlerChrysler merger, a visit to Berlin is highly recommended. I was there recently for the opening of Sir Norman Foster's Reichstag, a symbol of the new transparency of government. Looking out from the glass dome over a city dominated by whirring cranes, Berlin is a city in motion, and therefore ideally positioned to be the head-quarters of a company producing objects that move. The Potsdamer Platz, redesigned by Renzo Piano, is Europe's largest construction site. DaimlerChrysler, the development's main client, is a global maker of automobiles – one superlative enhancing the other.

The ochre yellow DaimlerChrysler building is rising fast into the sky, one of a total of 19 buildings, and it will dominate an historic square. The development speaks volumes about the merger itself; in a sense it is its visual representation. The merger between Daimler-Benz and Chrysler in October last year was seen as a triumph by the financial world and the automobile industry. Ann Marsh of *Forbes Magazine* spoke for everyone when she wrote: 'No, this merger isn't about savings. It isn't about blending German caution and Yankee freewheeling. It isn't about consolidation. It is about taking two splendid companies and transforming them into a truly multinational business…' The company has become the world's fifth largest car maker in volume and third largest in turnover.

The building, the company and the square stand for a new Millennium, in which hybridity, multi-ethnicity and multi-culturalism is celebrated. No longer can corporations exist in their ivory towers and produce their perfect products. Learning from others, being tolerant and open to outside influences, changing constantly while making products your own is considered essential in a world where distance has shrunk, speed has increased and information is crucial. The whole is more than the sum of its parts. Together we're more powerful, more global, more effective. With the arrival of the Internet, collaboration has become cool. Nobody can rule the world on their own – at least not in the fiercely competitive world of the global car industry.

"What does this mean?" my Mercedes-loving friends nervously ask. It's all very well merging and so on, but what's going to happen to those lovely gleaming limos we're so fond of being driven in, to premieres, dinners, launches, balls – will they stay the same? And what about German efficiency, will it stay reliable? The fact is, when it comes to cars, nationality still counts…for an awful lot. Merged companies have to be careful. Like in a successful marriage, the key is to unite without losing one's identity. Brands need to be nurtured like children. Consumers, like me, hang on to the old cliches: Germans are efficient, Italians are flashy, Americans are big…all that talk about collaboration goes right out the window. The secret is to preserve what's best about a car's origins and roots, and then put a global top-spin on it.

Together we're more powerful,
more global, more effective.
With the arrival of the Internet,
collaboration has become cool.

To find out what DaimlerChrysler thinks about nationality, I visited one of its chief designers, Murat Günak, in Sindelfingen. If I had to cast a car designer in a film, I would conjure up Murat Günak – an impressive, handsome, multi-lingual 38-year old. In fact, he's rather like the cars he designs; in the new brochure the S Class is described as a 'coupe-like saloon – a trim athlete with a lasting presence'. Günak is of Turkish origin, which makes him even more interesting in my eyes. To be Turkish in Germany is not easy. He must be very talented to have a job like his.

He studied design in Germany and at the Royal College of Art, and sounds like someone who has leapt over several cultural barriers. For him, the car is the ultimate object to design. "I can't think of anything as emotional as a car. It touches everybody, it is in our minds, it gives us motion." He credits the RCA for giving him crucial international and competitive skills, with different cultures coming together, working in the same studio at the college: "The demand was to stick together, and in every project there was a winner, a second and third place, and a loser. Very open, very visibly selective." He said the college taught students "to respect each other, despite the competition, and work as a team. This is crucial: the ability to be competitive. In design departments, designers work in competition, there is no way out of it. They have to hang their drawings on the wall, and the quality, the standard, the ideas are there for everybody to see. It's terrifying."

Asked how he feels about nationality, he says: "I have a German passport, and I was born in Turkey. But I feel European." There you have it, in a nutshell. It's valuable to be a melange, like many Americans are. The cars, however, are not a mixture – at least not yet. Both Americans and Germans state emphatically that the design process stays separate, as will the brands. But surely there will be an exchange of views, maybe even a joint project, prompted by the fact that there are already advanced design studios all over the world, and designers, like artists, are by definition international, and work internationally.

Nationalism may not be in demand as a feature of corporate style, but it is a crucial ingredient in brand loyalty. It's not only what the car looks like, but what it represents. A style seduces, but a pedigree clinches the deal. If one doesn't know the heritage of something or somebody, it's suspect, even dangerous. A car can kill, and we all want to drive one that is safe and secure. The combined DaimlerChrysler brand names deliver safety, and also promise worlds to aspire to – those of European charm or American pioneering spirit: Mercedes – meaning 'grace', named originally after a Viennese girl – or Jeep, Chrysler and Dodge. Elegant and sassy versus roomy and adventurous. Luxury segment versus specialist mass-market. Sophisticated European cities versus American wide open spaces.

"I can't think of anything
as emotional as a car.
It touches everybody, it is in
our minds, it gives us motion" – Murat Günak

CHRYSLER ATLANTIC
CONCEPT

CHRYSLER JAZZ CONCEPT

DODGE POWER WAGON
CONCEPT

DODGE CHARGER R/T
CONCEPT

Günak admits that roots are important for a car. He defines the positive sides of German-ness as "perfection, value, quality, continuity, long-termism." On the negative side, people have called the company 'arrogant, stiff, inflexible, cold, techno…' All this is now changing, as the company is dedicated to combining German-ness with being more flexible, more international, more honest: "Design is visualising this new brand culture. Design is the loud-speaker for this change. Before, design was there to clothe technology. Now we work hand-in-hand. We are part of shaping the future."

American values are completely different to traditional German ones. "There's a sense of adventure, an acceptance of the new, a pioneer spirit, and a return to nature," says Trevor Creed, Chrysler's vice-president of Advanced Design for Jeeps and Trucks. Creed is British, but has lived in the US for most of his life. It is an irony that he and Günak both have different roots from the car maker they represent. There's no mistaking why Creed works for an American company: "As a kid in Britain, I was fascinated by American cars. They were always much more dramatic. We had dull little black or grey saloons, and all of a sudden there were those fabulous two-tone machines. Americans have the space to look at their cars from afar," Günak says. "It's completely different in Japan, where cars look the same, but are extremely refined and different in detailing. In Japan, there is no space, and people always stand very close."

Germans don't stand very close – in fact, they are among the most formal people in the world, unlike the Americans. The two cultures, like their cars, are remarkably different, and the question is, how are they getting on? Chrysler in the US is coy about the cultural fusion – spokeswoman Amy Larkin told me that a merger team existed, but was disbanded shortly after the event. Journalist Michael Woodhead said in *The Sunday Times* at the time of the merger that 'the differences start in the boardroom and extend down to the production line'. He pointed out the powers of the German works councils, and quoted Karl Feuerstein, head of the Daimler-Benz works council as saying they would fight against the Americanisation of the company; 'which for them stands for cheap labour, poor job security and less union power', Woodhead wrote. He added that, privately, German union leaders admit they are fighting a losing battle to preserve 'the European model'. The American way, the global way, is the future in an industry which has to work hard to stay fit in a shrinking market.

MERCEDES-BENZ A CLASS SKETCH

MERCEDES-BENZ A CLASS PROPOSED CONCEPT MODEL

MERCEDES-BENZ A CLASS PROPOSAL ARTWORK

MERCEDES-BENZ A CLASS ALTERNATIVE PROPOSAL MODEL

Cultural fusion is not easy. In an ideal world, the joint leaders of the giant company, Daimler's Jürgen Schrempp and Chrysler's Bob Eaton, will take the best of both: German perfectionism and American adventure; German long-termism and American flexibility. Contrasts attract. They produce creative tension. I have worked both in the US and in Germany, and the main difference is that Americans are far more informal than Germans. People call each other by their first names, go drinking after work, and make spontaneous decisions. In Germany, there is the language barrier of 'Sie' (formal) and 'Du' (familiar); people adhere strictly to hierarchies have separate and closed offices, and don't tend to socialise with each other. If they do, they get sozzled on beer and tell you their entire life story, which is not what the doctor ordered.

This separateness is confirmed by the manual *Hidden Differences – How to Communicate with the Germans*, written by Americans Edward and Mildred Hall. The first paragraph is about time and space. For Germans, 'time is one of the principal ways of organising life. Promptness is almost an obsession. Space is sacred', they write. 'The German sense of privacy is much stronger; they stand and sit further apart than Americans do; they are formal, territorial, orderly. For the American in Germany, manners may be your most important asset – and their absence could certainly prove a great handicap'. I imagine it takes a little more than manners to create a successful fusion. Germany is small and old, the US huge and young. In its recent history, America has helped to defeat and rebuild Germany, leaving a lasting influence on both post-war generations. The current US-German relationship is close, but at times appears rather like a parent and rebellious teenager. Germany has grown up, and it needs to display the responsibility and self-confidence that goes with its new political status.

There is no-one better than the Americans to teach one about self-confidence. It's a can-do society. It celebrates individual achievement. It is brash and bold, which sometimes grates. One disenchanted advertising manager was quoted in the Hall manual as saying, 'it seems Americans always want to do things their way. But it doesn't work that way in Germany. The Association of Packagers had a convention in San Francisco. They had dancing girls and everything. Now they want us to have the same thing here. In Germany conventions are serious, tough and boring. It's strictly business. The dancing girls give the wrong image'.

In fact, America can teach the Germans to loosen up. Bring on the dancing girls, I say. Have fun at work. Collaborate openly. Be more interested in, and tolerant of, other cultures. "There is a new acceptance of other habits," Günak tells me. "In Stuttgart, for example, there are more foreign restaurants and cafes…it's a small thing, but it's important." He won't reveal any secrets about his car of the future, but acknowledges that it will have to reflect a changing world. There will be more comfort. Car interiors will be revolutionised as entertainment and office spaces while we're on the move. But cars will not lose their roots. The ones that do won't sell. Nationality is what defines us. It's our identity in a global world. It's a small thing, but it's important.

CHRYSLER CHRONOS CONCEPT

"Nationalism is a crucial ingredient in brand loyalty. A style seduces, but a pedigree clinches the deal. Americans care more about the overall look than the detailing. I believe this is because the country is so big, people have space to look at their cars from afar" – Murat Günak

MERCEDES-BENZ A CLASS

MERCEDES-BENZ A CLASS

22|31

A Citroën design reawakening at last: Donato Coco

Richard Bremner

The design of Citroëns has mellowed to a conformity that would be as shocking as the DS's 1955 debut, had it not occured so insiduously

CITROËN 2CV

→ It's a coincidence, of course. But on the notice-board behind the head of Donato Coco, the Italian ex-RCA designer responsible for the Citroën C3 concept car and the company's Xsara-sized cars, are scrawled two dates: 1948 and 1955.

The hieroglyphics beside them are inexplicable, and Coco cannot help because we are in a meeting room in Citroën's Boulevard Victor Hugo headquarters rather than his office. But the dates are significant. The first marks the birth of the Citroën 2CV, the second the launch of the DS, legendary cars that did much to cement the company's reputation for producing the most innovative and individual cars on the planet, cars admired not just by enthusiasts but by a wider world that has included artists, celebrities, and even intellectuals. Yet, until recently, Citroën has been actively disowning this history, almost trying to expunge a heritage that a Japanese or Korean company would happily redesign its badge around.

But now, things are changing. "Citroën is at a turning point," explains Coco. "It's starting a cultural revolution in its thinking and approach to products in the future. We've had very interesting designs stylistically and technologically in the past but, lately, we've been more preoccupied with product quality." And although he doesn't say it, this has been at the expense of originality, to say the least. Not only have Citroëns taken to looking much the same as every other car on the road, but in some cases they have ended up as mere clones of Peugeots. Good though it is, the Saxo supermini is near identical to the Peugeot 106 – the differences mere trifles. As a philosophy, this couldn't be more different from the days when Citroën built cars as other-worldly as the DS, as eccentrically practical as the 2CV and the Ami. But today's range, particularly at the lower end, is utterly conventional.

"That was in the past," says Coco. "We now want to change, we want more courage and pertinence in our products." And his use of Maoist phraseology like cultural revolution is more than a little apt, for in its attempts to move on Citroën has almost tried to rewrite history and exterminate its past. That (happily failed) attempt at extermination has been going on for years. From way back there are stories of spare Maserati engines for the beautiful SM coupé being dropped into skips from forklift trucks to destroy them and, more recently, tales of members of the design department rescuing irreplaceable archives and records from the rubbish bin.

CITROEN LNA

CITROEN AMI

More obviously, the design of Citroëns has mellowed to a conformity that would be as shocking as the DS's 1955 debut, had it not occurred so insidiously. The process began when conservative Peugeot bought the ailing firm from Michelin in 1974, the first offspring of this liaison being the barely remembered Citroën LNA, which was little more than a shamelessly reworked Peugeot 104 three-door. The Visa that followed, while decidedly more eccentric (as well as reassuringly ugly) was also a 104 sibling, and began a trend that has seen Citroëns become more and more conventional over the years, to look at, to drive and to own.

But as Coco points out, this policy has not been entirely disastrous. When Peugeot bought it, Citroën was losing money on complex, some-times unreliable products understood by too few people. Now, it is profitable, and has been for some time. And its products get bought – it has recently been setting sales records. "It is not good to talk negatively of the past," he says. "There is a time for everything, and Citroën need-ed to pass through a period of reconstruction, and get quality into its products, even if this approach was too low-profile for the stylists. We do well with the Saxo and Xsara, and I think these products are valid and a good basis, but now it's time for a change."

Of course, these conventional models have changed the type who buys a Citroën. As Coco explains: "It's hard to get under the skin of a customer, because you leave the reality of a company when you work inside it. But the people who buy a Citroën today fall into two categories: those who know Citroën, and are sentimentally attached from the period when we were producing singular cars, and a new category, younger, that has come from rival products to discover ours. These people are attracted by a certain elegance and dynamism, and good quality. Also, we're very competitively priced.

"But we accept we need to be different, and not just to be admired – that is not enough on its own." By which he means that it would be good if people actually bought the cars, something that has not always been the case with Citroën's more advanced models. Coco also believes we're in a different consumer age now too, in which people are more prepared for, and desirous of, being different. "More than ever, it's a time to give people something different. Not eccentric, but something more strong."

Of course, arch-rivals Renault, Fiat and others are doing just this. Coco's counter is that Citroën is doing it too, but the speed you go at depends on your starting point. "All the elements have been there and suddenly they combine, he says, likening creativity to a chemical reaction. And the catalyst for this has been the point at which Jean-Martin Folz took over as president of PSA from Jacques Calvet, and appointed Claude Satinet as director general of Citroën to oversee a strategy that will see it differentiated more effectively from Peugeot and, indeed, every other car company.

Encouragingly, Coco says there are great expectations of Citroën not just outside the company (although it has to be said that, after 15 years of producing very conservative models, with some exceptions, that expectation has diminished somewhat) but from within it, too.

"There's great experience among those who've known Citroën. It's like parents with a very clever child; you have a strong and creative spirit in front of you, but it should not be lazy." Which, by implication, Citroën has been of late.

So where is it heading? "That's difficult to answer because we are looking right now," he says. "But the C3 and C6 concept cars show the direction very well." The cute C3, for which Coco was responsible, represents his desire "to make a step with a new generation car of this class."

The C3 is innovative for its architecture – its height, which produces a cabin more spacious than any other in the category, allowing particular versatility in its seating arrangements. Of course, there's nothing radically new in this, but what's encouraging about the C3 is that it looks fresh, friendly and has a nose that faintly echoes those of budget Citroëns from yesteryear. And it achieves all this without appearing wilfully ugly, like most utility French cars (and not just Citroëns) from the past. Like the 2CV, the Dyane, the Ami and the Visa, it is a thoroughly practical and versatile machine, just like a good small Citroën should be. "It is a prefiguration of several different products which will be based on this new platform," says Coco. "And it is a new start, because this is a new platform."

CITROËN PICASSO

We're in a different consumer age now – people are more prepared and desirous of being different

CITROËN C6 LIGNAGE

CITROEN C3

CITROEN XSARA COUPE

The C3 looks fresh, friendly and has a nose that faintly echoes those of budget Citroëns of yesteryear

If the C3 was a sign of something stirring at Citroën, the elegant C6 Lignage, which debuted at the Geneva motor show this year, further confirms Citroën's creative reawakening. It's a top of the range luxury model, likely to cost more than £30,000 at today's prices, which will take it beyond the segment traditionally occupied by previous big Citroëns like the XM, CX and DS. And while it's possible to see a little of these cars in the C6, especially the DS, it is meant very much as a step forward.

Coco has strong views on the issue of retro designs and design that looks ahead. "It's a problem when you're creating – do I look at the past or the future? But I'm not so obsessed by this divide. The futuristic Citroëns were born like that because the people making them followed a certain thinking. When Flaminio Bertoni did the DS, it was for the first time – he was not looking back. But the history is very important – you have to have this in the back of your mind. It's like a family – we come from something. It gives a sense to the thinking. I don't believe the 2CV and the DS were designed just to have nice shapes. They were designed with a certain spirit and courage. That has been the catalyst for these cars. Each has been a singular adventure, a fight with the unknown. I don't think the future is to look in the mirror and take inspirations from old Citroëns."

There's no question that he reckons the best way to achieve this is through the designer's mindsets, by applying a philosophy. "If you think differently, you will be different. This applies to life in general, as well as the creation of a product."

Of course, there are constraints, not least of which is the fact that Citroëns must share the same platforms as their Peugeot cousins. That means they must be built using the same machinery, and share a great many components and sub-systems, running from heaters to entire engines and gearboxes.

Now, of course, part of what made Citroëns so different in the past was their mechanical configuration. This was particularly true of the 2CV, but also the DS and others. But since economic practicalities dictate that Citroën must share vehicle platforms with Peugeot – "it's the only safe way to make competitive products," says Coco – the scope for producing very different cars may be limited.

Our man, however, thinks not. "If you consider the Volkswagen Group and its platform strategy, you will see that the Golf and the Audi A3, both of which share platforms, are very different. And we are no different from them. Around 60 per cent of the Picasso is the same as the Xsara, but they look totally different. And the mechanical specifications of Citroëns and Peugeots are different, too; they don't feel the same because they are treated differently. Look at the Peugeot 605 and the XM, they were very different, but shared a lot of parts. They had different characters in every sense of the word."

Coco is keen there should be even more differentiation between Peugeots and Citroëns than VW achieves across its marques. "We don't want the same driving feel, as some of these models have. We want to push forward, and explode with creativity. We don't want to look like everybody else, we want different characters for our cars."

But, don't hold your breath if you're expecting radical Citroëns in the next couple of years. "The Picasso – Citroën's answer to the Renault Scenic – is not that, it's a car filling a space, a gap in the market," says Coco. "We intend to have a specific appearance for Citroën." And while the replacement for the Xantia, due in September 2000, promises to be attractive, it was nonetheless conceived under the old regime, and will doubtless have a strong conservative streak running through it as a result. Instead, it will be a few years before really fresh Citroëns appear in the showrooms. But for the first time in years, it looks as if Citroën, and Donato Coco, are really keen to get creative.

He is not the only ex-RCA designer at Citroën, there being five in total, of various nationalities and each with a different take on what Citroën means – a fact he regards as healthy: "If you put two designers in a room with the same brief, they will not come up with the same answer." That there are so many ex-RCA people bodes well. The college's ex-students are in no small part responsible for the bolder look of so many of today's designs, and those at Citroën will doubtless be keen to demonstrate at least as much imagination now that their creativity is being unfettered. So for those of you who had written Citroën off creatively – don't. You may be in for some surprises.

You can trace the DNA of the Porsche 911 back a remarkable 50 years – it is still the 'weekend sports car' envisioned by its creator.

23|31

Porsche 911: The Genetically-Modified Machine
Martin Pawley

EVOLUTION OF THE PORSCHE 911

PORSCHE 911 CARRERA 4

170

→ Tony Hatter is one of five ex-Royal College of Art graduate students working in the 35-strong Porsche design department in Stuttgart. He studied transportation at Coventry Polytechnic and then did two years post-graduate automotive design at the RCA from 1979 to 1981.

As Hatter remembers, it was his ambition even in his school days to design for Porsche, but the process of getting there was difficult.

"As soon as I graduated from the RCA I applied to the company but there were no vacancies at that time", he recalls, "so I tried elsewhere and worked for Opel for five years before approaching Porsche again in 1986. This time the company accepted me and I've worked in the design department ever since".

From 1995 to 1998 Hatter worked in the racing division. He designed the bodywork and paint-splash graphics of the three GT1 cars, including the winner of the Le Mans 24-hour race in 1997. He was also responsible for the "optical appear-ance" and livery of the racing division at that time. Today he looks back on the Le Mans effort as "the ultimate experience of my life".

Hatter has worked for years on 911 series cars. Of the current road-going version he says simply: "It's not a car to drive at 300kmh down an auto-bahn. It is a car for piloting swiftly along country roads. It enables you to enjoy a tremendous sense of achievement doing that".

He is deeply respectful of those responsible for the car's careful evolution.

"It is evolution, not revolution", he insists. "The car has always been the sum of incremental changes. You might say it lost its way slightly with the 964 model, but the 993 got it back on track. Now there's the water-cooled 996. The evolution of the 911 will never stop. It is based on a philosophy, not a style". As Ferry Porsche said, it was to be "driving in its purest form".

The difference between a philosophy and a style is a pattern of change. In the beginning it was a philosophy that enabled a tiny engineering company in post-war Austria, a country that had been occupied and divided after the Axis defeat in the Second World War, to produce a prototype sports car so much more advanced than those of other countries. It was a pattern of change that enabled it to become the most famous in the world within a generation.

The first Porsche car I ever saw was a 356. It was during a school trip to France which includ-ed the Palace of Versailles. The most memorable thing about the day was that silver shape moving slowly past the visitors in the gardens. I ran to see what it was and it drove right past me, its vestigial bumpers seeming only millimetres above the ground, its wheels with their huge chrome hub caps almost completely hidden from view, its exhaust note oddly clattering.

'Artifacts evolve using themselves as the point of departure: they contain the conditions for their own development. The structure of the object moves to match the future conditions in which it will be employed'
Gilbert Simondon
Du mode d'existence des objets techniques
Paris 1958

171

I had never seen anything like the 356. Nothing so small, so extreme or somehow so private. A ground-hugging exoskeletal creature of aluminium beaten into uncompromising curves.

That was in 1953, so it must have been a very early car. Coming from England, I had never seen anything like it. Nothing so small, so extreme or somehow so private. A ground-hugging exoskeletal creature of aluminium beaten into uncompromising curves.

It was many years before I properly understood how the Porsche philosophy of engineering and design had enabled that car to emerge from the wreckage of war-torn Germany, or what it was that made it so superior to its competitors. The elucidation came to me in part in a passage from Antoine de Saint Exupery's *Wind Sand and Stars* dealing with the clean appearance of the closed-cockpit, low-wing metal monoplanes with retractable undercarriages that had evolved out of the old strut- and wire-braced wooden biplanes of the early years of flight: 'It is a shock to realise that all visible evidence of invention has been refined out of these machines so that they look like products of nature', wrote Saint Exupery. 'They are objects so natural that they might be pebbles polished by the waves'.

The Porsche 356 in its time was just such a machine that looked like a product of nature, and so was its successor the Porsche 911. Like Simondon's artifacts that draw their future from within, the 911 grows out of its predecessors and thereafter not so much evolves as metamorphoses over a lifespan in excess of 35 years. During that time it has flaunted its inherited capacity to dissolve invention within itself so effectively that in its present manifestation, despite a very significant redesign, it retains enough of its historic purity of form to enable one to say, not that it has been changed, but that it has been born again.

There is no doubt that the Porsche 911 was the offspring of the Porsche 356, but in the taxonomy of machines, as in the taxonomy of natural species, there is no simple starting point. The entwined engineer/designer/driver DNA that was in the bloodstream of the 356 went through three changes in 17 years of production before it metamorphosed into the 911. Going further back, the prototype 356, the first ever Porsche, the 'weekend sports car' of 1948 with all but its body taken from the pre-war Volkswagen Beetle, contained even older genes. At the level of fundamental engineering the rear-mounted air cooled 'boxer' engine and the torsion bar suspension reached back to the 1934 Auto Union grand prix car and the NSU project 12 (an earlier design by Ferdinand Porsche for a people's car). From here the trail is harder to follow but still present. There must ultimately be some reference to the Austrian Paul Jaray's streamlining patents and the Porsche 'boxer' aero engine of 1912.

Unlike Saint Exupery's, the essence of Gilbert Simondon's insight is that not only inherited genes but predictive genes as well are present in the inanimate organism. Thus the Porsche 911 would not merely be descended from a cast of glorious ancestors: from its first 1964 production version onward it would have incubated its own future within its own cellular structure – together with the means to modify it.

In the world of plant and animal species, such genetic modification is achieved by inserting a construct that has three parts: a desired gene, a marker gene and a promoter or catalyst.

THE PORSCHE CLAN AT THE DRAWING BOARD

FERDINAND PORSCHE, HIS SON FERRY, AND THE FIRST 356

The marker gene enables the construct to select the correct cells for the modification, while the promoter inserts the desired gene. The incremental process of automobile design is a close analogue to this process. The desired outcome plays the part of the desired gene; the parts of the car affected by the achievement of this outcome play the part of the marker, and the promoter is not only the designer but the market maker and the driver. Because of this similarity, it is possible to compare the genetic modification that produces a pest-resistant strain of wheat, with the design modification that significantly enhances any aspect of the performance, safety or comfort of a car.

When dealing with a car with the long and illustrious pedigree of the Porsche 911 there are numerous instances of such designed modifications. They extend back from the present to the date of the car's introduction, and back before then to the design regime and the reigning technical ideas of the time when it acceded to the status of a project. This can be seen in the way the new-model 996 incarnation of the 911 possesses what could be called pre-foetal, foetal, infant, young, mature and senile elements side by side, all genetically blended into an indivisible whole.

In the car's bodywork, electronics and mechanical engineering there are not only buried assumptions that date back to before the revelation of the first version of the 911 in 1963, but also design features that have emerged much more recently – for example, as a result of new environmental legislation, changes in the customer base, or conditions of severe traffic congestion that in 1963 did not exist.

Were one to spread out all the images and documents necessary to take a synoptic view of the whole 35-year history of the Porsche 911, one would see this clearly. Put simply, it would become evident that half the car's life was spent getting bigger and heavier, gaining power and reputation, while the other half has been spent subtly divesting itself of the appearance of all these Darwinian attributes while retaining their substance in a concealed form. Thus the outrageously exhibitionist 1975 3-litre turbo – which must represent the fulcrum of road-going 911 hubris versus late model discretion – can be contrasted with both the modest original car and its wolf-in-sheep's-clothing present incarnation, the plain-looking model 996.

The 1975 car may boldly carry its American 5mph bumpers and whale tail like a bulldozer and backhoe, but the defiance does not last. From then on disarming emphases began to proliferate on all the road cars.

Brakes, for example, (which are philosophically as well as practically the antitheses of accelerators), were once considered of so litttle visual importance that they were hidden by steel wheels and chrome hub caps. Now they have become such powerful symbols of motoring survival that they are on ostentatious display, prowling like wild animals behind the spindly bars of their see-through alloy wheels.

In the same way the car's headlamps, once boldly raised to command the road and establish the aggressive lunge of the wings, now recline invisibly, dissolved into a rounder, flatter curve and deconstructed into busy, multi-purpose lamp clusters beneath a smoothly moulded transparent cover.

173

There are other examples of this metamorphosing of imagery. Austere painted steel, once proof of circuit mettle on even the most luxurious dash-board, is now banished in favour of leather, wood or (non-structural) carbon fibre. Air conditioning, once a power-sapping obstacle to sports car performance, is now standard even on open-top cars. Thin-rimmed steering wheels of huge diameter, made of extinct West German plastic, are now replaced by thick-rimmed, airbag-fat steering wheels of tiny diameter. Even the magnificent, horizontally-opposed, six-cylinder, air-cooled engines, once gloriously exposed simply by raising a metal cover, are now totally concealed under a cloak of accessories, electronics and water jackets.

Most drastic of all, the puissant flare of the front and rear wheelarches, introduced to accommodate wider tyres and subsequently seen at its most extreme in the various turbo versions up to and including the statuesque 959, is now dissolved into the deceptive blandness of a longer, wider car with gentle side modelling, more predictable curves, less aggression, more discretion, less promise, more concealment.

So much is this the case that only the fastback coupe roof and side windows, a styling cue held over from the model 993 (now regarded as the last of the 'old style' 911 cars), and the new racing shark's mouth air intake below the integral front bumper, enable the 996 to be seen as a reformed character rather than simply an anonymous one.

It is no accident that the science of genetics has assumed a burning importance in so many fields. Students, who shy away from traditional university subjects, queue up to study this important new discipline that promises massive change from microscopic interventions.

We are told that by genetic means desirable characteristics can be enhanced and undesirable characteristics diminished, with the result that species survival is ensured. Crops, livestock, fish and poultry, all line up for performance optimisation by this means. Why not cars too?

DNA is unique to an individual, and to any individual line. But for hundreds of years human beings have refined thoroughbred plants and animals in order to maximise beauty, performance and intelligence without understanding its mechanism at all. Ships, aircraft, buildings and other industrial products have been developed and steadily improved over time.

Today, at the end of a century that's seen industry evolve from the limits of steam and muscle power to the micrometric precision of the robot assembly line, we have products that are continually rendered more perfect in their relationship with their environment by design.

In the last half century, the harmful exhaust emissions of Porsche cars have been reduced by 95 per cent. The proportion of the car that is recyclable has risen to 87 per cent. The use of solvents, CFCs, heavy metals, non-reusable packaging and water in the production process and the product has been drastically reduced. And yet, at the same time, performance, fuel consumption, roadholding and comfort have been improved beyond measure.

In a conscious emulation of nature, design has created innumerable machine species, of which among the most prolific are cars – and perhaps the most successfully perfected of all cars is the Porsche 911.

Half the car's life was spent getting bigger and heavier, gaining power and reputation, while the other half has been spent subtly divesting itself of the appearance of all these Darwinian attributes while retaining their substance in a concealed form.

What can we expect
next from Patrick Le
Quément, the man who
brought you the Twingo?
Apparently, something big…

24|31

Made in France
Matthew Gwyther

YEARS SPENT MAKING VANS LIKE THIS...

...MEAN RENAULT AREN'T VERY GOOD AT BIG CARS, LIKE THIS

Le Quément believes French industrial and product design had a good few problems before the mid-1980s

For Patrick Le Quément, the challenges of life do not end with shutline width, grab handle spring resistance and cowl point height. Le Quément, head of design at Renault in Paris and a fairy godfather to many an RCA graduate, has never shirked from taking on the broader questions in life. An hour-long conversation with him is peppered with quotations – from Gropius to Antoine de Saint-Exupèry via Sir Denys Lasdun. For a car designer, he possesses an unusually broad and well-informed outlook.

"Many years ago during the time of our association with Volvo, there was a presentation about the differences between French and Scandinavian design," he recalls. "At the end of this our chairman, Louis Schweitzer, said: 'Mmm, that's interesting but what I've always wondered is what are the differences between French and Italian culture'."

How Le Quément's eyes must have lit up on hearing the boss wander in that direction. Such open-ended posers are obviously the stuff of life for the senior vice president (quality and design). "Well, I just got my gun out of my holster and gave it a shot," he says. "If you take the 10 greatest figures of the Italian renaissance, you'd have eight painters/sculptors and one each of a philosopher or poet. The 10 corresponding leading French figures of the Enlightenment, on the other hand, would produce eight writers or philosophers, one architect and one painter. That's because we're a very conceptual people in France. We've always gone for elegant, intellectual construction. A lightness of build quality. Look at Gustave Eiffel."

Before Le Quément arrived at Renault in 1987, via Ford and VW, that lightness more often than not translated into a quirky flimsiness. (If the Eiffel Tower had been built with wheels and moving parts it would have spent more time on the hard shoulder than the open road.) Le Quément believes French industrial and product design had a good few problems before the mid-1980s when the big shake-up occurred.

"Until that time, if you went into the kitchen equipment section of a French department store and looked for a coffee maker, for example, the result was usually the same.

"It would have some good, intelligent design features but a low perceived build quality. Our manufactured goods were just too approximative [sic]. I'd have said not 'Made in France' but 'Merde in France.' There was a great need to fill the gap between everyday goods and luxury industry products like Hermès or Louis Vuitton, where we excelled. That is one of the reasons why we never succeeded in producing a successful upper-segment car."

A sign of how things have changed is the Espace, now in an upper segment of sorts. Renault was way ahead of the game with the MPV and now the Espace has moved into its next generation the company is able, successfully, to premium-price it at a higher level than the opposition who were all forced to club together to produce two identical machines between six of them. The added bonus is that Espaces no longer come with that Renault trait of falling or rusting to bits after four years.

Le Quèment is driving an Audi A6 to remind him of the rules of the big segment quality game. "It's a great car, one of my favourites," he enthuses. "The fit and finish is excellent. I think Audi has become the new reference point for these areas. Far better than Mercedes"

RENUALT FIFTIE CONCEPT CAR

RENAULT FIFTIE CONCEPT CAR

RENAULT MEGANE SCENIC (LEFT) AND CLASSIC (RIGHT)

RENAULT TWINGO

What Renault has become good at is 'mould-breaking'; quite simply, excellent design ideas that take things forward. One suspects that this is achieved – and Le Quément does nothing to refute the suspicion – by denying the supremacy of the clinic or the 'focus group' in the design process and allowing the designer to use his or her imagination to the full.

"Some companies use market research to take decisions," says Le Quément. "You know – this scored eight and a half out of 10 so we'll go with it because the other two only got five or six. Well, this always reminds me of the old David Ogilvy saying: 'Market research is like the lamppost to the drunkard – it's there for support rather than illumination'.

"The problem with research is that if you push people into a corner and make them exert a choice then they tend always to choose what they know. If you show them six products where three are new and three are today's they'll always take refuge in the one that looks the most like the one they know and have driven. The result is that for far too long car manufactures have developed products which are DISliked by the least number of people. This is wrong. You need to accept that you'll always displease some but really go out to DELIGHT others. That's the difference of our approach – we want ice or fiery hot water, not something lukewarm in the middle."

As a result of this, Le Quément does not deny that a "productive tension" exists between his design department and his colleagues along the corridor in marketing. (The difference at Renault is that Le Quément reports directly to the chief executive.) "Of course, we have active disagreements with product planning but generally we fight the same battles," he says. "We do not abuse the autonomy we've developed."

And so how does the Renault way compare with how things are done in Japan? (Renault has just acquired a sizeable chunk of Japanese manufacturer Nissan.)

For once, Le Quément's flow stutters. What he's seen first-hand of the Nissan way has clearly perplexed him. "Well, let's say I wouldn't want to make a comment without having my lawyers present," he smirks. "What I would say is that the philosophy of consensus in design goes right against the expression of self. In Western Europe the individual still rules. In Japan they don't stand up and stand out. Jung said: 'To be in advance of others is always to invite a beating,' but everyone at Renault is expected to be innovative."

Le Quément took a fair old flogging with the Twingo. The supermini design that Le Quément and his designers came up with was regarded as a huge risk. Such adoration of futurism made the marketing boys' blood run cold. He won through. By contrast, the Megane Scenic seems so sensibly correct in the way it solves design problems that you wonder why nobody dreamt it up before. Actually asking children what they liked and did not like about sitting in the backs of cars seems a glaringly obvious start point to any outsider. "Yes, Sir Denys Lasdun understood that," says Le Quément. "He said: 'Our job is to give the client, on time and on cost, not what he wants but what he never dreamed he wanted. And when he gets it, he recognises that's what he wanted all the time'."

The 'all the time' bit is important. Because, although Renault has come miles since Le Quément's arrival, the cars remain visibly part of the same family and heritage. Purchasers are buying into something with a discernible lineage. "I do defend and like French design," says Le Quément, "and maybe that's because I'm half British." (His mother was from the UK and he was largely educated in this country and he taught on the RCA course.) One of his two chief lieutenants is a Brit, too. Anthony Grade is from the legendary showbiz family – Michael Grade is his brother. Grade A was responsible for the Laguna and Megane Scenic interior.

RENAULT ESPACE

That ability to look objectively at maintaining the heritage is important to Le Quément. There are 14 different nationalities in the Renault design studio and 50 per cent of the staff are non-French. "Foreigners have the ability to point out to us what 'Frenchness' is better than we can ourselves sometimes," he says. "It's like the man who walks by the river on a hot day and fancies a swim. 'What's the water like?' he asks a passing fish. 'What water?' replies the fish'."

Nationality and fish interrogation aside, one thing on which Le Quément is very keen is that his designers should get out of the studio and subject themselves to the influences of the world around them. For example, Renault organises 'missions' to cities for groups of four or five designers where they spend five days observing what makes the place tick and soaking up the atmosphere. On their return to Paris they produce a brochure and make a presentation outlining their findings: "We go and look how people do things. We go to the Milan Fair, we look at ships, yachts everything."

Thinking big means trying to solve that problem which Le Quément admits "nears an obsession" – a large car. What success Renault has enjoyed is despite the fact that it has consistently failed in the large car segment. The middle manager who covets a Safrane rather than a 5 Series BMW is a rare bird. (In this Renault has much in common with Fiat.) So what has gone wrong here, that has left the market to BMW, Mercedes and Jaguar?

"We had done well in the area of large, luxurious cars before the Second World War," says Le Quément. "But afterwards the French were subjected to state planning to reconstruct the country. We were kept out of the upper segment. We got light commercial vehicles and the 4CV only got through by the skin of its teeth, which made it the first step in a long generation of passenger cars. Also, our taxation system was harsh on large cars and so pushed us towards light, low consumption engines. You cannot do big cars without power and we did not have engines that were up to scratch." It's interesting that they did produce the best Formula One engine of its generation, but squeezing that into a Safrane proved beyond them.

"You cannot enter that segment unless you have all the fundamentals in place," says Le Quément. "I've felt very strongly for a long time that we should have a car of this type because it will improve and strengthen the image of the company. Indeed, it's the segment where you should be able to express the best you can do. And not having one is a tremendous handicap – we're without a flagship."

So far they have come up with the Avantime, a mangled piece of Franglais that has been given as a name to a sort of pleasure palace, super luxury Espace Coupe with a glass roof. (The interior was conceived by Stephan Janin, an ex-RCA student.) There have also been two concepts – the Initiale and the Vel Satis. All will be revealed in about two years' time. In the mean-time, Le Quément is driving an Audi A6 to remind him of the rules of the big segment quality game. "It's a great car, one of my favourites," he enthuses. "The fit and finish is excellent. I think Audi has become the new reference point for these areas. Far better than Mercedes."

The differences between French and German design and culture? There is another story…

"That's the difference of our approach – we want ice or fiery hot water not something luke-warm in the middle"

RENAULT VEL SATIS CONCEPT CAR

Volkswagen boss Ferdinand Piëch nurses a grand plan for the Group's products: just a few 'platforms' providing the raw hardware for its eight brands. Parts makers resent his cost-cutting measures but it's fantastic news for designers…

25|31

Now Arriving
on Platform One
Haig Simonian

STEFAN SIELAFF   PETER SCHREYER

→ "Seen that new Golf? Or was it an Audi?
Or a Seat, or a Skoda?"

A decade ago, such confusion would have
been unthinkable. Cars were identifiable at a
glance. Any doubts could be resolved instantly
by a quick peek at some distinctive feature like
the radiator grille.

Today, by contrast, brand differentiation risks
becoming a rarity as car-makers move towards
basing more of their products on common
components, in their drive to cut costs and
exploit economies of scale.

No manufacturer has pursued the idea of
commonality – known, in the car industry as
platform sharing – more vigorously than
Volkswagen. With four main, and often over
lapping, brands – VW, Audi, Seat and Skoda –
and a legacy of high costs in its core German
factories, Europe's biggest car company had all
the elements to experiment with shared platforms
to help resolve its financial and marketing
problems. All it took was the arrival of Ferdinand
Piëch, a gifted and hard-driven engineeer, as
chairman to provide the missing personal
chemistry. Now, with VW's profits mounting as
Piëch's vision nears fruition, other multi-brand
manufacturers are looking to VW and pushing
ahead with platform strategies of their own.

The idea of building vehicles on common basic
engineering structures is not new. Before the war,
the US 'Big Three' carmakers – Ford, Chrysler
and General Motors – produced families of cars
sharing certain mechanical underpinnings. In the
1980s, Fiat refined the art by devising one basic
underbody for products as diverse as the three-
and five-door Tipo hatchback, the foor-door
Tempra saloon and station wagon, the Alfa
Romeo 155 saloon and two Lancia models too.

But platform sharing as understood today –
using an array of common structural parts
across brand-spanning families of vehicles –
is very much a VW phenomenon. Last year,
about half the group's 4.5m cars were based
on shared platforms. The figure should rise to
nearly 100 per cent early next century.

The financial rewards have been stunning.
In spite of continuing high labour costs in
Germany, VW's profits have roughly doubled –
albeit from a very low base. The company has
turned itself from a virtual basket case, which
had to run at almost full capacity to turn a profit
at its overmanned German plants, into the envy
of the European motor industry. Platform sharing
has boosted earnings, released cash to plough
into better value mainstream cars and provided
the resources for image-enhancing niche products. The new model blitz has boosted VW's market share, and the group now accounts for almost
one in every five cars sold in western Europe.

But platform sharing as understood today – using an array of common structural parts across brand-spanning families of vehicles – is very much a VW phenomenon.

VOLKSWAGEN BEETLE

Developing common platforms to fit four main brands has taxed VW's engineers in the attempt to devise one-size-fits-all features for each family of vehicles. But it has put the group's stylists to an even tougher test. Shared platforms save their manufacturers money because one car's basic engineering architecture can be spread over a family of vehicles.

But with vehicles built on the same platform commonly sharing up to 60 per cent of their components, the danger has been to create lookalike products. It has been up to the designers to differentiate each model enough to convince customers they are different enough to warrant diverse badges and significantly different prices.

"Of course there's a difficulty of differentiation", admits Hartmut Warkuss, VW's 59-year old group design guru. "Our task in design is to convince customers by bringing out the characteristics of the different brands".

Since the launch of the Audi A4 in December 1994, each new group product has marked a further step in the strategy.

The A4's platform provided the basis for the 1996 Passat and the later Audi A6. The smaller Audi A3, launched in September 1996, inaugurated the new lower mid-sized platform which has formed the base for a breathtaking array of models, including the latest-generation VW Golf of October 1997 and the new Beetle. Vehicles sharing the same underbody include the Skoda Octavia, the VW Bora and the new Seat Toledo. as well as Audi's Bauhaus-inspired TT coupe and roadster. Add to that station wagon derivatives of the saloons and it is an impressive list. More is to come: a booted Toledo and a small people carrier, possibly for more than one brand, are not far off. Eventually, the lower mid-size platform will form the basis for 12 distinct vehicles, according to Piëch.

His plans will move into top gear later this year with the extention of shared platforms to VW's high volume superminis. The replacement for the ageing Skoda Felicia, due to be unveiled at the Frankfurt motor show in September, will be the first of a family of VW group models using a new small car platform. By about 2002, the same underbody will have formed the basis for a range of cars including the next generation VW Polo, the new Seat Ibiza and Cordoba and VW's top-selling Gol in South America.

Platform sharing is not limited to small cars – although the economies of scale involved mean that is where the biggest savings lie. Still to come is a new large car platform for the next generation Audi A8 and a likely VW-branded limousine. The platform could also provide the basis for the future medium-sized Bentley, which the Crewe, UK-based company hopes it has the resources to develop after being acquired by VW last year.

The potential money that can be saved by extending such commonality across VW's range is breathtaking. With parts and materials accounting for about two thirds of the manufacturing costs of a vehicle, developing linked families of products allows a car-maker to wrest huge discounts from suppliers in return for a contract for an entire platform over its lifetime. While the lowest volume product based on a platform may only account for 50,000 units a year – as with the Audi TT – production of the highest-volume vehicle, the Golf, could be 15 times that. The cumulative volume could approach 2m units a year – an astonishing figure compared with what were considered peak model output levels only a few years ago, and juicy enough to encourage even the biggest parts maker to cut prices. While the discount might amount only to a few *pfennigs* per component, the total could reach millions of *deutschmarks* over the life of a platform.

SEAT TOLEDO

VW BORA

Such economies explain why platform sharing has won over equity analysts and investors, who have ramped up VW's share price in recent years. But while it has entranced the financial community, it also carries significant risks. "The platform strategy has allowed us to design far more than would have been possible at a single brand manufacturer which only changes models once every few years", says Warkuss. "Designers have led the process of change in the group in recent years".

VW's product blitz has created unprecedented opportunities – and jobs – in design. Peter Schreyer, who became Audi's styling supremo in January 1994 after Warkuss moved up to become group design boss, has won international praise for a string of eyecatching new vehicles. He works closely with Stefan Sielaff. a genius at Audi interior design – witness the new TT. Dirk van Braeckel, the Belgian whose clever exterior styling has helped to revive Skoda by skillfully blending contemporary and traditional themes, has just transferred to Bentley to do the same there. His replacement, Erich Himmel, hopes to continue that work after having run the VW group's Spanish design centre for the past four years.

All four are ex-RCA students. Schreyer, 46, studied industrial design in Munich before moving to the RCA in 1979. Since then, his entire career has been with the VW group, switching between the VW and Audi brands, along with a stint in California at the group's West Coast design off-shoot. Van Braeckel, 41, is another lifelong VW group designer. After spending most of his career at Audi, he moved to Skoda in 1993 and was largely responsible for the revitalisation of the Czech marque's design credentials. Himmel, 42, also made his way up through Audi after leaving the RCA.

"No other car-maker can offer the range and variety we have", says Warkuss. "If we can't keep someone at Wolfsburg, we can offer him other opportunities at one of the brands or one of the group's styling centres in Spain or California".

But the range of VW's new models has created two big challenges for its designers. First, they have had to meet the sheer demand from four brands in the thick of model renewal programmes; secondly, they have struggled to distinguish each brand's cars sufficiently to make the platform strategy a commercial success.

SKODA OCTAVIA

"For a platform strategy to work, customers must believe cars built on common platforms are different enough to warrant stratified pricing. Emphasising brand identities has become crucial commercially, and not just a matter of aesthetics", says one leading automotive equity analyst.

"The platform strategy has given us much more work and elevated the role of the designer", says Warkuss. "The speed and spread of new model introductions has created unprecedented opportunities in design. And everyone knows how important design is not just to Mr Piëch but to the success of the platform strategy itself".

Design's importance looks set to expand given Piëch's apparently insatiable desire to buy more brands. The past year has seen the acquisition of Lamborghini, Bugatti and Bentley. Volkswagen also remains responsible for Rolls-Royce until the brand reverts to BMW in 2003 under a complex deal hammered out last year. And Piëch has made no secret of his wish to purchase a truck-maker – altough, presumably, its products would not form part of the platform strategy.

The additional workload has prompted a sharp rise in the group's design resources and staff. Studios have been expanded, especially at Skoda and Seat, which needed to catch up with the more established VW and Audi. To boost the Spanish marque, which Piëch sees as a rival to Alfa Romeo, VW head-hunted no less a luminary than Walter de Silva, the man whose stylistic thinking largely determined Alfa's new upmarket image. Products like the 156, Spider and GTV exemplify just the Latin characteristics of sportiness and passion Piëch wants to instill at Seat. Among VW's other alumni are J Mays, now vice president of design at Ford, who spent many years at Audi and at the California studio.

Warkuss argues the plaform strategy has let it develop more niche cars than would have been possible at any other manufacturer. Vehicles like the new Beetle – conceived by Mays in California – and the Audi TT bear witness to that. Even the most persuasive designer would have found it hard to justiify the economics of either model had it not been based it on an already developed and funded platform.

But there's another aspect to platform sharing which its exponents are less keen to publicise. Can shared platforms ultimately produce the claimed advantages over the long term, rather than just early on?

Platform sharing will only survive commercially if buyers believe the cars built on the same platform are really different. If an Audi and a Skoda share 60 per cent of their parts, including character-defining features like engines and gearboxes, customers may eventually opt for the cheaper brand rather than paying a hefty premium for an upmarket label.

Such differentiation may become even more difficult to maintain as each platform spawns ever more models Ultimately, platform sharing could start to be counter-productive as economies of scale prove self-defeating. While shared platforms promise immense savings, they also limit stylists' freedom of manoeuvre because of pre-determinded engineering hard points, like the location of an A pillar, which must be common to every model built on a given platform.

Car-makers planning platform strategies invariably reply that buying cars is as much about emotion as reason. While some motorists may reflect coolly on the preponderance of shared parts and make their purchases accordingly, most base their decision on a cocktail of factors, in which brand perceptions play a crucial part.

"Not every customer knows or cares what's under the bonnet", says Warkuss. "Car buying will always be a sociological thing. Whether rational or not, that is so. People buy what they want, and want to believe it's the best".

VW claims its research reveals very little cannibalisation between brands so far. Cases of customers buying a Passat rather than a dearer A6, or a Golf instead of an A3, are said to be relatively few and far between.

190

"No other car-maker can offer the range and variety we have"

The company also says it's as unconcerned about dangers that product proliferation will diminish its stylists' creativity. "I don't see any danger that all our cars will turn out looking the same", says Warkuss. "Each brand will find its own identitiy. It is true that, at the beginning, because we had to be quick, I was worried about the differences being too narrow. But now we've had more time to think things through, we've moved much closer to our targets." Those 'targets' for each brand's image are not held on complex computer programmes, or in massive tomes in a company vault, but on eight modest, glossy photo collages, with just five words per sheet.

Every leaf sums up all there is to be said about each of VW's eight brands (smaller, more recently acquired marques like Bentley, Rolls-Royce, Lamborghini and Bugatti are included alongside the mainstream brands. The five words synthesise what the stylists believe each brand stands for while the photo collage convey the visual elements of the message.

Seat, for example, is 'cheeky' and 'proactive', but also 'proud'. Its pictures convey passion and flamboyance, along with daring and colour. Skoda's words, by contrast, include 'classic', 'basic' and 'warm', with images of precision instruments like chronometers and Swiss Army knives to bring home the group's long engineering traditions, along with stripped down furniture to emphasise its no-nonsense, value or money side.

"We use pictures because that's the way designers think", says Warkuss. "And images speak a common language, unlike our designers.The sheets will be reviewed every year or two to keep the brand identities fresh, although the core words are unlikely to change in a hurry", he explains.

It is easy to deride such simplistic tools. Warkuss himself admits some brands also lend themselves to such treatment more than others. Finding the right images and words for the core VW marque was about the toughest task and provoked the most heated debate. "VW is the most difficult, because it is very broad. We had to go for more neutral images".

If such simple representations help Warkuss and his colleagues, they are to be welcomed. Car lovers around the world will favour the re-establishment of famous marques like Skoda or Bentley, and the creation of convincing new identities for more muddled brands like Seat. But the real test of the platform strategy, and the challenge it has posed for VW's designers, as for those from other manufacturers planning platform-based products, will come in the toughest arena of all – the market.

An Englishman working for an American-controlled Japanese car company in Germany, Peter Birtwhistle, chief designer at Mazda, represents the global meltdown of the car industry

26|31

One Car,
a Dozen Design
Directives – from
Across the World
Russell Bulgin

→ "What influences designers?" Peter Birtwhistle grins and wanders over to pick up a book, starts to rifle the pages. That this is a volume written by an Englishman about a German marque and translated into German may well be totemic: Birtwhistle is English, has worked in Germany for 21 years, and today is chief designer for the European arm of Mazda, a Japanese company controlled by an American multinational. His professional life is either wilfully cosmopolitan, or the way the car industry is today; perhaps both.

"See these hot air-vents for the turbo?" He points out a series of angled slots on the carbon fibre bonnet of a short-wheelbase Audi quattro Sport, a fearsome rally-derived confection from a German manufacturer, engineered in Switzerland, styled by an Englishman. This Englishman.

"That was the year the Formula 1 Ferrari used to have these distinctive vents on the side pods…" Angled slots, flushed into carbon fibre. A big grin. "I thought, 'oh, that's neat…'"

Downstairs at Mazda's European design HQ sit two ostensibly identical vehicles. These are sisters, sort of. The Premacy MPV, a production reality. And a full-size concept model. Squint and they morph indistinguishably. Birtwhistle can point out a subtle nose-job and some tweakery applied to the tail, but these two machines underline the fact European genesis and Japanese gestation can make for a convincing product, on-sale worldwide. And each iteration is, above all, neat.

"I studied, originally, exhibition stand design and interior design at Maidenhead College of Art," says Birtwhistle. "But I had a passionate interest in cars and on a college trip to the Royal College degree show, there was a small exhibition from the car design department, and that kind of sparked my interest."

But why cars? "What kicks that off, I've no idea. I've a twin brother who isn't interested in cars – he's an architect, he's creative. So I applied to the RCA, got sponsorship from Chrysler UK. Chrysler UK and Ford sponsored two students each – so it was a small group."

There's something faintly collegiate about Birtwhistle. His accent is English, Northern, his diction precise, his biography spun out modestly. "I graduated in 1973 and by that time Chrysler UK was down the pan… I met representatives from Vauxhall at my graduation show and I went for an interview at Luton.

"The design quality of Vauxhall, and of GM generally, was good. The studio was amazing, a big studio right in the middle of Luton. For a designer starting off it was a great place to work.

"Geoff Lawson [now chief of design at Jaguar] was there, Ken Greenley was there and John Heffernan. These were the people who guided my career at that early stage. It was an amazing place – there was a lot of showbiz. Bill Mitchell was still running GM Design worldwide. He'd turn up for design shows dressed for the occasion – he might wear jodhpurs and some kind of riding attire…"

"There are certainly features [in Mazda cars] which you see in Japanese art and architecture" – Peter Birtwhistle

MAZDA MX-3

"The awareness of
design is everywhere
– it's a global thing"
– Peter Birtwhistle

MAZDA XEDOS 9

Yet the role of Vauxhall was changing. Vauxhall cars were becoming visually re-configured Opels, with overall design direction handled at Russelsheim, Germany. Luton simply freshened up noses and tails for application to Opels: Ascona begat Cavalier as Kadett sired Astra. Birtwhistle stayed for four years.

He then followed Martin Smith to Audi, working on the original, ruthlessly aerodynamic 100 saloon. "There are certain designers who can stand by cars and say, 'I did that.' I don't think I can do that. I've been privileged to have worked with some significant companies and worked on some significant designs. I went to Audi as a junior staff member and I worked on the 100 programme, but the key player there was Hartmut Warkuss." A grin. There *might* have been a sketch on the wall of mine…"

Then again. "Actually, at Audi, I was hands-on with the short-wheelbase quattro," he says, almost surprised by the recollection. "It was developed by Audi Sport and being built at a company in Switzerland called Sieger & Hoffmann, who specialised in carbon fibre – they had worked for the ATS F1 team and Sauber in sports car racing.

"Basically, [lead driver] Hannu Mikkola wanted a shorter wheelbase and a steeper front screen for better visibility. It wasn't a shortened coupé – it was an Audi saloon with the rear of a coupé grafted on. I spent quite a few months out there working on it."

Six years at Audi was followed by a period at Porsche and then, in 1988, a move to Mazda. From Germany to Japan without leaving the country. Mazda wanted European input, and fast.

"The way it was originally was that these satellite studios were set up to offer an alternative proposal for Mazda headquarters," explains Birtwhistle. "I guess it was the influence of designers from Europe – and the obvious cultural things. It was also an opportunity to send designers to Europe and let them understand European requirements."

Europe didn't work in isolation – Mazda has studios in "Frankfurt, and Irvine, California and one studio in Yokohama, which is nearer to Tokyo, the trendy area – Hiroshima is a little away from the action in Japan.

"The process was that you could work on initial concepts here." Mazda's Xedos 6 and Xedos 9 executive contenders, plus the aborted Amati luxury brand, were conceptualised, sketched and modelled in Germany; the Xedos production designs were Japanese, incorporating cues and themes worked up at Mazda Europe.

The second generation MX-5 benefited from some extreme thinking from the Europeans. Concepts pasting motorcycle technology to post-modern Caterham 7s, with obligatory silly names: Lean Machine and Two For One. Then came Mark One – more conventional – and Mark One Alternative, while California cooked up the M-Speedster.

Back then, "We were like a consultancy in many ways," confirms Birtwhistle. "We tended to do a lot of concept vehicles here early on. Not necessarily for a motor show, but just to stimulate ideas. Some were wacky. But I think show cars should definitely be an indication of where you're going to be in the next few years. I would admire a good design, even if it is over-the-top, but if you have the opportunity to do a concept car you should use it to maximum effect."

Mazda had pursued niches, creating a product line dominated by what it nicknamed 'heartbeat cars': MX-5, MX-3, MX-6, with limited underskin commonality. Niche cars on niche platforms generated niche profits. Ford bought 34 per cent of Mazda and a heavy presence on the board.

"The decision process was complex – and this was something that worried Ford, when they started to take a more active involvement in our design process," admits Birtwhistle. "Ford is into market research. We were going down this path of selecting designs and there wasn't a *process* in place, which worried Ford – because sales didn't indicate these emotional designs were necessarily the right direction for our bread-and-butter products." Creativity focus was needed.

"That was when Ford said 'You've got to get into research.' This was a difficult thing for Mazda: they've never had that. And so the initial use of research clinics was very much new territory – and I think Mazda perhaps took the results of these clinics a little too literally…"

197

AUDI QUATTRO SPORT

MAZDA PREMACY

Ultimately, the result was Global One, a system which allies efficiency to imagination. "Global One is basically geared to the fact that the whole design process has to be speeded up and streamlined," says Birtwhistle.

"These days, with lead times down as low as 15 months from design sign-off, you can't afford to send models off to Japan, sending them back, refining them. It's too time-consuming. The whole design process has got to be speeded up. This involves data transfer and digital design."

Yet Global One is about more than parsing design to bits and bytes. "You have to handle the feasibility of the design where the car is engineered and manufactured. So Mazda wants to polarise design development in Japan – but it wants ideas from Europe or America. We'll be asked for initial ideas for virtually every programme, even if it's just sketches. Just to get the ball rolling. If there's a spark there and the designer can be sent over, that will happen."

Software and open communication, then, has freed Mazda designers. "The sense of ownership which every designer has in a design is very important – and Mazda understands that," confides Birtwhistle. "So it's necessary to keep the designer interested in his design right through to production.

"This is why, with a more global design organisation, if a design of ours [from Europe] is selected, then our designers would follow that through – involving a certain amount of time in Japan working on the project, reporting to the chief designer of that programme in Japan."

Mazda design is also set to integrate with Ford's global strategy. "The Ford connection isn't unusual when you're in the States or Asia where these joint programmes have been done for years.

"In Europe it's been different. The only programme where we've had an involvement is the little 121/Fiesta, which was a kind of kick-off for the relationship with Ford in Europe, getting to know the Ford process. Platform-sharing is what it's all about, and there will be future co-operation as the Ford family develops."

Slotting Mazda design into Ford is all about maximising resources and design intelligence across cultural boundaries. This, Birtwhistle understands. So what are the differences between, say, German and Japanese design?

"It's basically a question of time", explains Birtwhistle. "Especially if you've come from Porsche, where designers spend considerable time working on the surfaces, working on the highlights. BMW and Audi still take time refining their designs. They've also established a brand identity which they understand. They know where they are going."

Interiors are also worked differently in some Japanese studios. "They will create an image – a sculpture, if you like. When they've established that, then they will start to think about where they are going to put the switches. Then they might discover they can't do a vent this shape, because it's too expensive, so they will take another one... "There are certainly features which you see in Japanese art and architecture – they're comfortable with that kind of form and shape. You see it in a treatment of line or balance and proportion – that's where it's coming from. These days, though, design isn't just styling: it's brand, it's quality and it's design itself. Those three disciplines have an equal priority.

"The awareness of design is everywhere – it's a global thing." Which implies that Mazda Europe could, perhaps, design a product destined only to be sold in Japan. "Yes, in theory," says Birtwhistle, the Englishman working for an American-controlled Japanese car company in Germany. "There's no reason why not."

Slotting Mazda design into Ford
is all about maximising resources
and design intelligence across
cultural boundaries

MAZDA 121 (BACKGROUND), 323F (LEFT) AND 626

Nothing handles
better than a rented car.
PJ O'Rourke
1987

Cars are
rolling sculpture
Arthur Drexler
1951

→ Predictions

Stephen Bayley

27|31

Working Backwards

from the Future

Designers live in the present, but have to think in the future.

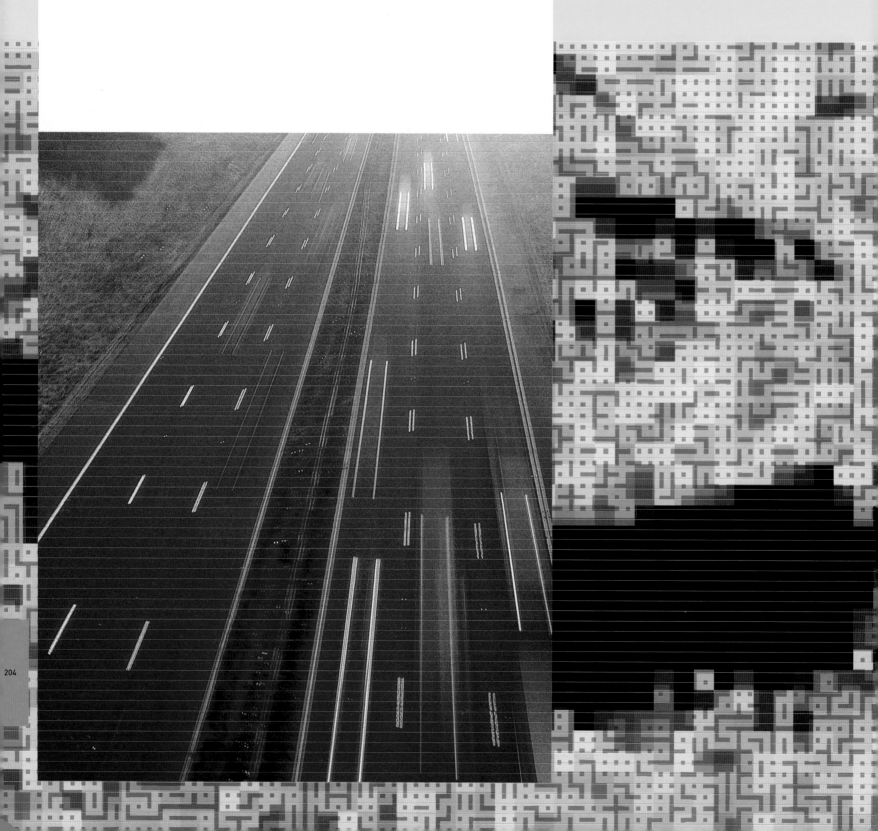

→ Designers live in the present, but have to think in the future.

There's a famous illustration from Norman Bel Geddes, one of the pioneers of the design profession, from the period in the 1930s when he had a consultancy with the Graham-Paige car company. He stretched his imagination to the absolute maximum to envisage the car of the future and eventually produced a shape that satisfied his considerable artistic vanity.

However, he knew the design he foresaw was way too advanced for the tastes of the conservative engineers who ran Graham-Paige. So what Bel Geddes did was work backwards from his imagined future in easy annual stages, in a sort of decadent canon, to get to a safe point Graham-Paige would accept. This was the concept he would present and if it was accepted then Bel Geddes had acquired not just another professional job, but a path to the future… designed by himself.

In all essentials, car designers still work in the same way. Harley Earl told his team to go artistically all the way they could, then just pull back (somewhat) to the point of popular accept-ability. When the public began to appreciate what was going on, this process gave the professional designer the reputation of being a prophet, some-thing eagerly adopted by, for instance, Raymond Loewy who exploited the media via energetic press agents to persuade his clients that he had privileged insights into the future.

This requirement that the designer has a predictive vision, that he can anticipate progress and give meaningful shape to it, remains one of the defining characteristics of a profession which has developed parallel with manufacturing industry. The act of prophecy may lead design to be excitably confused with art, but car design is an overwhelmingly practical matter.

The revolution that began in 1927 with the sett-ing-up of General Motors' Art and Color was a simple one: for the first time, creative people were integrated into the manufacturing process. Hitherto, body designers had been coachbuilders who knew little more about production technology than a hammer and a dolly and a wheeling machine. Now, they were exposed to more advanced techniques: it was when one of Harley Earl's designers saw what could be done with deep-draw sheet metal forming (a process used in chassis manufacture for years) that cars began to assume more moulded, sculptural form.

The car designer occupies a diplomatic – some might say ambivalent - position between the consumer and technology. A creative idea might push him forward, but popular taste (mediated by market research) might hold him back. New tech-nologies might inspire imaginative solutions, but Affordable Cost Targets have a retarding effect on many innovations that are technically feasible. Designers have to look both ways, using micro-scopes and wide-angle lenses.

It is true that when a new car is presented to the public, the planners and designers already have a very good idea of what the replacement of its replacement will be like. These are people who think two product generations ahead, but must also appreciate the vectors of contemporary taste. Of course, this tests traditional notions of novelty. Your 'new' car is, in fact, the one they designed perhaps eight years ago. Peter Stevens, who designed the body of the McLaren F1, says it is absurd to consider cars as 'art'. If asked, Roman engineers would have said the same about the Pont de Gard.

Car designers may not in fact have the prophetic qualities of the authentic artist, they need to be pragmatic people. But they need to be aware of the imminent innovations in technology or impending social changes which will simultaneously inspire and constrict change.

Will the car of the future be much the same as today's, or will it be very different? No-one really knows, but one thing is certain: the car of the future will still have to be 'designed.' Today's designers are working backwards from that future right now.

As recently as the early 1980s, futurologists were predicting that by the end of the century we would have viable electric cars and automated roads. Viable electric cars are still a very long way off. No solutions are in sight for the problem of low power density in the batteries: a vicious circle of weight, low performance, short range, and the inconvenience of long-charging times militates against the pure electric car (although hybrid vehicles have some potential for urban use). Solar power is an interesting, if marginal, sustainable energy source for the future car. One immediate opportunity here (with clear implications for design) is that solar panels can provide auxuiliary power for ventilation and other systems while parked. Presently, these devices are very cumbersome, but it is easy to see how new technology thin-film photovoltaic panels might be acquired for the designer's vocabulary of style.

Against the time-consuming nuisances of the pure electric car, the simple benefits of petrol are easily overlooked: taking on sufficient fuel for a journey of up to, perhaps, 500 miles need take no more than a few minutes.

While the internal combustion engine will most likely be around for as long as the concept of the car remains popular, and will eventually achieve figures equivalent to 200mpg, alternative fuels are a legitimate current research topic. Plant-based fuels are a real possibility: hemp is a source of environmentally friendly ethanol-based fuel.

The idea of the automated, or 'intelligent' road running at traffic densities and speeds beyond the response ability of the average person remains a possibility…although a distant one. The US Intermodal Surface Transportation Efficiency Act of 1991 optimistically aimed for testing an automated road by 1997. Some of the key technologies do already exist, satellite navigation and proximity radar, for instance, but the genuine intelligent road is still a long way off, even if it has some appeal to those wearied by the tedium of the motorway.

The intelligent road would offer the following experience. After approaching the motorway via an access ramp, the car is fed into the traffic stream and then follows a programmed course managed by a central computer. At the exit nearest the destination, the driver re-assumes control of the car. The expensive infrastructure of the intelligent road makes it unlikely and the implied authoritarianism of this traffic management denies the central principle of individual mobility so keenly appreciated by Henry Ford.

Equally, unrestricted self-driving vehicles are only a futurologist's daydream, at least until machine vision improves.

There are few realistic prospects of new materials. Plastics may have the advantage of light weight, but carry heavy disadvantages in the areas of cost, noise-suppression and fastening, the last being notoriously problematic. They are also expensive to recycle. Toughened glass and sheet metal will continue to dominate the architecture of the car, although there are some indications the actual categories of car types are mutating. It is clear, for instance, that the idiosyncratic, but very popular, off-road format and the ingenious, but less popular, MPV are mutating into a single type which will probably be resolved into a large, tall, one-box format with ever more flexible seating and storage.

Another trend is unambiguously apparent: the private car is becoming a communications platform. Since 1996 Lincolns have been fitted with a RESCU system, essentially a factory-fit phone that can be used to alert emergency services. Electronic voice commands are already available on certain Jaguar and Mercedes-Benz models. Head-up displays for driver information will be available soon and sat-nav will eventually become as familiar as a radio. As traffic gets worse, in-car food and drink preparation becomes daily more likely.

The development time for a new car has fallen dramatically. It was 52 months for the Sierra. It will be nearer 24 for the next generation Mondeo. Doing it fast, as the chairman of Motorola recently remarked, means you have to do it right. The rapidly improving efficiencies in production bring big gains in tangible 'quality' to mass-market cars, increasingly an important factor in consumer psychology. Significantly, Renault's Patrick Le Quément is called the Chef du Design et Qualité.

Stephen Bayley

The Literary Digest in 1889 predicted the price of horseless carriages would probably fall, but it was unlikely ever to become as popular as the bicycle. So much for predictions. The ordinary car of 1999 is an astonishing technical achievement, a fine industrial reconciliation of poetry and pragmatics. For less than £10,000 you can buy a safe, comfortable, quiet machine that will rapidly transport four adults plus luggage at a seat-mile cost that makes a mockery of public transport economics and will do so for about five years or 100,000 or so miles without complaint or failure.

But the same practical genius that made the car such a useful, attractive and popular machine is also the source of increasingly ferocious criticism.

The great travel writer Wilfred Thesiger said in 1994: "I despair of the deadly technical ingenuity of modern man. When the first men landed on the moon, I had a terrible feeling of desecration. Looking round me, I feel there will be no human life at all on our planet in 100 years. Once every Chinese has a car, we're finished. The internal combustion engine has been a profound misfortune. What have we gained from it?"

Freedom and wealth are the answers, but the problem with Thesiger's argument is that while perhaps the philosophy of Henry Ford is not well-known in China, as the Chinese economy becomes more liberal consumer appetites are demanding that promise of independence and mobility that the Model T first realised. Only an authoritarian regime of the very type they are struggling to escape would deny the Chinese their new cars.

WH Auden was critical of the car. In a 1974 poem he said, somewhat apocalyptically:

Dark was that day when Diesel
conceived his grim engine that
begot you, vile invention…
Metallic monstrosity,
bale and bane of our Culture,
chief woe of our Commonweal.
…You poison
the lungs of the innocent,
your din dithers the peaceful,
and on choked roads hundreds must
daily die by chance medley

The influence of the car on contemporary life is almost indescribably profound, although in 1964 Marshall McLuhan explained what it had done to the urban geography of the United States: 'The motor car… exploded each city into a dozen suburbs, and then extended many of the forms of urban life along the highway till the open road seemed to become non-stop cities… As the city filled with mobile strangers, even next door neighbours became strangers… The car, in a word, has refashioned all the spaces that unite and separate men."

Even the keenest apologists for the car accept that while it is a humane benefit of indefinite utility and relevance, our use of it will have to change. The amazing machine which offered ordinary people aristocratic freedoms is now throttling their cities and congesting their countryside. Restrictions on traffic volume in cities are inevitable, although there is vigorous debate on the means of achieving them. The Japanese have a partial solution: there you cannot own a car unless you also own off-street parking.

Perhaps the future use of the car is the biggest creative challenge to designers.

Nearly 30 years ago Buckminster Fuller said: "Making the world's available resources serve 100 per cent of an exploding population can only be accomplished by a boldly accelerated design revolution to increase the present performance per unit of invested resources. This is a task for radical technical innovators, not political voodoo-men."

Apologists for the car are not environmentally irresponsible or negligent of nature. On the contrary, the pursuit of engineering targets is a process of perfection in harmony with the environment rather than in opposition to it. The quest for technical efficency is a positive benefit to nature: engineers dislike noise, heat and pollution because these are wasted energy. This is one of the many things Henry Ford meant when he said in *My Life and Work*: 'We shall learn to be masters rather than servants of nature.'

Will the car of the future be much the same as today's, or will it be very different? No-one really knows, but one thing is certain: the car of the future will still have to be 'designed.' Today's designers are working backwards from that future right now.

'I believe the designer's real task begins once functional and behavioural needs have been satisfied. We create objects not only because we hope to satisfy the pragmatic needs of man, but mainly because we need to satisfy the demands of our passions and imaginations'

Emilio Ambasz, Designer and Curator, New York Museum of Modern Art

28|31

Royal College of Art
Vehicle Design:
The Course Philosophy
Professor Ken Greenley

209

'I think that cars today are almost the exact equivalents of the great gothic cathedrals; I mean the supreme creation of an era conceived with passion by unknown artists and consumed in image, if not in usage, by a whole population which appropriates them as a purely magical object'
Roland Barthes, academic, structuralist and author of Mythologies Paris 1957

In 1951 the Museum of Modern Art in New York held an exhibition entitled Eight Automobiles. The exhibition selected eight key cars including the Cisitalia 202 and the Cord 810, which were then visually deconstructed and discussed by leading art critics, one of whom, Arthur Drexler, commented that "cars are rolling sculpture."

The quotations by Ambasz (previous pages), Barthes and Drexler collectively embrace the core philosophy and ambitions of the course. Vehicle Design and Automotive Design have been studied at the RCA since 1967. The course, under its various titles, has provided over 250 graduates, 98 per cent of whom are successful automotive design practitioners, some of whom have subsequently developed careers in academic institutions, related to the undergraduate study of transportation design in Europe and the Far East.

Vehicle Design graduates are not employed as technical or engineering professionals, nor as material technologists, aerodynamicists or ergonomists, although they have an understanding of these issues and, in many cases, can be successful contributors.

Their primary activity is to create, manipulate and sophisticate the three-dimensional volumes which constitute the exterior and interior design of a modern, functional and manufacturable vehicle. The skill of the vehicle designer is to communicate to the observer in subliminal ways the values, issues and functions of the design. Some of these values are related to its quality and status, its technology and performance, the cultural and social context, and historic lineage.

The issues that are three-dimensionally communicated can describe a contextual aspect, gender or age issues, private sector, municipal or industrial usage, and also the relationship to the environment and society.

The visual description of the vehicle's function is usually more obvious, but in the most successful designs this can also be delivered subliminally; for example, in the visual reduction of bulk in a large vehicle, or the application of protective imagery to a small family city vehicle.

In the delivery of a successful design, the designer will have passed through a rigorous and detailed investigation of the object, through a comprehensive dialogue in three dimensions. During this process the student designer will demonstrate his/her creative intelligence through application and appropriateness. The designer will also use a high degree of critical wisdom in the 'reading of the object', and the ability to develop self-critical judgements.

The three-dimensional programme is the core activity of the course. Through the programme the student will develop sculptural competence, which will lead to sculptural confidence.

Through the three-dimensional programme, the student will set critical design parameters, by researching and interpreting historical, cultural, contextual, social, technological, emotional, romantic, poetic, humorous and sometimes pragmatic values appropriate to the design of the subject vehicle.

These parameters become the targets by which the design will be judged.

The core mission of the course to produce professionally independent graduate designers. The majority of students entering the course have progressed through their undergraduate degree with a predictably high level of tutorial direction and instruction. It is the ambition of the course to produce post-graduate designers who possess high levels of creative intelligence, sophisticated and professional skills, sculptural confidence, an understanding of their professional contribution, a high degree of social and moral responsibility, and a well developed level of critical wisdom. They should therefore be well equipped to practise as professional vehicle designers.

Aims of the course. The primary aim of the course is to develop, sophisticate and deliver a programme of study appropriate to the requirements of future vehicle designers.

•The course aims to investigate the individual requirements of each student, identify the most appropriate activities and projects relevant to each individual, and develop a programme of study designed for potential examination, graduation and career success.
•The course aims to provide a high level of pastoral care to each student, to support the ambitious, promote confidence, subdue arrogance, and develop moral and social responsibilities.
•The course also aims to anticipate the future product requirements of society and the vehicle manufacturing industry, and introduce the study of these vehicle types into the course curriculum.
•The course intentionally aims to provoke, influence and inspire the vehicle design profession, by the public presentation of the students' project work and the delivery of the course's design philosophy.
•The course intends to produce vehicle design graduates who have developed a high level of independence.

Course objectives. The main objectives of the course are to realise the aims in relatioin to individual students:

The course aims to work for the benefit of: students of vehicle design, the vehicle design course, the School of Architecture and Design, the Royal College of Art, vehicle design graduates, professional vehicle designers, the vehicle design profession, the vehicle manufacturing industry, national and international cultural, contextual, environmental and social issues, the College research programmes, the MPhil/PhD Programme, the Post-Experience Programme.

To advance learning, knowledge and the professional skills related to the vehicle design profession. To understand, evaluate and critically appraise historic and current examples of vehicle design. To develop the students' ability to 'read' the design intentions, execution and effects in examples of vehicle design. To develop the students' ability to create inspirational 'narrative' and subsequent 'vocabulary' selection to form a design brief, design development guidelines, and the criteria for evaluation. To enhance and develop the studio skills required by students in the execution of the design process. To anticipate the requirements of both society and the vehicle manufacturing industry. To promote and increase the awareness of the course, and enhance its reputation through the exposure of the post-graduate design activities. To develop,

through the core activity of the three dimensional modelling programme, the students' sculptural competence. The course will endeavour to graduate students with a high level of professional independence. The course is committed to developing its reputation within the Royal College of Art, by promoting and explaining the intellectual depth of its activities. The course will endeavour to develop the critical wisdom of its students, related to their own work and that of their work of professional practitioners. The course will continue to maintain a multi-national and multi-cultural balance in its student intake. To develop the students' abilities to communicate design intentions, design development and the final design presentation. To encourage student participation in the design debate, and to increase student confidence in the promotion of personal aspirations.
To increase student awareness of new design methodologies, and tools pertinent to vehicle design activities and, where possible, simulate the methods and familiarise the student with the tools To record and collate the students' work. To accumulate a 'body of knowledge' related to previous activities that will preface future design briefs. To develop the partnership between student and tutor, a mature. relationship could lead to the joint authorship of a design solution. To encourage students to develop their confidence, and accelerate their design maturity, so they can become self-motivated, with the confidence independently to select and edit their own concepts and ideas

"I love art and I love painting. When I started working in the car industry, it wasn't by choice, even though I liked cars. Then I started to feel the emotion and pride of knowing how to create, on a stylistic level, an object with a primarily technological and functional purpose"
Giorgetto Giugiaro,
Founder of Ital Design

Royal College of Art
Vehicle Design Graduates
The names, the years they
graduated, what they do now
and details of previous employment

— **PETER STEVENS**
Graduated: 1969
Peter Stevens Design – director
(BMW 1999 Le Mans car, Subaru Impreza Rally
Car, Tag McLaren Audio – HI.IP., Lambourghini
Jota SV, Jaguar XJR-15, Aston Martin, Audi,
Benneton, Bentley, Chrysler, Citroen, ERF Trucks,
Ford, Hyundai, Panoz, Prodrive, Subaru, Toyota.
Formerly worked for: McLaren (Designer F1 Road
Car), Lotus (Excel, Esprit, Elan, Isuzu 4200R) Ogle
(Seddon Atkinson Cab), Ford Dunton

— **DAWSON SELLAR**
Graduated: 1969
Applied Sweepers – designer
Formerly worked for Lansing Linde, BMW,
Porsche, Ford

— **JOHN HARTNELL**
Graduated: 1970
Ford USA – design manager
(Libre, MC2, MC4, Indigo concepts,
Cougar interior). Formerly worked for Ford UK
(Puma, 1993 Escort, 1996 Fiesta interior, 1992
Mondeo interior, RS200)

— **PAUL GEBBETT**
Graduated: 1970
Ford UK – design manager (1996 Mondeo
interior, 1994 Galaxy interior, 1995 Escort interior,
1992 Scorpio interior, 1982 Concept Cargo truck)

— **CLIFF PICKERING**
Graduated: 1971
Ford UK – design manager
Formerly worked for Chrysler UK, Triumph

— **LAWRENCE MARTIN**
Graduated: 1971

— **CLIVE POTTER**
Graduated: 1971

— **GRAHAM HULL**
Graduated: 1971
Rolls-Royce & Bentley – chief stylist (Silver
Seraph/Bentley Arnage, Bentley Continental SC
Sedanca, 'Pinnacle' Silver Spur/Bentley, Bentley
Continental T, 1996 Silver Spirit/Spur/Bentley
Turbo R, Bentley Java concept, Bentley
Continental R, Bentley Turbo R, Silver
Spirit/Spur/Bentley Mulsanne)

— **STEPHEN FERRADA**
Graduated: 1972

— **GEOFF MATTHEWS**
Graduated: 1972

— **DAVID ARBUCKLE**
Graduated: 1972
Rover – studio director (Freelander, Discovery II,
second-generation Rover 800). Formerly worked
for Volvo (FL6 truck), Chrysler UK (Horizon,
Alpine)

— **JONATHAN SAVILLE**
Graduated: 1973

— **MARTIN SMITH**
Graduated: 1973
Opel – chief designer (Speedster). Formerly
worked for Audi (quattro, Avus), Porsche,
Vauxhall/Bedford

— **PETER BIRTWHISTLE**
Graduated: 1973
Mazda – chief designer, Germany (mainly concept
cars). Formerly worked for Porsche, Audi
(1982 100, 80, quattro Sport), Vauxhall (Chevette
2300HS)

— **JEAN NAHUM**
Graduated: 1973

— **DAVID EVANS**
Graduated: 1973
Freelance – principal (Jeep Cherokee Orvis
special edition, Chrysler Neon GLS special
edition). Formerly worked for Land Rover
(Discovery, Range Rover), Chrysler UK (Talbot
Tagora Interior, Alpine II interior, Horizon specials)

— **BOB CARROL**
Graduated: 1974

— **LIONEL CHEW**
Graduated: 1974

— **PETER HORBURY**
Graduated: 1974
Volvo – design director. Formerly worked for MGA

— **FERGUS POLLOCK**
Graduated: 1975
Jaguar – design manager (XK8, XJS, XK180)

— **IAN CAMERON**
Graduated: 1975
BMW – design manager. Formerly worked for
Iveco, Pininfarina, Ogle

— **RYUZO HOSINO**
Graduated: 1975

— **MEHMET OZOZTURK**
Graduated: 1975
Rover – principal designer
(Land Rover Freelander)

— **ANDERS CLAUSAGER**
Graduated: 1976
British Motor Industry Heritage Trust –
archivist. Formerly worked for Volkswagen
(Polo MkII), Rover

— TONY CATIGNANI
Graduated: 1976
Saab – chief designer. Formerly worked for Ogle
Design, Ford

— ROB POWELL
Graduated: 1976
BMW Technik – chief designer
(Z13, Just 4/2, Z22). Formerly worked for
Porsche, Leyland Trucks

— ELIO NICOSIA
Graduated: 1976

— SIMON BURY
Graduated: 1976

— JAN FELLSTROM
Graduated: 1976

— SIMON BURY
Graduated: 1977

— TAKASHI HASUMI
Graduated: 1977

— BILL ASLETT
Graduated: 1977

— GERRY MCGOVERN
Graduated: 1977
Rover – chief designer (Land Rover Freelander,
MG*F*, Rover 200 Coupe, 200 Cabriolet, second-
generation Rover 800, MG EXE show car exterior,
Rover CCV show car)

— CLIFF WILKINS
Graduated: 1977

— TOSHIAKI MIZUTANI
Graduated: 1977

— GEOFF WARDLE
Graduated: 1977

— DAVID SHERRIFF
Graduated: 1977

— KEITH HELFET
Graduated: 1977
Jaguar – principal designer (F-type, XJ220, XJ6/8,
XK8)

— GRAHAM THORPE
Graduated: 1978
BMW – studio manager (3 series IV). Formerly
worked for Audi (Avus, A4), Ford (Sierra interior)

— ROLAND STERNMANN
Graduated: 1978
Porsche – senior designer (944 cabriolet,
911 cabriolet). Formerly worked for Mazda
Germany (323F/C)

— RICHARD OAKES
Graduated: 1978
Freelance – principal

— ROB SUNDENE
Graduated: 1978

— THOMAS PLATH
Graduated: 1978

— IAN CALLUM
Graduated: 1979
TWR – chief designer. Formerly worked for Ford

— JIM KELLEY
Graduated: 1979

— ROBIN AUSTIN
Graduated: 1979

— LUC LANDYUT
Graduated: 1979
Renault – designer. Formerly worked for BMW,
Ford

— ALAIN JAN
Graduated: 1979

— RANJIT BHAMBRA
Graduated: 1979
Porsche – designer (959)

— JOSE DE LA VEGA
Graduated: 1980
Volvo – designer (interiors)

— ALEX SANTOS
Graduated: 1980

— JOACHIM STORZ
Graduated: 1980
Design A Storz – principal

— SIMON LUNN
Graduated: 1980

— PINKY LAI
Graduated: 1980
Porsche – design manager (1996 911 Carrera
coupe/cabriolet). Formerly worked for BMW, Ford

— TOM JARA
Graduated: 1980

— PETER SCHREYER
Graduated: 1980
Audi

— GERT HILDEBRANDT
Graduated: 1980
Mercedes-Benz

— KEITH RYDER
Graduated: 1980
Peugeot – project leader (205, 106, Oxia, 406 and 206 interiors)

— STEVE HARPER
Graduated: 1980

— CHRIS JOHNSON
Graduated: 1981

— LUCIANO D'AMBROSIO
Graduated: 1981
Bertone – design director. Formerly worked for Ital Design (Seat Toledo, Ibiza), Ford (Escort, Sierra)

— CHRIS BIRD
Graduated: 1981
Ford

— TONY HATTER
Graduated: 1981
Porsche – designer (993 Turbo, GT1) Formerly worked for Opel (Omega/Carlton)

— JONG SUH PARK
Graduated: 1981

— ADRIAN GRIFFITHS
Graduated: 1981

— MIKIO FUJITO
Graduated: 1981

— CORNELIUS STEENSTRA
Graduated: 1982
Foresee Car – chief executive (Toyota, Mitsubishi, Honda, DAF Trucks. Formerly worked for Mazda Germany (626, 323 Bingo, K Car, Supersports, 929 interior), Mercedes-Benz, Volvo

— MARTIN LONGMORE
Graduated: 1982

— VALENTIN SIRILOV
Graduated: 1982

— MIKE DICKENS
Graduated: 1982

— ERWIN HIMMEL
Graduated: 1982
Design Centre Europe (VAG) – managing director (Seat Bolero, Formula). Formerly worked for Audi (quattro Spyder)

— PETER HUTCHINSON
Graduated: 1982
Ford – chief designer, Japan (all Fords for Asia-Pacific based on partner platforms). Formerly worked for Ford Australia (Telstar, Fairlane, LTD), Ford UK (Cargo, Transit, Fiesta)

— ROLAND HEILER
Graduated: 1982
Audi. Formerly worked for Porsche (C88 China car, 968, 928GTS)

— MORAY CALLUM
Graduated: 1982
Ford USA – chief designer (large cars). Formerly worked for Peugeot, Ghia

— BRUCE BRYANT
Graduated: 1982

— OLIVIER BOULAY
Graduated: 1982

— MURAT GUNAK
Graduated: 1983
DaimlerChrysler – design director. Formerly worked for Peugeot, Mercedes-Benz, Ford

— NIKOLAUS VIDAKOVIC
Graduated: 1983
Volkswagen

— DAVID WILKIE
Graduated: 1983
Ghia – designer (Via, Connecta, Lagonda Vignale, Arioso, Turing Ka, Zig)

— STEVE MURKETT
Graduated: 1983
Porsche – design manager (Boxster, 996 concept, 1991 Targa, 1993 GT2 993, RS 993, Panamericana, 964/911 facelift, 959)

— STEVE SYKES
Graduated: 1983

— JONG CHA
Graduated: 1983

— HOWARD GUY
Graduated: 1983

— AAMER MAHMUD
Graduated: 1983

— GUNVANT MISTRY
Graduated: 1984

— ED JAMES
Graduated: 1984
Peugeot Citroën – deputy chief designer (Xsara)

— **LOUIS SANTOS**
Graduated: 1984

— **HANS-HARALD HANSEN**
Graduated: 1984
DaimlerChrysler – design director, Italy.
Formerly worked for Daimler-Benz
(C-class W202, S-class coupe C140)

— **DONATO COCO**
Graduated: 1984
Citroën – chief designer (C3, Xsara, Picasso)

— **LAURENT ROSSI**
Graduated: 1984

— **KEN MELVILLE**
Graduated: 1984
Renault – project manager (Concept Zo, Clio II).
Formerly worked for Mercedes-Benz (SLK),
Citroën (Xanthia, Concept Activa I)

— **DIRK VAN BRAECKEL**
Graduated: 1984
Bentley – director of styling. Formerly worked for
Skoda (Octavia Combi, Octavia limousine, Felicia
facelift), Audi (A3 concept, A8 concept, Cabriolet
concept, 80 Avant)

— **JULIAN THOMSON**
Graduated: 1984
Design Centre Europe (VAG) – design director
(1999 Seat Formula). Formerly worked for Lotus
(1989 Isuzu 4200R, 1992 Lotus Esprit S4, 1992
Asia Motors Neo Mattina, 1995 Elise), Ford

— **ULRICH LAMMEL**
Graduated: 1984

— **HEUNG SIK KIM**
Graduated: 1985

— **RICHARD CARTER**
Graduated: 1985

— **DOUGLAS BARBER**
Graduated: 1985

— **HELMUD SCHMID**
Graduated: 1985

— **ROBERTO GIACHIN**
Graduated: 1985

— **PATRICK STUYVERS**
Graduated: 1985

— **KARL ELMITT**
Graduated: 1985

— **JAMES DAVIES**
Graduated: 1985

— **HEINZ-GEORG ABBING**
Graduated: 1985

— **BILL BARRANCO**
Graduated: 1986

— **INATOSHU KUSAMA**
Graduated: 1986

— **SHUJI TAKANO**
Graduated: 1986

— **PIERRE TERREBLANCHE**
Graduated: 1986
Ducati motorcycles – design director

— **MARK ADAMS**
Graduated: 1986
Ford UK – designer (Focus, Ka interior). Formerly
worked for Ford USA (MC4, Indigo show cars)

— **ANDREW MCGEACHY**
Graduated: 1986

— **DONG-YONG LEE**
Graduated: 1986

— **MARK LLOYD**
Graduated: 1986
Citroën – design manager (C6, Xanae, Activa II).
Formerly worked for Jaguar (XJ220)

— **SYLVIAN POTTIER**
Graduated: 1986
Peugeot – designer (interiors)

— **SIMON COX**
Graduated: 1986
General Motors – design director (Cadillac Icon).
Formerly worked for Isuzu (VX2, Amigo/Frontera II,
Deseo, VehiCross, Como), Lotus (Elan, Esprit)

— **SEON HO YOON**
Graduated: 1986

— **MICHAEL FARNEY**
Graduated: 1986

— **CHRIS MILBURN**
Graduated: 1987

— **IAN MATTHEWS**
Graduated: 1987

— **MATTHIAS KULLA**
Graduated: 1987
Porsche – designer (Boxster, 989 Carrera).
Formerly worked for Audi (A8)

— **ANTHONY LO**
Graduated: 1987
DaimlerChrysler – design manager
(F200, Maybach concepts). Formerly worked
for Audi, Lotus

— **ALEX PADWA**
Graduated: 1987

— **MICHAEL ANI**
Graduated: 1987

— **LIONEL DEAN**
Graduated: 1987

— **WILLIAM FRANKE**
Graduated: 1987

— **JAN HETTLER**
Graduated: 1987
BMW – designer (1998 V12 Le Mans car)

— **YOSUKE YAMAMOTO**
Graduated: 1987

— **HARRY UDEN**
Graduated: 1997

— **RICHARD KILLGREN**
Graduated: 1987
Lotus – designer

— **JULIAN QUINCEY**
Graduated: 1988
Rover – principal designer (MGF)

— **NEIL SIMPSON**
Graduated: 1988

— **JANET MERCER (NÉE STEVENS)**
Graduated: 1988
Rover – principal designer
(200, MGF, Land-Rover Freelander)

— **DAVID CUTCLIFFE**
Graduated: 1988

— **TADEUSZ JELEC**
Graduated: 1988
Jaguar – principal stylist (XJ8, S-type, X300, XJ6).
Formerly worked for Dove Design (XJR-15),
Holden, Mazda, Lotus

— **ABDUL RASHID RAHMAN**
Graduated: 1988

— **YOU SUP YI**
Graduated: 1988

— **IAIN ROBERTSON**
Graduated: 1988
Freelance – principal
Formerly worked for Caterham (21), Autocar, JCB,
Sunseeker

— **ANDREW DYSON**
Graduated: 1988

— **NICK TALBOT**
Graduated: 1988
Seymour Powell – senior designer
(Nexus light bike)

— **LAURENCE CUTTS**
Graduated: 1988
MSX International – design Leader.
Formerly worked for Volvo (LG platform),
MSX International (Heathrow Express),
Peugeot (S16 Roadster), Panther

— **FRANCIS CUSH**
Graduated: 1988
Cush Design – director (Ultima GTR, Spectre
R45, limousine project, Marlboro Ferrari Formula 1
Team, Marlboro Yamaha)

— **CHRIS LIGHTFOOT**
Graduated: 1988

— **PAUL GIBSON**
Graduated: 1989
Ford – senior designer, Italy (show cars)
Formerly worked for Ford USA (2000 Taurus,
1999 Windstar, Mercury Villager), Ford Australia
(EBIII Falcon, Bathurst Falcon racer, Falcon GT)

— **NICK COUGHLAN**
Graduated: 1989

— **MARK OLDHAM**
Graduated: 1989
Daewoo – exterior design team leader, UK.
Formerly worked for TWR (Nissan R390 Le Mans
car, Holden HSV), Mazda Germany, Vauxhall

— **ERIC BELLINGER**
Graduated: 1989

— **HELEN THOMPSON**
Graduated: 1989

—— BART VAN LOTRINGEN
Graduated: 1989
Volvo – designer (S80, S40/V40 interiors)

—— MALCOLM WARD
Graduated: 1989
Opel – chief designer

—— TONY PETTMAN
Graduated: 1989

—— RAINER ZIMMERMANN
Graduated: 1989

—— ABDUL ABDULLAH
Graduated: 1990

—— ALFRED PHILLIPS
Graduated: 1990

—— ARAM KASPARIAN
Graduated: 1990
Design Research Associates – designer.
Formerly worked for Rover

—— TAE WAN KIM
Graduated: 1990

—— STEFAN SIELAFF
Graduated: 1990
Audi – design director (AL2, TT coupé
and roadster)

—— SVEN MORRIS
Graduated: 1990

—— DANY GARAND
Graduated: 1990

—— NEIL MCCABE
Graduated: 1990

—— IVANOV LAMPKIN
Graduated: 1990
BMW – senior designer (Mini AGV 30
show car interior). Formerly worked for Audi
(Avus show car interior)

—— MARTIN FROST
Graduated: 1990

—— JOO HYUN CHUNG
Graduated: 1990
Hongik University. Art College, Korea –
department of Industrial Design. Formerly
worked for Daewoo (electric vehicle, Lanos),
Samsung (compact car), SsangYong (4x4),
ATT (electric vehicle), Hyundai (Atoz)

—— JENNY WATERSON
Graduated: 1990
Jenny Waterson Design – director. Formerly
worked for Citroën, Mazda Germany

—— NEIL WOODFORD
Graduated: 1990

—— MARK BUTLER
Graduated: 1991
Rover – designer. Formerly worked for Omni
Design (Rolls-Royce Silver Seraph/Bentley
Arnage Interior)

—— WON CHOL CHO
Graduated: 1991

—— ALLEN CRAWFORD
Graduated: 1991

—— NORMAN EDWARDS
Graduated: 1991

—— HERVE FOLLIOT
Graduated: 1991
Saab – designer. Formerly worked for Renault
(concept cars, buses), NYA Porspektiv Design

—— GEOFF GARDINER
Graduated: 1991

—— WAYNE GRUNDY
Graduated: 1991

—— THOMAS INGENLATH
Graduated: 1991
Volkswagen – exterior designer. Formerly worked
for Audi

—— SIMON LOASBY
Graduated: 1991

—— NIELS LOEB
Graduated: 1991
Opel – assistant chief designer (Astra
coupe/cabriolet). Formerly worked for Lotus
(Opel Speedster), Bertone (Opel Signum
concept), Saab (9-5)

—— DANTE LUPINI
Graduated: 1991

—— PETER NAUMANN
Graduated: 1991
Naumann Design – director. Formerly worked for
BMW (C1 scooter)

—— MAREK REICHMAN
Graduated: 1991

—— GEERT SCHELLEKENS
Graduated: 1991

— JULIAN WILTSHIRE
Graduated: 1991

— JORDAN BENNETT
Graduated: 1992

— CHRIS SWENSEN
Graduated: 1992

— GILES TAYLOR
Graduated: 1992
Jaguar – Project leader. Formerly worked for
Citroën (Xsara exterior), Ford (Ka),
Mercedes-Benz

— GLEN THOMPSON
Graduated: 1992

— DAVID WOODHOUSE
Graduated: 1992
General Motors – assistant chief designer, UK.
Formerly worked for Rover (MGF Supersports,
Land Rover Freelander, Land Rover Megacity
Cab), BMW (motorcycles)

— SIN YONG WOOK
Graduated: 1992

— KEUN LEE
Graduated: 1992

— JEREMY LENG
Graduated: 1992
Renault – designer. Formerly worked for Hawtal
Whiting

— STUART COOPER
Graduated: 1992

— CLAUDIO FASSINI
Graduated: 1993

— GAVIN HARTLEY
Graduated: 1993
Rover – designer (Discovery II)

— MARCUS HIRST
Graduated: 1993

— SUNG HWAN HONG
Graduated: 1993

— SOTIRIS KOVOS
Graduated: 1993
Toyota – assistant chief designer,
Belgium (MR-J, Funtime, Yaris)

— JASON LESKOS
Graduated: 1993

— ALEXANDRE MALVAL
Graduated: 1993
Design Centre Europe (VAG) – designer

— KARL NEUBOLD
Graduated: 1993

— KARL-HEINZ ROTHFUSS
Graduated: 1993

— JAMES WATKINS
Graduated: 1993
Rover – designer

— MARK WHITELEY
Graduated: 1993
Redman Whiteley Design – partner (yachts)

— PATRICK WONG
Graduated: 1993

— PAUL AKINTUNDE
Graduated: 1994

— KURT BEYER
Graduated: 1994
Opel – designer

— EDUARDO CARCAMO
Graduated: 1994

— GUY COLBORNE
Graduated: 1994
Daewoo – designer, UK (Mirae show car).
Formerly worked for Technicon (Opel Astra, Zafira)

— ALESANDRO, MESONENO-ROMANOS
Graduated: 1994
Design Centre Europe (VAG) – senior designer
Formerly worked for Seat, IDD
(electric car exterior)

— STEVEN CRIJNS
Graduated: 1994
Lotus – design leader (Opel Speedster, 340R
show car, sports boat, Esprit V8, GT3 interior,
Elise Sport 190 show car)

— JOHN DERBY
Graduated: 1994

— TONY FOX
Graduated: 1994

— PATRICK GIRAUD
Graduated: 1994

— ALEJANDRO MESONERO
Graduated: 1994

— CESAR MUNTADA
Graduated: 1994

— **ALFONSO BELLOD**
Graduated: 1995

— **SCOTT BROOKES**
Graduated: 1995

— **JONATHAN DALE**
Graduated: 1995
Ford – designer. Formerly worked for Volvo, Audi

— **DEAN DICKINSON**
Graduated: 1995

— **STUART JAMIESON**
Graduated: 1995
Daewoo – designer, UK (utility vehicle for
release 2001). Formerly worked for Mazda
(SW-X concept interior)

— **MYUNG-KI LEE**
Graduated: 1995

— **HENRY MORSEHEAD**
Graduated: 1995

— **ADRIAN MORTON**
Graduated: 1995
Benelli – designer (superbikes). Formerly
worked for Cagiva (MV Agusta motorcycles)

— **HUGO NIGHTINGALE**
Graduated: 1995
Ghia – designer (Saetta and Lincoln Sentinel
concepts)

— **STEPHEN POTTER**
Graduated: 1995

— **FRANK RIMILI**
Graduated: 1995

— **JOHAN STENUIT**
Graduated: 1995

— **DANIEL WALKER**
Graduated: 1995
Seymour Powell – designer

— **JOLYON YATES**
Graduated: 1995

— **JEREMY ASTON**
Graduated: 1996

— **MATTHEW BEAVEN**
Graduated: 1996
Design Centre Europe (VAG) – designer

— **JIM DAS**
Graduated: 1996

— **BART GROESBEEK**
Graduated: 1996

— **PAUL HANSTOCK**
Graduated: 1996
Rover – designer (Land Rover concepts).
Formerly worked for BMW

— **SUNG KON KIM**
Graduated: 1996

— **ANDRE KRUGER**
Graduated: 1996
Sani Design – designer
(Sani MK2 three-door interior)

— **EDUARDO LANA**
Graduated: 1996
Renault – designer. Formerly worked for
Volkswagen

— **EDUARDO MARCHENA**
Graduated: 1996

— **MAXIMO RUBIO**
Graduated: 1996

— **LEE ROBINSON**
Graduated: 1996
Eggshape. Formerly worked for Volkswagen,
MGM/Castle Rock/Pinewood Studios, Sony, PSD

— **KOICHI SAIKYO**
Graduated: 1996

— **RICHARD WINSOR**
Graduated: 1996

— **PAUL WRAITH**
Graduated: 1996
Daewoo – designer, UK. Formerly worked for
Hyundai, Germany (Euro 1 interior), Ford

— **PETER WOUDA**
Graduated: 1996
Volkswagen – exterior designer

— **BERTRAND BACH**
Graduated: 1997
Opel – designer

— **MATTHEW HILL**
Graduated: 1997
Lotus – design engineer (340R interior, Elise 190R
Motorsport). Formerly worked for LTI, Ford

— **STEPHANE JANIN**
Graduated: 1997
Renault – designer

— **LEE MORAN**
Graduated: 1997
Ford UK – designer

— **CHANG HYUP BAEK**
Graduated: 1997
Design A Storz – designer

— **JOZEF KABAN**
Graduated: 1997
Volkswagen

— **MIKE LEADBETTER**
Graduated: 1997

— **XITIJ MISTRY**
Graduated: 1997
Volkswagen

— **PASI PENNANEN**
Graduated: 1997
Jaguar – stylist (XK180)
Formerly worked for Sisu Trucks

— **JOSE RUBAU SOLA**
Graduated: 1997
Volkswagen – designer

— **GEORGE SARIDAKIS**
Graduated: 1997
Toyota – designer, Belgium

— **PER IVAR SELVAAG**
Graduated: 1997
General Motors – designer, UK

— **NOBUHIRO SUGIMOTO**
Graduated: 1997

— **EARL BECKLES**
Graduated: 1998

— **KYUNG-SIL CHO**
Graduated: 1998

— **CLARENCE BS KIM**
Graduated: 1998
Saab – designer

— **SVEN DELCOUR**
Graduated: 1998

— **BORIS FERKO**
Graduated: 1998
Volkswagen

— **JOAQUIN GARCIA SANCHIS**
Graduated: 1998
Renault – designer

— **ANDREW JONES**
Graduated: 1998

— **CORADIN FABIEN**
Graduated: 1998
Audi – designer (exterior)

— **JEA-SOO KIM**
Graduated: 1998
Audi – designer (exterior)

— **MARTIN KROPP**
Graduated: 1998

— **MATTHIEU MASSONNEAU**
Graduated: 1998

— **JORDAN MEADOWS**
Graduated: 1998
DaimlerChrysler – designer, USA

— **MATTHEW NOONE**
Graduated: 1998

— **CHARLOTTE SCHIFFER**
Graduated: 1998

— **DANIEL SCHMITT**
Graduated: 1998

— **MARC TARLING**
Graduated: 1998
Ford – designer, UK

29|31

225

Glossary
The Visual Language of Car Design is Completely Eclectic, its Sources International; the Written Language is Transatlantic
Stephen Bayley
Peter Stevens
Giles Chapman
Illustrations by Peter Stevens

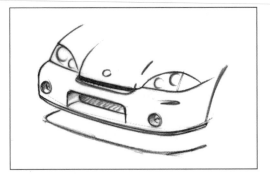

AIRDAM

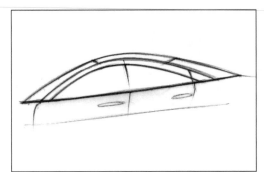

BELTLINE

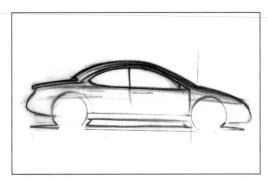

CAB-FORWARD

In the 1950s, American designer Virgil Exner helped establish a major transatlantic current of exchange, with collaborations between the old Torinese *carrozzeria* of Ghia and Detroit's Chrysler, much to the benefit of each. Two decades later, General Motors was exploiting Italian design both unconsciously and explicitly: the fine-lined 1973 Camaro was clearly influenced by Pininfarina, while the 1988 Cadillac Allante was actually manufactured in Pininfarina's Grugliasco plant. But sometimes the influence flows the other way: as chief designer of Porsche in the early 1980s, Anatole Lapine's responsibility was to maintain the hard, bright flame of German technical superiority and find a poetic expression of it. Lapine had been trained in Detroit under Harley Earl's disciple, Bill Mitchell.

The spoken and written vocabulary of design is similarly transatlantic, a curious mixture of Piedmontese artisan slang and American neologisms. The development of the vocabulary is inseparable from the evolution of design: if you have a word to describe, say, the precise radius of curvature of the transverse baseline of the windscreen, then the chances are you will pay very special attention to refining that radius to the best possible effect.

ABS
Affordable Business Structure, a management term used in defining the budget for a new programme.

ACT
Affordable Cost Target, a management term used to determine the cost of individual components. The industry speaks of 'real dollar costs': designers often work to financial disciplines of a fraction of a cent.

AERODYNAMICS
The scientific study and measurement of airflow over a moving body, usually in a wind tunnel. Pioneer investigators included Rumpler, Jaray and Kamm. The resistance of a body to airflow is known as drag and is scientifically expressed as Cd (for 'drag coefficient' in Britian or Cx in Europe). Low drag means better penetration, less friction and therefore more efficiency, but often leads to poor dynamic stability. This requires furthur study and development to balance lift forces (Cy) at the front and rear of the car, and to control aerodynamic side forces (Cz). The science of aerodynamics has been absorbed into the aesthetics of design as 'streamlining'. Today, the technical study is often known as…

AIRFLOW MANAGEMENT

AIRDAM
A transverse lip or bib at the lowest point of the front of a car intended to control airflow under the car and, hence, reduce drag and front lift forces.

AXIS
See Co-ordinates

BAFFO
Protective wheelarch extensions. From the Italian *baffi* – for moustaches.

BECQUET
An overhanging transverse ledge or indentation over the top of the rear glass, which may have some aerodynamic value but is more often used for visual emphasis.

BELTLINE
The longitudinal frontier between the car's main mass and its greenhouse.

BERLINA
Originally a closed coach for fast, long-distance travel, with four wheels, four seats and two or four doors. A **BERLINETTA** is a coupé (qv) version of this.

BOCCA DI COCCODRILLO
Literally 'crocodile's mouth,' a rear hinged bonnet generally triangular in plan.

BONE LINE
Designers often use natural metaphors to describe body shapes, talking of hard muscle under soft flesh. A bone line is a suggestion of solid structure beneath the car body's surface.

BOX
One of the major volumetric components of a car's architecture. In a traditional saloon there are three boxes: one for the engine, one for the passengers, and one for the luggage. In Italian, three-box is *tre volumi*. A hatchback, missing a boot, is a two-box car, or *due volumi*.

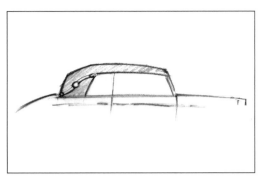

CABRIOLET

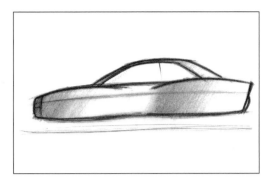

COKE BOTTLE CURVE

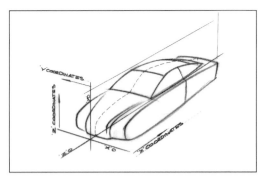

COORDINATES

BRAKE (BREAK)

A European term, now rare, for an estate car or station wagon. Originally horse-drawn for transporting staff and equipment, often for sporting functions.

SHOOTING BRAKE (BREAK)

Specifically for carrying sporting dogs and so on.

BROADBRUSH

An informal metaphorical term for the stage of the design process when no firm decisions about a new car's character have been made and its engineering specification has not been finalised.

BUCK

A buck was originally the body of a cart. A styling buck is the full-size framework on which creative modelling is developed in the studio. In practice, an interior buck is the passenger cell minus the anterior and posterior boxes, often without roof.

CAB-FORWARD

The position of the passenger cell with respect to the whole is one of the most significant ways of determining a car's stance. A cab-forward design tends to suggest dynamism, while cab-backwards gives a vehicle a more relaxed posture.

CABRIOLET

A carriage originating in France – an open two-seater with a groom perched on a platform at the back, having a folded roof with external 'irons' for folding. As a car, the folding roof would also have exposed external 'irons'.

CADENINO

The decorative edging, or piping, on seat upholstery.

CAID

Computer Aided Industrial Design.

CAMPANATURA

The angle between the vertical and the greenhouse (qv) when seen from the front. Tumblehome in English.

CANT RAIL

The longitudinal roof frame running above the tops of the doors.

CARROZZERIA

A coachbuilder. The great Italian design houses, mostly developed from Torinese coachbuilders.

CLAY

Hard styling clay (soft when warmed in an oven – hardens as it cools and can then be sculpted) used for simulating panels and components. 'Clay' is also the generic name for full-size models of the entire car which designers use to demonstrate their thinking. More effort is put into clay models than rendering and, even when computers dominate studios, production of a clay (often using antique manual skills) is still the most important part of the design process.

CODA

Tail.

CODA DI SEPPIE

Literally 'cuttlefish tail,' an anterior box given a sleekly rounded diminishing sculptural form.

COFANO

The hinged lid of an engine or luggage compartment.

COKE BOTTLE CURVE

A belt line that is prominently kicked-up in a sinuous curve just forward of the rear wheelarch. Inspired by the classic 1916 6.5oz Coca-Cola 'contour' bottle (itself inspired by a kola nut), the Coke bottle curve was first seen on Raymond Loewy's 1961 Studebaker Avanti and soon became a dominant motif in 1960s styling. Coke bottle curves appeared on the 1964 Mustang, 1965 Camaro and 1968 Escort.

CONCEPT CAR

In the 1950s General Motors presented travelling roadshows known as Motoramas to test (sometimes extravagant) ideas on the public. Nowadays, most major manufacturers present concept cars at the international motor shows: today, concept cars are often intended to prepare public acceptance of new models.

CO-ORDINATES

A system for defining any point on, or in, the car. The longitudinal axis of the car is described as 'X' axis. Normally, the front axle centre line is defined as X1000. X numbers increase rewards measured in millimetres. 'Y' co-ordinates are either side of the longitudinal centre line known as 'Y'O. The height above a nominal horizontal 'Z' plane produces the Z co-ordinates. On a flat-floored car such as a race car, the underside of the floor is ZO. CAD systems are unable to work with negative numbers, so XO and ZO must be outside the car envelope.

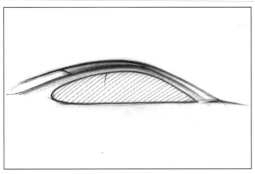

DLO

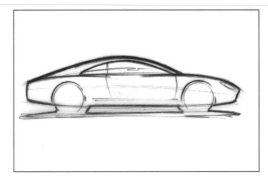

FASTBACK

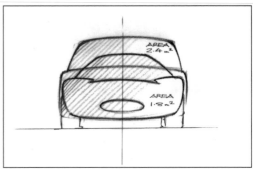

FRONTAL AREA

COUPÉ

A closed carriage, the front part of which has been coupé (cut off in French), leaving the rear still covered. In horse-drawn coachbuilding it applied to the part of the carriage between the front 'box' and the rear 'trunk,' or 'boot.' The term has evolved to mean two- or four-seat bodywork which has been stylishly foreshortened or cut-back.

COWL OR SCUTTLE

The structural transverse beam below the windscreen that usually carries the screen wiper assembly.

CUE

A detail copied from, or inspired by, another car.

CURVANO

The anterior or posterior transverse curve of the passenger cell glass when seen from above.

DCA

Design Cost Analysis is a stage in the design process. Designers are trained to discipline their creative work to strict cost implications.

DECK

Anterior or posterior horizontal surfaces (deck lid, US for boot lid).

DIGITISER

Electronic measuring devices 'read' designers' clay models and translate measurements into data for machine tools, or CAD screens.

DLO

Daylight Opening, or window intended to be a distinctive design feature of the car's side view.

DRAG

See Aerodynamics.

DUFLUNKY

The father of styling, Harley Earl, was famous for convoluted, odd, but expressive language. Lacking a precise vocabulary to describe certain body parts or specific aesthetic gestures, he invented it. No-one was ever certain exactly what a duflunky was, but it excited useful creative speculation among the studio staff. See Rashoom and Zong.

EPOWOOD

A synthetic modelling material.

FAIRING

In general, any smooth surface effect which covers an opening, such as a wheelarch. More specifically, a feature that connects the rear of the glasshouse with tail, known as *pinne* in Italian.

FASTBACK

Now rather out of favour, rooflines sloping dramatically rearwards first appeared in the General Motors cars for the 1948 model year. This fastback roofline was adapted for Bentley's Continental throughout the 1950s and became a popular motif in the next decade with the 1965 Ford Mustang and Plymouth Barracuda of the same year.

FEATURES LIST

The original document issued by product planners, a dispassionate description of every component of a car (continuously revised during the car's gestation). It is the job of designers to interpret a Features List as a practicable vehicle.

FENDER

American for bumper, *paraurti* in Italian. Now redundant as cars tend to be conceived as integral shapes with the function of the bumper assumed by body-colour impact-absorbing plastics.

FIGURINO

A rendering, or coloured sketch. Even with CAID, designers tend to prefer drawing by hand as a primary means of visualising a new car.

FINIZIONE

The final stage of finishing a model or prototype.

FLUSH GLAZING

A technique, originally in the cause of aero dynamic efficiency and first seen on the 1982 Audi 100, which has the glass forming an unbroken surface effect between door panels, pillars and roof.

FRONTAL AREA

The maximum cross-sectional area of the car which, when multiplied by the Cd, (drag coefficient) give the CdA of the car. A major influence on drag. The less the frontal area the better will be performance and economy.

FUNCTIONAL BUILD

The first metal car to be made with production tools.

GREENHOUSE

Upper part of the passenger cabin comprising the DLOs (qv). *Padiglione* in Italian.

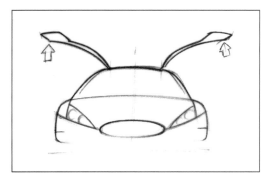

GULLWING DOOR

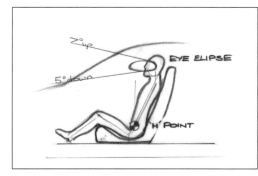

H-POINT

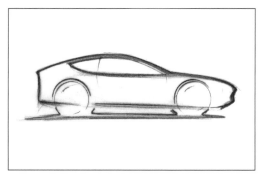

KAMM TAIL

GT

Now archaic, an abbreviation of the Italian *gran turismo* to suggest a type of car with the comfort of a saloon and the performance of a sports car well suited to long-distance travel.

GULLWING DOOR

A passenger door that swings upwards so that, when both are raised, they assume the shape of the wings of a gull when landing. Key feature on both the Mercedes-Benz 300SL and De Lorean DMC-12.

HARDPOINTS

Hardpoint has an actual and a metaphorical meaning. It is the stage of design after Broadbrush, or conceptual phase. Hardpoints are also the fixed or frozen positions of, for example, the top of the radiator, top of the engine, top of the scuttle, suspension top mounts and so on. Hardpoints might include greenhouse pillar sections, spare tyre location or side glass surface at driver's eye level. Hardpoints are used in continuous comparative evaluation of competitors.

HARDTOP

Properly, a detachable, rigid, weather-proof roof for cabriolets, sports cars and roadsters. In the 1950s, some American designers, including Virgil Exner at Chrysler, developed the motif of an 'apparent' (in fact, fixed) hardtop to give a racy aspect to otherwise pedestrian cars. This sublime artifice was eloquent of US styling at its most gloriously absurd.

HEADER

A header rail is the transverse structural beam above the windscreen.

HIGHLIGHTS

Designers test their models in different visual environments to see how light falls on the shape's surfaces. Such niceties are strong determinants of a car's overall aesthetic effect. Some say a car's character depends on whether a model is tested in natural or artificial light. The prominent effects of light falling on the surface are known as Highlight Lines.

H-POINT

A theoretical point (R-point in Europe) from which critical dimensions relating to legislation are measured. The H-point is approximately in line with the driver's hip joint. The position of the 'eye elipse' is derived from the H Point; the eye elipse is used to generate legally required vision lines.

KAMM TAIL

Wunibald Kamm was an Aerodynamics (qv) pioneer. His belief was that a sharply truncated tail created dynamic value by exploiting the benefits of the low-pressure area behind a moving vehicle. Zagato's 1965 Alfa-Romeo GTZ had a classic Kamm tail, as did Pete Brock's 1965 Shelby Daytona Cobra.

KICK PLATES

A strip of bright metal on the outer edge of the door sill, usually revealed when the car door is open. A throwback to coachbuilding days, when it would have protected the hand-made wooden threshold of a carriage, kick plates are now a feature supposed to confer prestige.

LIMOUSINE

An archaic term from coachbuilding to describe a large, closed car of four or more doors where the person in charge of the vehicle sits in the back. Now a form used to describe a formal saloon car often stretched in length (limo!).

LUXOTRUCK

Sports Ute (qv) with material indulgences and effects more often found in a Limousine (qv).

MASCHERONE

The full-size wooden Buck (qv) on which prototype panels are tested and formed.

MICROCAR

Now redundant, a term derived from the German *kleinwagen*, used to describe the often ingenious miniature cars that were the motor industry's response to the rationed economy of the 1950s.

MILLING

A machine tool process. ANC (Numerically Controlled) Milling Machine interprets math ematical data from a Digitiser (qv) and sculpts a 3D model from wood or clay. A five-axis milling machine is used to form anything from a 1:1 vehicle exterior to a small component measuring just a few centimetres. The latest machines can move at speeds of 20msec-1 with a positioning accuracy of 0.15mm within a working cube of 9m x 3m x 3m.

MINIVAN

A coinage by Chrysler to describe the new type of vehicle that came between the old minibus and today's MPV (qv). Chryslers 1984 Minivans just anticipated the Renault Espace as hybrids offering exceptional passenger accommodation together with unexpectedly sophisticated dynamics.

MODANATURA

A sculptural moulding.

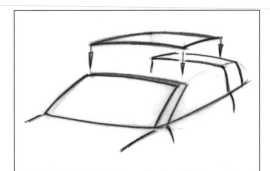

SPOILER

TARGA ROOF

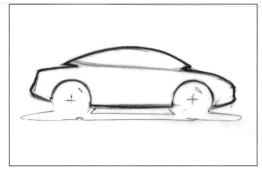

THREE-BOX

MONTANTE
The pillars and posts of the Padiglione (qv), what in architecture would be called glazing bars.

MPV
Multi-Purpose-Vehicle.

NOTCH-BACK
As opposed to Fastback (qv), a car with a clearly defined rear Deck (qv).

ORGANIC
An approach to design that derives its inspiration from the expressive curves and lines of vegetables and animals. In an organic design, there are no straight lines.

OVERHANG
The parts of a car anterior and posterior to the wheelarches.

PACKAGE
A term for what in architecture and engineering is known as the 'general arrangement.' The most demanding part in the design of any car is to achieve the maximum interior space within the smallest exterior. This is the package.

PADIGLIONE
See Glasshouse.

PARAFANGO
Italian for mudguard.

PILLAR/POST
Identified by the letters A,B,C,D ('A' pillar being the foremost or windscreen pillar), as they move rearwards through the glasshouse, the vertical (almost always angled) members of the bodywork that support the roof, the equivalent of glazing bars in architecture. *Montante* in Italian.

PINNE
A sort of Fairing (qv), an element sometimes structural, more often aesthetic, that joins the *padiglione* with the *coda*. Pinne are a favourite motif of Pininfarina's, seen most memorably on 1960s Ferraris, notably the Dino 246.

PLANCIA
An instrument panel.

PLATFORM
The invisible, but elemental and expensive, basic structure of a modern car. It is the contemporary task of car designers to achieve maximum aesthetic diversity from a single platform.

PROGRAMME
The general term for the entire creative process of making a modern car, from market research to product planning through design, research, engineering, prototyping and testing.

PROSCIUTTO
Known in England and US as the Column Shroud. The bulky plastic moulding, often housing functional stalks, shrouding the steering column between the steering wheel and the Plancia (qv).

PROFILE
A side elevation.

RASHOOM
See Duflunky.

RAZOR EDGE
The origami school of car design, where sharp, geometrical forms and angles dominate the overall shape.

ROADSTER
Originally a US term that initially meant a drop-head with three-abreast bench seat, but is now synonymous with open two-seat sports-type cars, but usually more civilised than sports cars.

ROCKER PANEL
In US English, the body part between the bottom of the doors and the ground. See Sill.

SALOON
One of the most enduring terms in the design vocabulary, a completely enclosed fixed-head vehicle with four or more seats.

SCOCCA
A steel body shell.

SGUSCIO
A concave longitudinal depression with a minor structural and major aesthetic function.

SHUT LINE
The line between panels and doors. The precision and economy of these lines is a matter of intense competition between manufacturers and is a serious test of manufacturing finesse. The way the shut lines are articulated by designers is an unconsciously powerful influence on the customer's perception of the car's character.

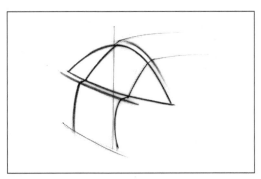

TUMBLEHOME

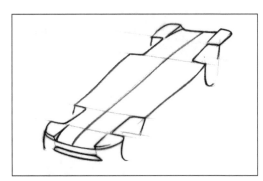

UNDERBODY OR FLOORPLAN

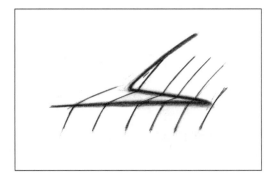

ZORRO

SILL
British English for Rocker Panel (qv).

SOAK TIME
The time given to assimilating a 'shocking' new car design, since the best are often the most outlandish.

SOGLIA
The perimeter of any hinged aperture.

SPIDER
Originally, an open two-seater carriage, now synonymous with open sports cars. Actually, a very light four-wheeled vehicle whose intention was to show off elegant horses.

SPOILER
A transverse (usually) posterior device intended to interrupt the airflow and enhance stability through Aerodynamic (qv) downforce, at the rear.

SPORTS CAR
Nowadays an anachronism, but an expression powerfully redolent of automobile culture at its peak. An open two-seater intended solely for pleasure and performance. See also Cabriolet, Roadster, Spider and Targa.

SPORTS UTE
A four-wheel drive vehicle, inevitably with expressively blocky masculine aesthetics, for recreational more than agricultural use.

SURPRISE & DELIGHT
An informal expression, loosely derived from an aesthetic credo of architect Sir John Soane, used to describe the emotive power of a novel solution.

SWAGE LINE
An emphatic crease in a metal panel.

TAPE DRAWING
At an early stage in the Programme (qv), designers do full-size 'drawings' using adhesive tape on clear acetate over a package drawing.

TARGA
A coinage by Porsche in honour of its own successes in the Sicilian Targa Florio road races: a Sports Car (qv) with a removable and storable roof panel.

TGR
Things Gone Right, a management term used in discussion at all stages in the Programme (qv). Its cognate is TGW for Things Gone Wrong (sometimes, but not often, prefixed with Zero).

TUMBLEHOME
See Camoanatura.

UNDERBODY OR FLOORPAN
The structural floor of a car, usually a fairly untidy surface since it doubles as a mounting surface for suspension, exhaust system, gearbox, fuel tank and so on. It is aerodynamically beneficial to keep this surface as smooth as possible to reduce drag, but not always practical. The McLaren F1 road car, like recent Ferrari models, was designed with a smooth underbody.

VOLUMETRIC IMAGING
1:1 computer-generated colour hologram.

VOLUMI
See Box.

WCR
Worldwide Customer Requirements, a management term used in consideration of how the global Platform (qv) might best be adapted to local requirements.

WHEELARCH
The aperture containing the wheels, *arco ruota* in Italian.

X
Ingredient X, the X Factor, Project X, Generation X, call it what you will, this letter finds its way on to almost all concept cars to denote them as 'ex'-tra special, 'ex'traordinary or 'ex'traterrestrial. X, however, rarely marks the spot when it comes to actually making them – most are never seen again. 'X' only ever sees a showroom attached to the end of 'GL' or 'SL', to denote some arcane trim level.

ZONG
See Duflunky.

ZORRO
A highlight effect on the surface of a car that looks like an elongated letter 'Z', a much admired result of skillful modelling.

231

→ Bibliography

Despite the enormous social, economic and cultural significance of the car, its literature is thin. Designers who can make metal speak eloquent volumes, are rarely great communicators in other media: there is still no great autobiography by a car designer. In addition, the urgency of manufacturing, the pressure of competition, the dominating rhythms of the production cycle govern the industry: maintaining the sort of archival resources historians need to write proper books is not a priority for the motor industry. Indeed, the problems of storing the vast amounts of sketches, models and data generated in the design of a car usually lead to manufacturers junking superb source material as soon as a vehicle is in production. In addition, propriety does not allow the release of the commercially sensitive information researchers need to write academic studies: an authoritative 'standard' work on car design may never be realised. But there has been a handful of books which capture some of the glamour, fascination, quirky genius and dizzy power of car design.

C Edson Armi: *The Art of the American Automobile*. Penn State University Press, Philadelphia, 1988. Armi, author of *Masons and Sculptors in Romanesque Burgundy*, was one of the first mainstream art historians to concern himself with car design. This is a book of scholarly interviews, mainly with General Motors designers.

Stephen Bayley: *Harley Earl and the Dream Machine*. Alfred Knopf, New York, 1983. An impressionistic account of the most influential designer of them all – the man who styled America's golden age.

Battista Farina: *Nato con l'automobile*. Turin, 1968. The autobiography of the founder of Pininfarina emphasises the vernacular origins of Italian car design.

Henry Ford *My Life and Work*. Garden City Publishing, New York, 1922. Written with Detroit journalist Samuel Crowther, Ford's autobiography is a compelling testament of faith.

Nick Georgano *Art of the American Automobile – the greatest stylists and their work*. Prion Books, 1995. The best book (yet) on the subject lavishly illustrated with Nick Wright's superb photographs.

Vittorio Gregotti *Carrozzeria Italiana – cultura e progetto*. Alfieri, Milan, 1978. A superbly illustrated book based on an exhibition about Italian car design.

Ralf J Kieselbach: *Stromlinienautos in Deutschland: Aerodynamik in Pkw-Bau 1900 bis 1945*. Kolhlhammer, Stuttgart, 1982. A unique illustrated account of the period when aero dynamic research dominated German car design.

L'Idea Ferrari (exhibition catalogue). Fabbri Editori, Milan, 1990. A superbly illustrated catalogue of the Ferrari exhibition held at Florence's Forte di Belvedere in 1990.

Raymond Loewy: *Never Leave Well Enough Alone*. Simon & Schuster, New York, 1951. A swaggering masterpiece of myth-making, and self-aggrandisement, Loewy's fascinating book describes his influential work for Hupp and Studebaker.

Doug Nye: *Ferrari in Camera*. Palawan Press, London, 1995. A sumptuous album of gorgeous photographs by Geoffrey Goddard: nothing better evokes the romance of the Italian automobile.

John B Rae: *The American Automobile – a brief history*. The University of Chicago Press, Chicago, 1965. The best academic account of its subject to date.

Alfred Sloan: *My Years with General Motors*. Doubleday, New York, 1964. The portentous autobiography of the man who turned a loose confederation of disparate industries into the world's biggest manufacturing corporation.

Tom Wolfe: *The Kandy-Kolored Tangerine Flake Streamlined Baby*. Farrar, Straus & Giroux, New York, 1965. The brilliant account of California hot-rodding that launched Wolfe's career.

Christopher Frayling: *The Royal College of Art – 150 Years of Art & Design*. Barrie & Jenkins, London, 1987. Puts the edcucational side of car design in context.

234

→ Index

ADVERTISING – p75
ALFA ROMEO GIULIETTA SPRINT – p25
AMBASZ, EMILIO – p22
ANDERLONI, CARLO – p27
ART AND COLOR DEPARTMENT, GM – p92
AUDI A3, A4 – p188
AUDI ADVANCED STUDIO – p132
AUDI AVUS – p132
AUDI QUATTRO SPORT – p194, p197
AUSTIN MINI – p28
AUSTIN-MORRIS 1100/1800 PROTOTYPES – p28

BARTHES, ROLAND – p44
BEL GEDDES, NORMAN – p24, p205
BENTLEY – p25
BENZ, KARL – p22
BERTONE – p24
BIRD, CHRIS – p72, p74, p75
BIRTWHISTLE, PETER – p194, p197, p198
BLACK, MISHA – p15
BMW 507 – p27
BODY ASSEMBLY – p59
BOULANGER, PIERRE – p25
BRAND MANAGEMENT – p139
BRITISH LEYLAND – p140, p141
BUGATTI ATALANTE – p92
BUICK Y-JOB – p147

CALLUM, IAN – p68
CALVET, JACQUES – p164
CHABONNEAUX, PHILIPPE – p28
CHAPMAN, COLIN – p27
CHAPMAN, NIGEL – p14
CHEVROLET CORVAIR – p28
CHEVROLET CORVETTE – p24
CHRYSLER 300 – p27
CHRYSLER UK – p14
CISITALIA – p25, p26, p27, p210
CITROËN DS – p163, p165
CITROËN 2CV – p163, p165
CITROËN C3 - C6 – p164, 165
COCO, DONATO – p163, p164
COLOUR TREATMENTS – p94
COMPUTER AIDED DESIGN (CAD) – p59
CORD – p25, p92, p210
COX, SIMON – p146, p147, p148
CREED, TREVOR – p156

D'AMBROSIO, LUCIANO – p121
DA SILVA, WALTER – p190
DAIMLERCHRYSLER – p154
DARRIN, HOWARD – p27
DE LA VEGA, JOSÉ – p115
DREYFUSS, HENRY – p24

EARL, HARLEY – p24, p26, p205, p226
EATON, BOD – p157
ELECTRIC CARS – p206
ELLIOT, ALAN – p57, p59, p60
EPINOSA, CATHRYN – p96
EXNER, VIRGIL – p27, p226

FERRARI 166 BARCHETTA – p27
FIGONI & FALASCHI – p25
FIORAVANTI, LEONARDO – p28
FISHER, LARRY – p24
FOLZ, JEAN-MARTIN – p164
FORD MUSTANG – p26
FORD THUNDERBIRD – p24
FORD, HENRY – p22, p23, p72
FRUA – p24

GENDER AND CARS – p100
GENERAL MOTORS – p23, p24
GHIA – p24
GIACOSA, DANTE – p25
GM ART AND COLOR – p205
GOERTZ, ALBRECHT – p27
GRADE, ANTHONY – p181
GRAHAM-PAIGE – p205
GREENLEY, KEN – p15, p16, p17
GÜNAK, MURAT – p155, p156

HANSON, HANS-HARALD – p66
HARROW, DALE – p15
HATTER, TONY – p69, p170
HEFFERNAN, JOHN – p96
HEIGHT, FRANK – p15
HELFET, KEITH – p69
HORBURY, PETER – p111, 1113, p114, p115
HULL, GRAHAM – p67

INTELLIGENT ROADS – p206
ISSIGONIS, ALEC – p25, p28
ISUZU VEHICROSS – p147, p148

31|31

JAGUAR E-TYPE – p25, p104
JAGUAR E-TYPE – p52
JAGUAR MK11 – p27
JAGUAR S-TYPE – p50
JAGUAR XK140 – p52
JEEP – p25
JEEP WAGONEER – p28
JUST-IN-TIME COMPONENT DELIVERY – p60

KAISER FRAZER SEDAN – p27
KAREN, TOM – p14, p28
KING, CONRAD – p96

LAI, PINKY – p65
LAWSON, GEOFF – p48, p50, p51, p52, p194
LE QUÉMENT, PATRICK – p15
LINCOLN CONTINENTAL – p25, p74
LOEWY, RAYMOND – p24, p26, p28
LOTUS 7 – p27
LOVEGROVE, ROSS – p123
LUPINE, TONY – p132
LUTHE, KLAUS – p28
LUTZ, ROBERT – p45
LYONS, WILLIAM – p27

MAYS, J – p18
MAZDA MX5, MX3, MX6- p197
MAZDA PREMACY – p194
MCGOVERN, GERRY – p141
MELVILLE, KENNETH – p68
MERCEDES-BENZ A-CLASS – p139
MERCEDES-BENZ SS – p25
METALLIC PAINT – p94
MG TC – p25
MICHELOTTI – p24
MITCHELL, BILL – p28, p94, p194, p226
MOBIUS, WOLFGANG – p132
MODEL T – p23. p72
MOTORAMA – p147
MUSEM OF MODERN ART – p25

NICKLES, NED – p28
NSU RO80 – p28

OGLE – p14
OLDSMOBILE TORONADO – p28
OLSEN, CARL – p14
OPEL/VAUXHALL SPEEDSTER – p134
OPEL/VAUXHALL ZAFIRA – p94

PIËCH, FERDINAND – p186
PININFARINA – p24
PLATFORM SHARING – p186, p190
POLLOCK, FERGUS – p66
PORSCHE 356 – p172
PORSCHE 911 – p170
PORSCHE 928 – p132
PORSCHE, FERRY – p25

RANGE ROVER – p143
RELIANT SCIMITAR GTE – p28
RENAULT 16 – p28
RENAULT AVANTIME CONCEPT – p182
RENAULT INITIALE CONCEPT – p182
RENAULT MEGANE SCENIC – p181
RENAULT VEL SATIS CONCEPT – p182
ROVER 75 – p56
ROVER GROUP – p140

SALVAAG, PER IVAR – p146
SATINET, CLAUDE – p164
SAYER, MALCOLM – p52, p104
SCAGLIONE, FRANCO – p27
SCHOOL OF INDUSTRIAL DESIGN – p13
SCHREMPP, JÜRGEN – p157
SCHREYER, PETER – p189
SELLAR, DAWSON – p14, p15
SIELAFF, STEFAN – p189
SLOAN, ALFRED – p23
SMITH, MARTIN – p131, p132, p197
SOCIETY OF MOTOR MANUFACTURERES
AND TRADERS – p13
SODERBURGH, DICK – p132
SOVUNUZZI, GIOVANNI – p27
STEERING WHEELS – p96
STEVENS, BROOKS – p28
STEVENS, PETER – p14, p15
STUDEBAKER AVANTI – p28

TAYLOR, GILES – p66
TEAGUE, WALTER DORWIN – p24
TERREBLANCHE, PIERRE – p122
TOURING – p24

VAN BRAECKEL, DIRK – p189
VIGNALE – p24
VOLVO 960 – p111
VOLVO ECC CONCEPT – p113
VOLVO P444 – p113
VOLVO S80 – p113

WALKER, GEORGE – p23, p26
WARKUSS, HARTMUT – p188, p191, p197
WILTSHIRE, JULIAN – p146
WOODHOUSE, DAVID – p146
WOODHOUSE, DAVID – p65
WOOLLEY, RICHARD – p56, 57

ZAGATO – p24
ZOOM ZOOM SCHOOL – p13